ELECTRIC MOTORCYCLE CHARGING INFRASTRUCTURE ROAD MAP FOR INDONESIA

OCTOBER 2022

ASIAN DEVELOPMENT BANK

 Creative Commons Attribution 3.0 IGO license (CC BY 3.0 IGO)

© 2022 Asian Development Bank
6 ADB Avenue, Mandaluyong City, 1550 Metro Manila, Philippines
Tel +63 2 8632 4444; Fax +63 2 8636 2444
www.adb.org

Some rights reserved. Published in 2022.

ISBN 978-92-9269-474-6 (print); 978-92-9269-475-3 (electronic); 978-92-9269-476-0 (ebook)
Publication Stock No. TCS220426
DOI: http://dx.doi.org/10.22617/TCS220426

The views expressed in this publication are those of the authors and do not necessarily reflect the views and policies of the Asian Development Bank (ADB) or its Board of Governors or the governments they represent.

ADB does not guarantee the accuracy of the data included in this publication and accepts no responsibility for any consequence of their use. The mention of specific companies or products of manufacturers does not imply that they are endorsed or recommended by ADB in preference to others of a similar nature that are not mentioned.

By making any designation of or reference to a particular territory or geographic area, or by using the term "country" in this document, ADB does not intend to make any judgments as to the legal or other status of any territory or area.

This work is available under the Creative Commons Attribution 3.0 IGO license (CC BY 3.0 IGO) https://creativecommons.org/licenses/by/3.0/igo/. By using the content of this publication, you agree to be bound by the terms of this license. For attribution, translations, adaptations, and permissions, please read the provisions and terms of use at https://www.adb.org/terms-use#openaccess.

This CC license does not apply to non-ADB copyright materials in this publication. If the material is attributed to another source, please contact the copyright owner or publisher of that source for permission to reproduce it. ADB cannot be held liable for any claims that arise as a result of your use of the material.

Please contact pubsmarketing@adb.org if you have questions or comments with respect to content, or if you wish to obtain copyright permission for your intended use that does not fall within these terms, or for permission to use the ADB logo.

Corrigenda to ADB publications may be found at http://www.adb.org/publications/corrigenda.

Notes:
In this publication, "$" refers to United States dollars.
ADB recognizes "China" as the People's Republic of China.

On the cover: Electric mobility can help make transportation more sustainable. Many elements, charging stations, batteries, operators must come together to enable the electric transport transition.

Cover design by Claudette Rodrigo.

Contents

TABLES, FIGURES, BOXES, AND MAPS	v
ABBREVIATIONS	viii
WEIGHTS AND MEASURES	ix
ELECTRIC TWO-WHEELER DEFINITIONS	x
SUMMARY	xi
1 INTRODUCTION AND BACKGROUND	**1**
2 FOCUS OF THE REPORT	**3**
2.1 Vehicle Category Focus	3
2.2 Geographical Focus	4
3 CLIMATE CHANGE BACKGROUND	**5**
3.1 Greenhouse Gas Emissions	5
3.2 National GHG Commitments and Electric Vehicle Policies	6
3.3 Electricity Generation	7
4 ASIA'S EXPERIENCE WITH ELECTRIC MOTORCYCLES	**9**
4.1 Experiences with Promotion Policies for Electric Motorcycles	9
4.2 Experiences with Charging Infrastructure for Electric Motorcycles	12
5 ELECTRIC TWO-WHEELER USER CATEGORIES	**21**
6 MOTORCYCLE CLASSIFICATION AND COMPARISON	**23**
6.1 Private Users	23
6.2 Commercial Users	28
6.3 Summary Electric Two-Wheeler Usage Type	30
7 CONVERSION OF GASOLINE MOTORCYCLES AND BATTERY STANDARDIZATION	**32**
7.1 Conversion of Motorcycles	32
7.2 Battery Standardization	33
8 ELECTRIC MOTORCYCLE PROJECTIONS	**34**
8.1 Official Scenarios	34
8.2 Scenario Modelling	36
8.3 Impact of Decreasing Electric Motorcycle Prices	37
8.4 Impact of a Carbon Tax	38
8.5 Conclusions on Business-As-Usual Development	39
8.6 Subsidy Scenario	39
8.7 Regulatory Scenario	41

8.8	Comparison of Electric Motorcycle Deployment of Scenarios in JABODETABEK and Bali	42
8.9	Viewpoint of Manufacturers	43

9 ELECTRIC MOTORCYCLE CHARGING SYSTEMS FOR INDONESIA — 47
9.1 Battery Swapping Infrastructure — 47
9.2 Battery Charging Infrastructure — 54

10 GRID IMPACTS — 58
10.1 Impact of Charging Electric Motorcycles on the Power System — 59
10.2 Connections — 66
10.3 Quality of Power Supply — 70
10.4 Summary and Conclusion on Grid Impact — 73
10.5 Investments Required — 74

11 REUSING AND RECYCLING BATTERY — 75
11.1 International Electric Vehicle Battery Standards — 77
11.2 Regulations in Indonesia — 79

12 PROPOSED POLICIES AND ACTIONS — 80

13 OUTLINE ROAD MAP FOR ELECTRIC MOTORCYCLES IN INDONESIA — 88
13.1 Environmental and Economic Benefits — 97

APPENDIXES
1 Standards — 99
2 Data Details — 100

FURTHER READING — 108

Tables, Figures, Boxes, and Maps

TABLES

S1	E-Motorcycle Characteristics for Urban Usage	xiii
1	Main Components of Taipei,China's E-Motorcycle Road Map 2018–2022	10
2	Technical Properties of a Typical Swappable Electric Vehicle Battery and a Typical Swap Station	19
3	Sample of Electric Two-Wheelers Sold in Indonesia	23
4	Main Features and Cost Components of Gasoline and Electric Motorcycles	24
5	Cost Comparison Electric and Gasoline Motorcycle Indonesia, 2021	26
6	Cost Components of High-Powered Electric Scooters for Urban Usage	26
7	Cost Comparison of High-Powered Electric Scooters and Gasoline Motorcycles in Indonesia, 2021	27
8	Are E-Motorcycles Attractive for Clients?	28
9	Cost Components of Commercial Electric Motorcycles for Urban Usage	28
10	Cost Comparison between Electric and Gasoline Motorcycles for Commercial Usage, 2021	29
11	E-Scooter Characteristics	30
12	E-Motorcycle Characteristics	31
13	Tentative Target of Electric Two-Wheeler Production and Sales in Indonesia	34
14	Electric Vehicle Deployment Target Based on the Draft Grand Strategy for Energy	35
15	Electric Vehicle Deployment Target Based on the Public Launching Commitment	35
16	Core Elements and Impacts of a Carbon Tax on Fuels	38
17	Estimated Subsidy Requirement to Achieve Target of 2.1 Million E-Motorcycles by 2025	39
18	Subsidy Level versus Economic Benefits of Emission Reductions per E-Motorcycle	40
19	Projected Population	41
20	Projected Number of E-Motorcycles with Regulatory Interventions	41
21	Projected Number of E-Motorcycles in JABODETABEK with Different Scenarios	42
22	Projected Number of E-Motorcycles in Bali with Different Scenarios	43
23	Docking Station Plans Swap Energi	46
24	General Assumptions for Swapping and Charging Infrastructure	48
25	Overview JABODETABEK	49
26	Scenarios for 2025 in JABODETABEK	49
27	Projected Number of Swapping Stations in JABODETABEK under Scenario 2	50
28	Overview of Bali	51
29	Scenarios for 2025 in Bali	51
30	Projected Number of Swapping Stations in Bali under Scenario 2	52
31	Potential Size of Charging Locations	55
32	Number of Chargers in JABODETABEK and Bali in 2025 for E-Motorcycle Scenarios	57
33	Projected Electricity Usage of E-Motorcycles with Regulatory Interventions	59
34	Limit of Harmonic Distortion – Flow in Indonesian Distribution Code CC3.0	72
35	Impact of Chargers on the Electricity Network	73

36	Expected Investment Related to Charging Infrastructure for E-Motorcycles in Indonesia	74
37	Overview of Central Government Agencies' Roles and Responsibilities Related to the Transport Sector	81
38	Derivative Regulations from Presidential Decree 55/2019	82
39	Other Relevant Regulations Concerning Electric Vehicles	83
40	Local Government Regulations on Electric Vehicle in Jakarta and Bali	84
41	Expected Regulations Concerning Electric Vehicles to be Released	84
42	Summary of Incentives for Electric Vehicles	85
43	Targeted Electric versus Gasoline Motorcycles for Private and Commercial Urban Usage	90
A2.1	General Parameters used for Calculations of the Impact of E-Motorcycles	100
A2.2	Environmental Impact per E-Motorcycle Lifespan	100
A2.3	Cost of Gasoline Fueled Motorcycles	101
A2.4	Projections of Cost of E-Motorcycles of Same Power as Gasoline Motorcycles Used Currently	101
A2.5	Impact on Total Cost of Ownership of Applying a Carbon Price in Indonesia	101
A2.6	Projected Number of E-Motorcycles in Total Indonesia with a BAU Scenario, an Urban Regulation Scenario and a Financial Incentive Scenario	102
A2.7	Motorcycle Total and E-Motorcycle Sales Projections	103
A2.8	Estimated Subsidy Requirement to Achieve Target of 2.1 Million E-Motorcycles by 2025	103
A2.9	Scenarios of Number of Swapping Stations for E-Motorcycles in JABODETABEK	104
A2.10	Scenarios of Number of Swapping Stations for E-Motorcycles in Bali	104
A2.11	Destination Chargers	105
A2.12	Scenario Calculations	105
A2.13	Scenario Calculations	105
A2.14	Charging Infrastructure	106
A2.15	Scenarios for 2025 in JABODETABEK	107
A2.16	Scenarios for 2025 in Bali	107

FIGURES

S1	User Categories and Charging Infrastructure	xii
S2	Projected E-Motorcycle Market in Indonesia	xvi
1	Vehicle Registration in Indonesia, 2015–2019	3
2	Greenhouse Gas Emissions in Indonesia, 1990–2018	5
3	Greenhouse Gas Transport Emissions in Indonesia, 1990–2018	6
4	Source of Electricity Generation in Indonesia, 2019	7
5	Development of the National Carbon Grid Factor in Indonesia, 2000–2016	8
6	Electric Vehicle with Swappable Batteries without an On-Board Charger	12
7	Swapping Station with Charger	13
8	Overview of Electric Vehicle Charging Infrastructure	14
9	Mode 1 Charging	15
10	Mode 2 Charging	15
11	Mode 3 Charging	16
12	Mode 4 Charging	16
13	Connectors for Mode 3 Charging (IEC 62196)	17
14	Electric Two-Wheeler User Categories	21
15	Usage of Electric Two-Wheelers	30
16	E-Motorcycle Scenarios for Indonesia	36
17	Price and Cost Comparison of Higher Powered Electric versus Gasoline Motorcycles	37

18	Required Subsidy for E-Motorcycles versus Potential Revenue from Carbon Tax on Gasoline Fuel	40
19	E-Motorcycle Scenarios in JABODETABEK	42
20	E-Motorcycle Scenarios in Bali	43
21	Indonesia Battery Corporation Production Plans	44
22	Projected Service Area per Swap Station with Non-Standardized Batteries, JABODETABEK	50
23	Projected Service Area per Swap Station with No Standardization, Bali	52
24	Typical Charging Profile of Swap Station with 20 Docks of 1 kW Each	53
25	Indicative Charging Pattern for Home Charging	55
26	Indicative Charging Pattern for Small Area Charging	56
27	Indicative Charging Pattern for Medium- to Large-Sized Area Charging	56
28	Simplified Overview of Power System and Connection Level of Charging Sites	58
29	Electricity Usage of E-Motorcycles for Scenario 2 and Forecasted Total Electricity Sales in Indonesia	60
30	Net Peak Demand Projections Compared with Generation in the Power System of Bali and Java	61
31	Reserve Margin for Bali and Java	61
32	Total 150-Kilovolt Transformer Capacity Projections, 2019–2028	63
33	Typical Distributions Network for JABODETABEK	64
34	Distribution of Connection Capacity of PLN Customers in Jakarta and Bali in 2021	68
35	Power Ratings of Selected Household Appliances Applied in Indonesia	69
36	Reliability of Power Supply Indicators SAIDI and SAIFI, 2014–2019	70
37	Used Battery Options	75
38	Electric Two-Wheeler User Segments	89
39	Projected E-Motorcycle Market in Indonesia	92
40	Projected E-Motorcycle Market in JABODETABEK and Bali	92
41	Projected Destination Electric Vehicle Charger Market	93
42	Projected E-Motorcycle Battery Swap Station Market	94
43	Reduced Emissions Due to E-Motorcycles in Indonesia	97
44	Reduced Emissions Due to E-Motorcycles in JABODETABEK	98
45	Reduced Emissions Due to E-Motorcycles in Bali	98

BOXES

1	An Introduction to Smart Charging	65
2	Smart Charging in Indonesia	66
3	What is Harmonic Distortion?	72

MAPS

1	Java-Bali Electricity Transmission Map	62
2	Potential Initial Location of Swap Sites in JABODETABEK	95
3	Potential Initial Location of Swap Sites in Bali	96

Abbreviations

ADB	Asian Development Bank
BAPPENAS	Badan Perencanaan dan Pembangunan Nasional (National Development Planning Agency)
BAU	business-as-usual
BMS	battery management system
CO_2	carbon dioxide
CAGR	compound annual growth rate
CAPEX	capital expenditure
CNG	compressed natural gas
DEN	National Energy Council
EU	European Union
GHG	greenhouse gas
GSE	Grand Strategy for Energy
IEC	International Electrotechnical Commission
JABODETABEK	DKI Jakarta, Bogor, Depok, Tangerang, and Bekasi
MEMR	Ministry of Energy and Mineral Resources
OPEX	operational expenditure
PRC	People's Republic of China
PLN	PT Perusahaan Listrik Negara
RUEN	Rencana Umum Energi Nasional (Ministry of National Development Planning)
SoH	state of health
SOE	state-owned enterprise
TCO	total cost of ownership

Weights and Measures

km	kilometer
kg	kilogram
kV	kilovolt
kW	kilowatt
kWh	kilowatt-hour
tCO_2	ton of carbon dioxide
V	volt

Electric Two-Wheeler Definitions

Electric vehicle. This is any vehicle using 100% electricity (battery electric vehicle) including all types of electric two-wheelers.

Electric two-wheeler. This includes all types of electric vehicles with two wheels such as electric bicycles, electric scooters, and electric motorcycles.

Electric bicycle. This is an electric two-wheeler with a support engine but with the possibility to also use muscular power to move the vehicle.

Electric scooter. This is an electric two-wheeler with limited engine power and speed (25–35 km/h maximum), which does not need vehicle registration. In some places such as the People's Republic of China, electric scooters may have pedals, although they cannot be used. There are countries that do not classify vehicles with pedals as motorcycles, thus they can still be allowed even if motorcycles are restricted.

Electric motorcycle. This is an electric two-wheeler or e-motorcycle with an engine power above 500W and maximum speeds higher than 35 km/h. Such vehicles require registration as a motorcycle.

Note: This publication focuses on electric motorcycles. The term "electric two-wheelers" applies to electric scooters as well as electric motorcycles.

Summary

Background

More than 120 million motorcycles operate in Indonesia, of which an estimated 12,000 are electric motorcycles. The numbers continue to grow. Motorcycles are used for private as well as commercial purposes including ride-hailing and delivery services. Electrification of motorcycles would result in improved air quality and reduced greenhouse gas (GHG) emissions, fuel imports, and noise. Indonesia therefore aims to increase the share of electric motorcycles or e-motorcycles.

The report focuses on Greater Jakarta, i.e., DKI Jakarta, Bogor, Depok, Tangerang and Bekasi (JABODETABEK), and Bali. This allows for developing the characteristics required for a charging infrastructure for an urban area, as well as for a densely populated nonurban area. Results from these "typical" areas can then be extrapolated to other areas of the country, differentiating between urban and nonurban zones.

The total GHG emissions of Indonesia in 2016 were 1,458 metric tons of carbon dioxide equivalent ($MtCO_2e$). Transport GHG emissions in 2018 are estimated at 154 $MtCO_2e$, representing 16% of total emissions excluding land use change and forestry emissions, or 26% of energy emissions. Emissions from motorcycles are estimated to contribute around 20% of total transport emissions.

In its nationally determined contribution (NDC), Indonesia has committed to reduce its GHG emissions unconditionally by 29% compared to a business-as-usual scenario by 2030. To achieve this, Indonesia focuses on land use change and forestry emissions and the energy sector. E-mobility is on top of the political agenda in Indonesia to achieve the NDC target. The focus of the e-mobility strategy is on electric two-wheelers and on electrifying public transport buses.

Details on objectives, study focus, and climate change background can be found in Chapters 1–4.

Types of Motorcycles

Three distinct types of electric two-wheelers exist: (i) electric bicycles with a support engine plus the possibility to use muscular power to move the vehicle; (ii) electric scooters with a limited engine power and speed (25–35 kilometers per hour [km/hr] maximum), which do not need vehicle registration; (iii) e-motorcycles with an engine power above 500 watts (W) and maximum speeds higher than 35 km/h, which require registration as a motorcycle. E-motorcycles are differentiated from electric scooters, which have a limited engine power and speed and generally do not require vehicle registration. Converted e-motorcycles can be of any category. The focus of this report is on e-motorcycles.

Standard motorcycles as purchased in Indonesia are 110 to 150 cc (cubic centimeter), with a maximum power of 6.5 to 12 kilowatts (kW) (9 to 16 horsepower [HP]). A same power e-motorcycle requires a 2.5x higher initial investment. This incremental investment is not recovered during the e-motorcycle lifespan. Urban trips could, however, be made just as quickly and conveniently with a lower-powered e-motorcycle of around 2,000 W with speeds of 70–80 km/h. This type of e-motorcycle has sufficient power to comply with urban requirements and can thus be considered comparable in terms of convenience or usage value to a fossil-fuel-based motorcycle. The initial investment for such an e-motorcycle is 40% higher than for a gasoline motorcycle. This incremental investment is recovered during its lifespan due to having 80% lower operational expenditures. However, this type of e-motorcycle is not in line with the aspirations of customers concerning power and speed and additionally has range issues. Technology trends and lower battery costs will not resolve this customer preference issue.

Based on a purely rational purchase choice, lower-powered e-motorcycles are financially attractive and sufficient for urban trips. From a societal point of view, e-motorcycles are beneficial due to reduced air and noise pollution. Therefore, it could be justified that the government introduces regulations that swap the emotional benefits of high power and speed for reduced environmental pollution and improved health outcomes. As lower-powered e-motorcycles are profitable, this would not result in an additional financial cost to users, and it would generate considerable economic, social, health, and environmental benefits.

Details on motorcycle types, costs, and operation conditions are found in Chapter 7.

User Categories and Charging Infrastructure

E-motorcycles can be differentiated based on user category (private or commercial) and usage purpose. This results in different two-wheeler types and charging systems relative to user and usage purpose.

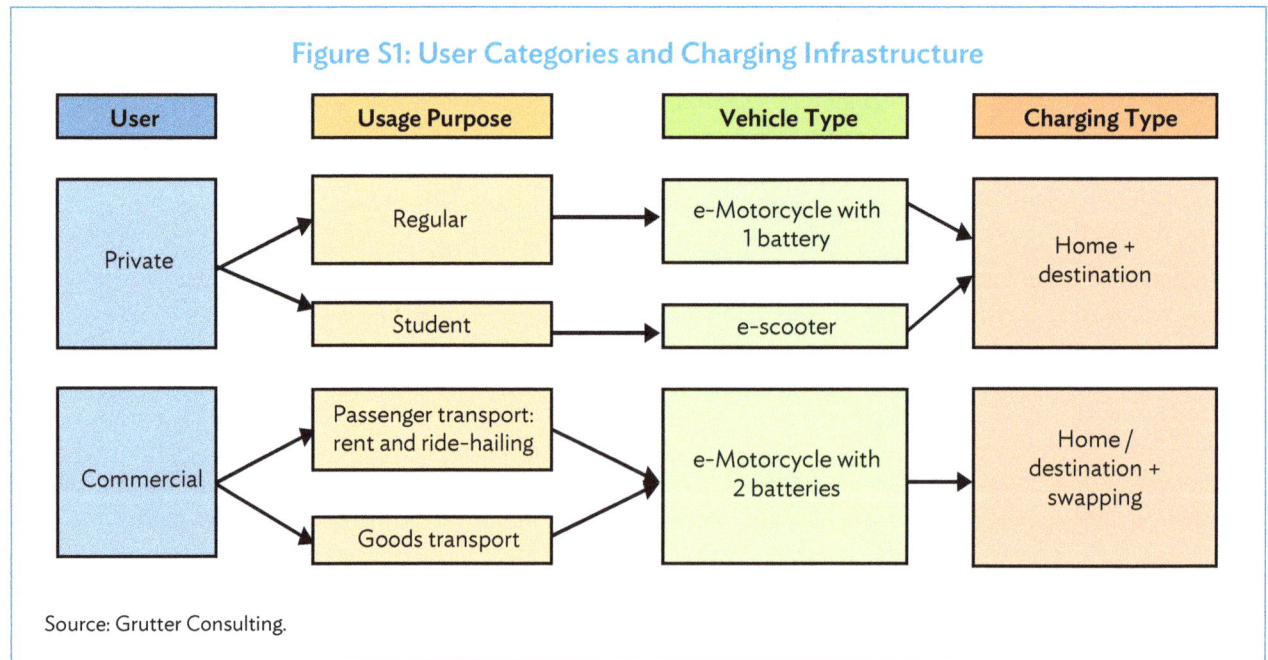

Figure S1: User Categories and Charging Infrastructure

Source: Grutter Consulting.

Private users can be differentiated in regular or standard electric two-wheeler users and students. Regular owners use their vehicle for daily trips to work, shopping, visiting friends, or other activities. The average trip length is 9–13 kilometers (km) in the urban area of Jakarta. Students are an important segment of the motorcycle user population. Low-powered and low-speed e-scooters are popular among students as they do not require a license. In practice, low-powered e-scooters often replace bicycles, ride-hailing services, or public transport. Private e-motorcycles will be charged at home and at the destination. Battery swapping is not a necessity or a big advantage for private users except for long-distance rides. Charging facilities at work or school (so-called destination chargers) are critical to reduce range anxiety issues of private users.

Commercial users can be divided into ride-hailing services for passengers, rental services, and goods transport. On average, commercial users drive 80–100 km per day. Commercial clients would therefore purchase an e-motorcycle with two batteries. For commercial users, battery swapping has an advantage as daily mileage is higher and it reduces the recharging time. The batteries of e-motorcycles cannot receive a high-powered charge and therefore require a minimum charging time of 1–2 hours, far too long for commercial applications; thus, battery swapping is an ideal option for commercial users to not have range issues and to allow for short "charging" times.

Table S1: E-Motorcycle Characteristics for Urban Usage

Parameter	Private Usage	Commercial Usage
Average engine power (watt)	1,800–2,500	1,800–2,500
Maximum speed (kilometer per hour)	70–80	70–80
Driving range (kilometer)	50 (one battery)	100 (two batteries)
CAPEX e-scooter	Rp24 million (with one battery)	Rp29 million (with two batteries)
Battery cost per unit	Rp5 million	Rp5 million
Electricity usage (kilowatt hour per kilometer)	0.025	0.025
Average daily trip length (kilometer)	45	80

CAPEX = capital expenditure.
Source: Grutter Consulting based on market assessment.

Details on user categories and necessities of former can be found in Chapters 6 and 7.

Experience of Economies in Asia

The electric two-wheeler market is estimated at around 300 million units by 2030. The People's Republic of China (PRC) dominates the electric two-wheeler market, with around 90% of both vehicle stock and sales. In many economies, a large share of electric two-wheelers are electric scooters with a maximum speed of 25 km/h which are not registered, making official data difficult to obtain.

Taipei,China has been subsidizing e-motorcycles since 1996. Since 2013, the subsidy level is $240 for electric scooters and up to $1,200 for e-motorcycles, with a slight decline since 2020. Swapping-cum-charging stations are also subsidized, with up to 50% of construction costs and free publicly accessible land. Battery swap sites are placed every 500 meters in urban Taipei,China, and turn up every 2–5 km in rural areas. Nonfinancial incentives include exclusive parking spaces, preferential parking fees, and prohibition for two-strokers in certain areas. The large subsidies had a positive impact on e-motorcycle sales but have not resulted in a paradigm change. The market share of e-motorcycle sales grew from 3% in 2017 to 15% in 2019 but dropped back to 10% in 2020. This loss of market share came at the same time as subsidy levels were decreased.

In the **PRC**, electric two-wheelers dominate the market without massive subsidies, with more than 200 million units, the majority of which are deemed to be electric scooters. Nearly every major PRC city has banned gasoline-powered motorcycles. Thus, the driver of the electric two-wheeler boom in the PRC has been the local motorcycle bans.

As of 2014, **Viet Nam** had around 43 million registered motorcycles. The electric two-wheeler market peaked in 2016 and then dropped again, basically due to frustration of users over the low quality of vehicles. Most units in Viet Nam are low-powered e-scooters used by students as they do not require a license and have a lower cost.

Promotion of e-motorcycles has only had limited success in other economies to date, although at first glance e-motorcycles seem to be comparable in purchase costs and have lower operational costs. Viet Nam only achieved very limited sales of e-motorcycles, with the market only taking up low-powered electric scooters used primarily by students. In Taipei,China, massive subsidies in swapping stations and vehicles have resulted in a stagnating market share of 10% of e-motorcycles. The only success case for widespread adoption of electric two-wheelers is the PRC, where gasoline units have been replaced with electric ones due to banning fossil-fuel-based motorcycles in most cities.

In the absence of either high financial subsidies or regulations, customers will prefer to purchase gasoline motorcycles, which have more power and speed than their same-cost electric equivalents. While the limited driving range and the absence of charging infrastructure is a challenge, it is not the core issue with e-motorcycles. This is clearly shown, for example, in Taipei,China, which has established a very dense swapping network without e-motorcycles increasing their market share beyond 10%–15% and still requiring massive subsidies. The core critical point for why customers prefer gasoline units is the "need for speed."

Some lessons from other economies concerning the promotion of e-motorcycles are clear: (i) without government intervention, the market for electric two-wheelers in the next few years will focus on low- powered e-scooters that do not replace primarily gasoline motorcycles but bicycles and public transport; (ii) financial incentives need to be (very) high to persuade customers to choose e-motorcycles; and (iii) regulations limiting the usage of gasoline motorcycles result, on the other hand, in a swift uptake of electric units.

Details on the experiences of other economies can be found in Chapter 5.

Conversion Kits

Trials have been realized in Indonesia to convert used gasoline motorcycles to electric units. The conversion kit includes the engine, the battery pack, a main controller, and a speed regulator.

The client receives an old motorcycle with an outdated chassis, brakes, lights, etc., combined with new electric components without the original manufacturer guarantee. The resultant e-motorcycle costs as much as a new gasoline motorcycle. For a 50% additional investment (RP24 million), the client could get a same-powered new e-motorcycle with brand-new components and a manufacturer warranty. For a similar price, the client could purchase a 2- to 3-year used e-motorcycle or a new gasoline motorcycle. Converted e-motorcycles are therefore not considered to be a technically and commercially attractive option for clients and subsidizing such efforts is not recommended as a strategy to increase the uptake of e-motorcycles. Conversions, offered initially in Viet Nam, have not proven to be popular. The same is also true for all other electric road vehicles, where initially some conversions were made but as soon as manufacturers started mass-producing electric units, the market for such backyard ventures disappeared.

Details on conversion from fossil-fuel-based -fuel to e-motorcycles can be found in Section 8.1 of Chapter 8.

Battery Standardization

Indonesia has plans to standardize batteries for two-wheeler usage. Standardized batteries have the advantage of allowing for easy interchange and for a higher density of swapping stations as all motorcycles would have the same battery. Taipei,China included standardization of batteries in its road map without achieving this target. Standardization of batteries had also been tried in the PRC when battery swapping was made with buses and passenger cars; however, the PRC also dropped this approach.

Battery standardization is problematic due to the dynamics of market forces. The battery is a core element of an e-motorcycle and a main competitive distinction and cost parameter. Standardization reduces competition between e-motorcycle/battery manufacturers, which diminishes the innovation speed and again results in fewer price decreases. Standardization can thus hamper instead of promote the uptake of e-motorcycles.

Standardization is only required for battery swapping not demanded by private users, i.e., by commercial clients with long driving distances that want to recharge or swap batteries within minutes. However, commercial customers can realize a cooperation agreement with a manufacturer to standardize their fleet and thus have a sufficient e-motorcycle density with identical batteries to warrant the set-up of battery swap stations. The analysis also showed that the required number of identical e-motorcycles for efficient battery swapping is not very high and can be achieved quickly.

Details on battery standardization can be found in section 8.2 of Chapter 8.

Policies for Promoting Electric Motorcycles

From a market perspective, e-motorcycles will succeed if they offer a higher value than a conventional unit. Without government intervention, the share of e-motorcycles is marginal, since fossil-fuel-based units have lower costs and are more convenient. Sticker price parity of an electric and a gasoline motorcycle will only be achieved by around 2030. The impact of a planned carbon tax of Rp30,000 per ton of carbon dioxide (CO_2) will be negligible as it influences cost structures by less than 1%.

Without massive financial subsidies or restrictions on fossil-fuel-based motorcycle usage, the e-motorcycle market will not grow; Indonesia will not achieve its e-motorcycle targets by 2025.

An estimate of the required subsidies to achieve the target (2.1 million e-motorcycles operating in 2025) results in a price tag of around \$1.1 billion (Rp$1.6*10^{13}$), most of which would be subsidies for motorcycles and a smaller part for charging stations. This subsidy would be around Rp7.5 million per e-motorcycle. The economic value of emission reductions is less than the subsidy cost, i.e., from an economic viewpoint, the subsidy is not justified.

Instead of subsidies, the government could make regulations favoring e-motorcycles and restricting the usage of fossil-fuel-based motorcycles. The regulatory scenario would prescribe that motorcycles need to be electric to enter specific zones or areas from a given year onward. The regulatory scenario requires no subsidies. Swapping stations can be established without subsidies as they can cover service costs due to having a captive demand. Lower-powered e-motorcycles would be chosen by the people and commercial agents as they can fulfil the urban transport demands. Ride-hailing and delivery service companies could be obliged to gradually increase the share of electric kilometers driven. Regulations would affect neither private nor commercial users financially due to comparable total costs of ownership of electric and gasoline units. For low-income residents that live within or commute to areas with restrictions and are dependent on their motorcycle, the government can establish an initial purchase subsidy paid against scrapping of the fossil-fuel-based motorcycle on a one-time basis.

Details on policies can be found in Chapters 9 and 13.

Proposed Road Map for Electric Motorcycles for Indonesia

E-motorcycles will outpace fossil-fuel-based units in terms of market share of newly sold units by 2030. E-motorcycles result in less air pollution, climate gases, and noise compared to fossil-fuel-based units. This improves the health and social well-being of citizens. The Indonesian motorcycle industry can profit by having a strong and growing domestic market demanding e-motorcycles thereby positioning themselves in a future growth market.

The projections are based on following a policy clearly favoring e-motorcycles by restricting usage of fossil-fuel-based motorcycles, initially in urban areas and thereafter also in rural areas. The following figure shows the projected market share of e-motorcycles for Indonesia until 2030 under the stated strategy. By 2030, 80% of newly sold motorcycles would be electric and the share of e-motorcycles in the total stock of vehicles would be around 45%, representing some 55 million units.

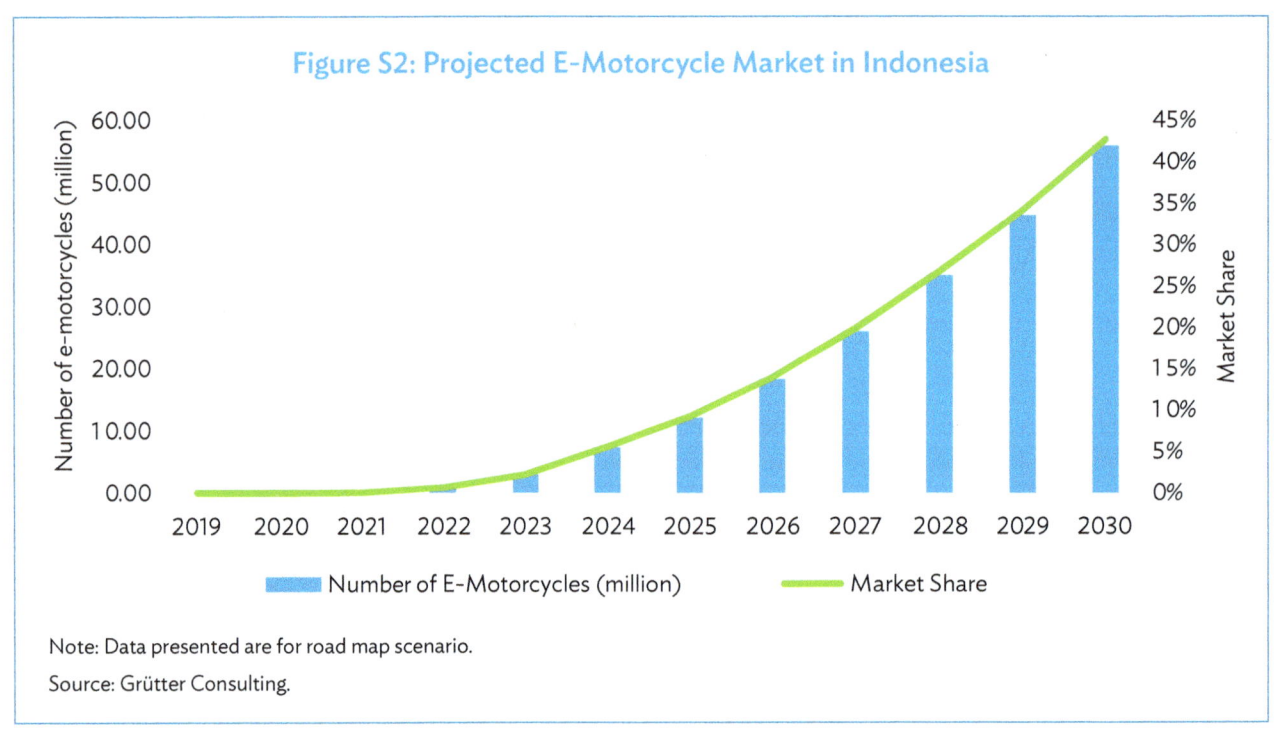

Note: Data presented are for road map scenario.
Source: Grütter Consulting.

Charging is divided into home charging, destination charging, and battery swapping, with the latter being used predominantly by commercial users. Home charging is a feature of all e-motorcycles. However, not all e-motorcycles are charged simultaneously and every day. Charging at home or at work could be done just by plugging into a wall socket, with no need for a dedicated charging infrastructure. In total, some 5.5 million destination chargers would be required by 2030 to meet the projected e-motorcycle numbers. Battery centers allow swapping a low-energy battery with a new, fully loaded battery. This system is predominantly used by commercial users. It is feasible to operate with various battery types and sizes, either within the same battery swapping site or at different locations if the number of e-motorcycles is large enough. Typically, such sites handle 10–30 batteries and are densely distributed, having a swap point every 4–6 km. Business models used for swapping often include monthly subscriptions or payments per swap, with batteries often owned by the swapping company or the motorcycle manufacturer.

Policy steps proposed to restrict area usage of fossil-fuel-based motorcycles would start in 2023. Motorcycle rental services in Bali and other selected islands should be obliged to have an electric fleet that is a minimum of 20% of their total offered for rental. For ride-hailing and delivery services, a certain minimum share of e-motorcycles operating in urban areas should be requested. An initial target for 2023 could be that 10% of each ride-hailing or delivery company's motorcycles in JABODETABEK and in Bali must be electric. Restricting the usage of fossil-fuel-based motorcycles is justified in economic and social terms as: (i) trips can be made also with e-motorcycles with comparable convenience levels; (ii) e-motorcycles have a comparable cost or are even less expensive than fossil-fuel-based units over their entire lifespan; (iii) the environmental impact of fossil-fuel-based motorcycles is highly negative due to emission of air pollutants, climate gases, and high noise levels; and (iv) in the absence of such policies, private and commercial users will continue using fossil-fuel-based motorcycles.

There are numerous **environmental and economic benefits** of e-motorcycles under the road map scenario for Indonesia. By 2030, e-motorcycles could reduce 39 million tons of CO_2, 10,000 tons of particulate matter 2.5 ($PM_{2.5}$), and 65,000 tons of nitrogen oxides. This results in economic benefits of Rp50,000 billion ($3.4 billion) annually due to reduced emissions. Reducing GHG emissions by 39 $MtCO_2e$ is highly relevant for Indonesia considering that 2018 total transport emissions were 154 $MtCO_2e$

INDONESIA'S ROAD MAP ON ELECTRIC MOTORCYCLE CHARGING INFRASTRUCTURE

TARGET
By 2030: **E-motorcycles** shall outpace fossil units in terms of market share of newly sold units.

FOCUS
Private and commercial users (ride-hailing and delivery services)

POLICY
- The Government of Indonesia takes decisive steps to increase significantly the market share of **e-motorcycles** based on a phased approach.
- Access to urban areas being limited to **e-motorcycles** with a gradual expansion of these spatial areas.

E-MOTORCYCLES

By 2025: **12 million units** in Indonesia
- 1.7 million in JABODETABEK
- 0.4 million in Bali

By 2030: **55 million units** in Indonesia
- 8 million in JABODETABEK
- 2 million in Bali

CHARGING INFRASTRUCTURE
- Home charging
- Destination charging
- Battery swap for commercial users

BENEFITS

By 2030
- 38 million tons CO_2 less emitted
- 10,000 tons $PM_{2.5}$ mitigation
- 65,000 tons NO_x reduction
- **$3.4 billion savings** due to reduced emissions

and would be around 301 MtCO$_2$e by 2030, assuming the same average annual growth rate as in the period 1990 to 2018; this would represent a 13% reduction relative to a business-as-usual GHG scenario.

Total additional **electricity demand** in 2030 due to e-motorcycles would be around 21 terawatt-hours, or 4% of the national consumption. The grid impact is limited. Additional investments for generation or transmission are only required after 2025. Total investments until 2030 for grid upgrades are estimated at less than $9 billion while being able to sell an additional 21 terawatt-hours of electricity per year. Investments will primarily be required in upgrading home connections. Smart charging flexibility could reduce loads and reduce the need for upgrades.

Details on the road map can be found in Chapter 14.

1. Introduction and Background

More than 120 million motorcycles currently operate in Indonesia, and the number continues to grow. Motorcycles are used for both private and commercial purposes, including ride-hailing and delivery services. The electrification of motorcycles would improve air quality and reduce greenhouse gas emissions, fuel imports, and noise. Indonesia, therefore, aims to significantly increase the share of electric motorcycles or e-motorcycles in the coming years.

The issuance of Presidential Decree 55 of 2019, which provides the framework legislation for the introduction of electric vehicles, charging infrastructure, and battery technology, is an important initial step in promoting electric vehicles in Indonesia's transportation system. Charging infrastructure will be developed based on projections for electric transportation deployment, the availability and reliability of grid-based electricity service, and conducive tariffs for electric transportation.

The Ministry of Energy and Mineral Resources' release of Ministerial Regulation 13 of 2020 specifically regulates the provision of charging infrastructure, from private to public charging stations, including battery swapping facilities. The State Electricity Company (PLN), has been tasked with kickstarting the deployment of charging stations across the country, starting with the capital city of Jakarta.

To provide the technical framework and assistance for charging infrastructure, Indonesia, represented by the Ministry of Energy and Mineral Resources, requested the Asian Development Bank (ADB) to study a realistic road map for the deployment of e-motorcycles. ADB supports Indonesia's ambitious plan for e-mobility, as it is consistent with multiple Sustainable Development Goals, as well as the operational priorities set forth in ADB's Strategy 2030. This report was prepared under the technical assistance grant to Indonesia for Electric Transportation and Charging Infrastructure and was administered by ADB with grant-based financing from the Republic of Korea's e-Asia and Knowledge Partnership Fund.

This report highlights best practices and assesses lessons learned in the implementation of e-motorcycle charging infrastructure experiences elsewhere in Asia. The report proposes policies and a strategy to foster electric motorcycle usage in Indonesia in line with governmental targets, focusing on private and commercial uses. It does not cover other electric vehicle categories due to differences in technologies, policies, strategies, and targets. The study area focuses on Greater Jakarta (DKI Jakarta, Bogor, Depok, Tangerang and Bekasi) and Bali, so characteristics for both urban areas and a densely populated nonurban area can be identified and incorporated in planning.

Focusing on e-motorcycles, the report covers (i) experiences elsewhere in Asia, (ii) projections on deployment, (iii) strategies and a conceptual plan for a charging infrastructure road map, (iv) grid impacts of charging infrastructure, (v) an analysis of different battery policies, (vi) policies and strategies for the promotion of charging infrastructure, and (vii) core elements of a road map for the deployment of charging infrastructure.

Indonesia has taken steps to promote the deployment of electric vehicles in its transportation system. Presidential Decree 55 of 2019 provides the framework legislation for the introduction of electric vehicles, charging infrastructure, and battery technology in Indonesia. Of key importance is the development of charging infrastructure based on projections for electric transportation deployment and the availability and reliability of grid-based electricity service, as well as conducive electricity tariffs for electric transportation.

The Ministry of Energy and Mineral Resources (MEMR) has released Ministerial Regulation 13 of 2020 that specifically regulates the provision of charging infrastructure, from private to public charging stations, including battery swapping facilities. As a state-owned enterprise (SOE), the State Electricity Company (PLN) was given the task to kickstart the deployment of charging stations across the country, starting from the capital city of Jakarta.

The Asian Development Bank (ADB) is supportive of Indonesia's ambitious plans for e-mobility, as it is consistent with multiple Sustainable Development Goals, as well as the operational priorities in ADB's Strategy 2030. The MEMR has requested a study on a realistic road map for the deployment of e-motorcycles and charging infrastructure.

The report was prepared under the technical assistance (TA) grant to Indonesia for Electric Transportation and Charging Infrastructure. The TA was administered by ADB with grant-based financing from the Republic of Korea's e-Asia and Knowledge Partnership Fund.

2. Focus of the Report

2.1 Vehicle Category Focus

Charging infrastructure is linked with specific vehicle categories. Buses, passenger cars, or motorcycles each need different types of chargers, as well as business models related to the charging infrastructure. The focus of this report is on charging infrastructure for e-motorcycles. This includes privately as well as commercially used e-motorcycles, which might require different types of charging infrastructure.

Indonesia has a total population of around 256 million, with an expected population in 2030 of 294 million.[1] In 2019, the country had some 134 million vehicles, 84% of which (113 million) were motorcycles. Motorcycles also have the largest increase in vehicle numbers, with an annual increase between 2015 and 2019 of 6.2% (Figure 1).[2] This clearly shows the importance of initiating the electrification of motorcycles in the country.

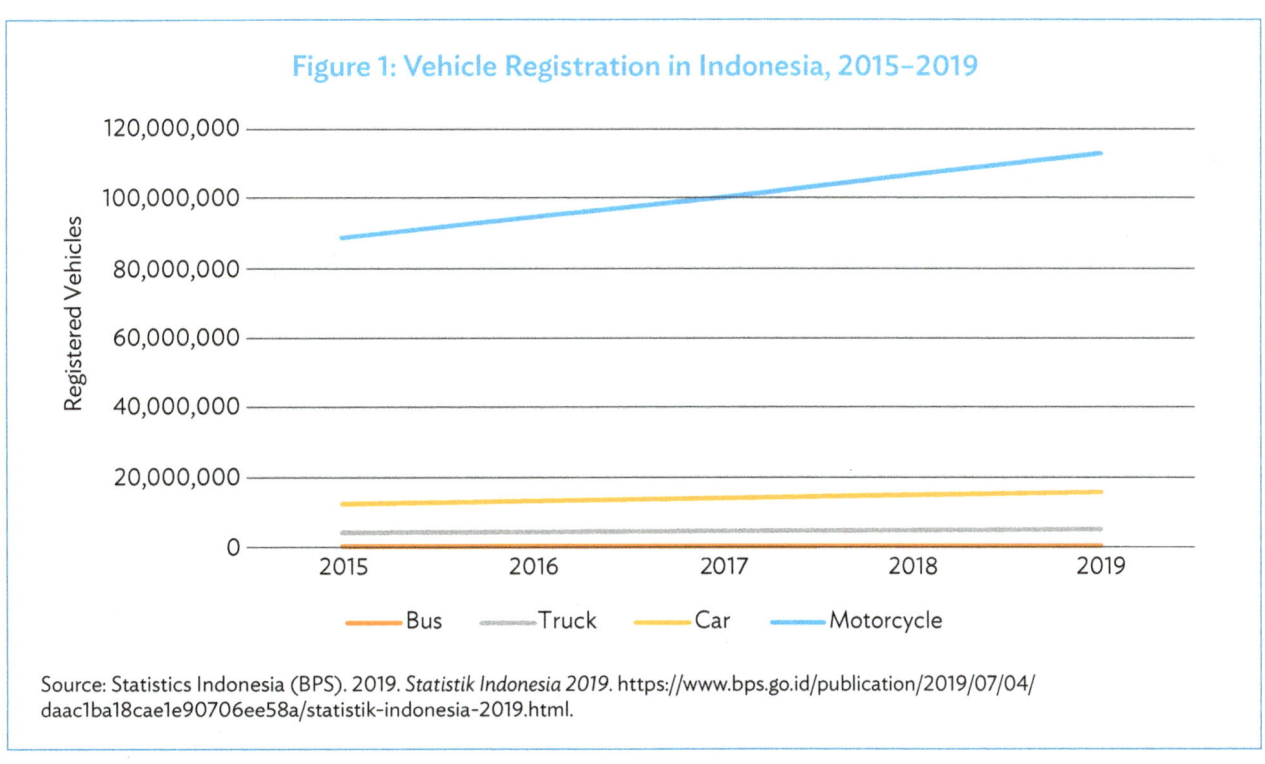

Figure 1: Vehicle Registration in Indonesia, 2015–2019

Source: Statistics Indonesia (BPS). 2019. *Statistik Indonesia 2019*. https://www.bps.go.id/publication/2019/07/04/daac1ba18cae1e90706ee58a/statistik-indonesia-2019.html.

---

[1] National Development Planning Agency (BAPPENAS), Statistics Indonesia (BPS), and United Nations Population Fund (UNFPA). 2018. Indonesia Population Projection 2015-2045. UNFPA Indonesia | Indonesia Population Projection 2015-2045.

[2] BPS. 2019. *Statistik Indonesia 2019*. https://www.bps.go.id/publication/2019/07/04/daac1ba18cae1e90706ee58a/statistik-indonesia-2019.html.

The actual operating number of motorcycles is probably significantly lower than the official registration statistic as the annual sales figures of new motorcycles in Indonesia prior to the coronavirus disease (COVID-19) was 6–6.5 million units and is expected to reach 9.5 million units by 2025.[3] This is an indication of a total market of operational motorcycles of around 70–80 million units (the lifecycle of motorcycles is estimated to be at a maximum of 15 years). Based on actual motorcycle sales statistics, it is estimated that perhaps 30% of the registered motorcycles are either not operating anymore or are seldom operated, with a very low mileage. This is a common phenomenon in vehicle registration data if not based on annual vehicle taxes, as old vehicles are not taken out of registries.

2.2 Geographical Focus

The report focuses on (i) Greater Jakarta: DKI Jakarta, Bogor, Depok, Tangerang, and Bekasi (JABODETABEK); and (ii) Bali. This allows developing the characteristics required for a charging infrastructure for an urban area, as well as for a densely populated nonurban area. Results from these "typical" areas can then be extrapolated to other areas in the country differentiating between urban and nonurban zones.

JABODETABEK has an estimated population of 35 million in 2020, around 30% of which is in DKI Jakarta, 27% in Bogor, 23% in Tangerang, and 20% in Bekasi. By 2030, the population is expected to be at 42 million, with 89% of households owning at least one motorcycle, 36% owning two, and 11% owning three or more.[4] Greater Jakarta has some 20 million motorcycles responsible for 63% of all trips and 76% of all motorized trips in 2018 (footnote 4). This is thus clearly the dominant transport mode. The number of ride-hailing motorcycles in Greater Jakarta is estimated at 1.25 million units.[5]

Bali has an estimated population of 4.3 million in 2020, with the city of Kota Denpasar having some 0.7 million residents (17% of the total) and the rest distributed in eight districts.[6] By 2030, the population is expected to reach 4.9 million. More than 6 million tourists also visit the island annually.[7] This could result in around 100,000 additional visitors to the island during the peak season.[8] As of 2019, Bali had some 3.7 million motorcycles operating.

---

[3] Association of Indonesia Motorcycle Industry (AISI). Statistic Distribution. Jakarta: AISI. https://www.aisi.or.id/statistic/ (accessed 5 July 2021); Statista. Motorcycles - Indonesia. https://www.statista.com/outlook/mmo/motorcycles/indonesia (accessed 5 July 2021).
[4] Japan International Cooperation Agency (JICA). 2019. Annex 02: JABODETABEK Urban Transportation Master Plan.
[5] Government of Indonesia. 2021. Accelerating e-Mobility Adoption and GESI Mainstreaming in e-Mobility Adoption. Presentation. 9 March. Jakarta: Ministry of Transport.
[6] Sensus Penduduk 2020 BPS. Jumlah Penduduk Hasil SP menurut Wilayah dan Jenis Kelamin, Indonesia 2020. https://sensus.bps.go.id/topik/tabular/sp2020/83 (accessed 5 July 2021).
[7] R. Woods. 2020. A Brief Review of Bali Tourism in 2019. *Hotel Investment Strategies*. 4 February. http://hotelinvestmentstrategies.com/a-brief-review-of-bali-tourism-in-2019/.
[8] Based on peak month of arrivals of tourists 2018 and 2019 with around 620,000 arrivals (July) and average stay of 5 days. Bali Hotels Association. Visitors Statistics. https://www.balihotelsassociation.com/media-centre/stats/ (accessed 5 July 2021).

3. Climate Change Background

3.1 Greenhouse Gas Emissions

Total greenhouse gas (GHG) emissions of Indonesia were 1,458 metric tons of carbon dioxide equivalent (MtCO$_2$e), in 2016, 538 MtCO$_2$e of which were from the energy sector.[9] The country is one of the world's largest GHG emitters. Energy sector emissions increased between 2000 and 2016 by a factor of 1.7. Transport GHG emissions in 2018 are estimated at 154 MtCO$_2$e, representing 16% of the total, excluding land use change and forestry emissions (LUCF) or 26% of energy emissions (Figure 2). Land transportation accounted for more than 90% of total transport emissions.

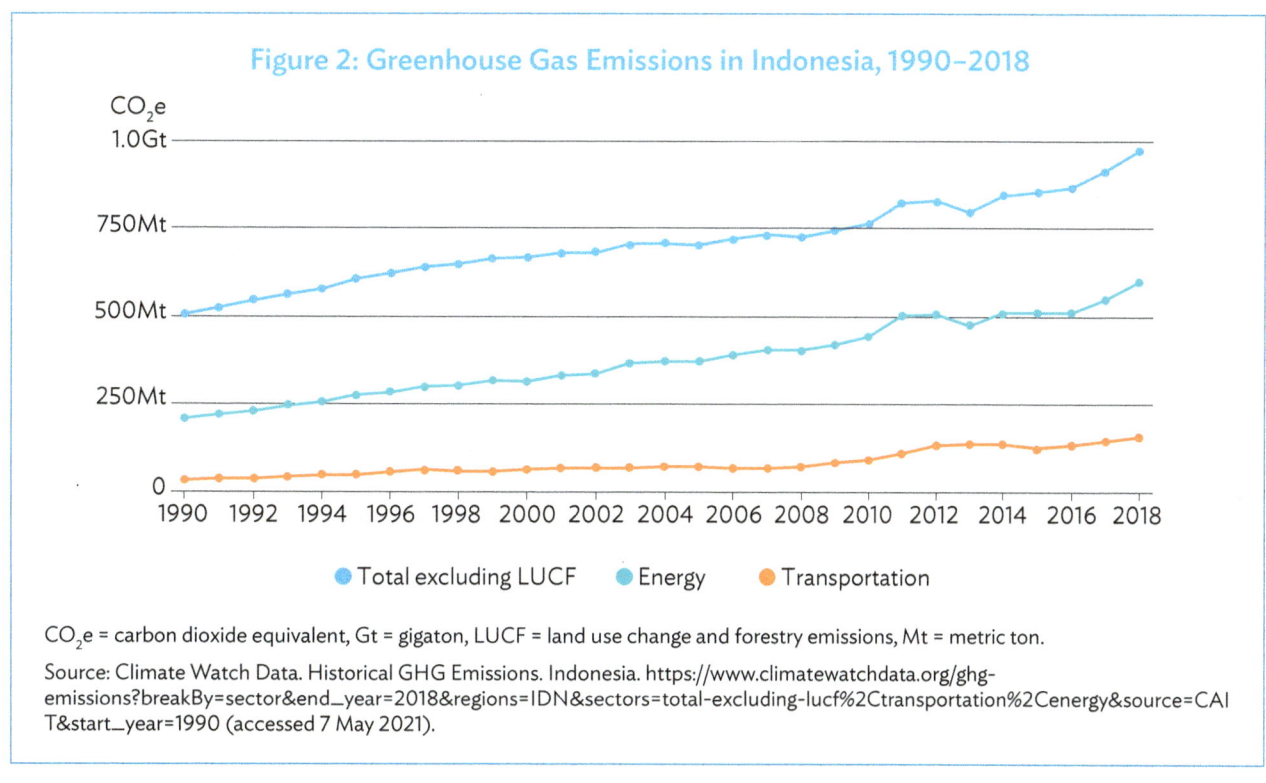

Figure 2: Greenhouse Gas Emissions in Indonesia, 1990–2018

CO$_2$e = carbon dioxide equivalent, Gt = gigaton, LUCF = land use change and forestry emissions, Mt = metric ton.
Source: Climate Watch Data. Historical GHG Emissions. Indonesia. https://www.climatewatchdata.org/ghg-emissions?breakBy=sector&end_year=2018&regions=IDN&sectors=total-excluding-lucf%2Ctransportation%2Cenergy&source=CAIT&start_year=1990 (accessed 7 May 2021).

Figure 3 shows how transport emissions in Indonesia have grown fivefold, or with a compound annual growth rate (CAGR) of nearly 6%, since 1990. Energy emissions in the same period have "only" grown by 4% and total emissions by 2%, i.e., the share of transport emissions is clearly growing.

---

[9] Government of Indonesia. 2018. *Second Biennial Update Report*.

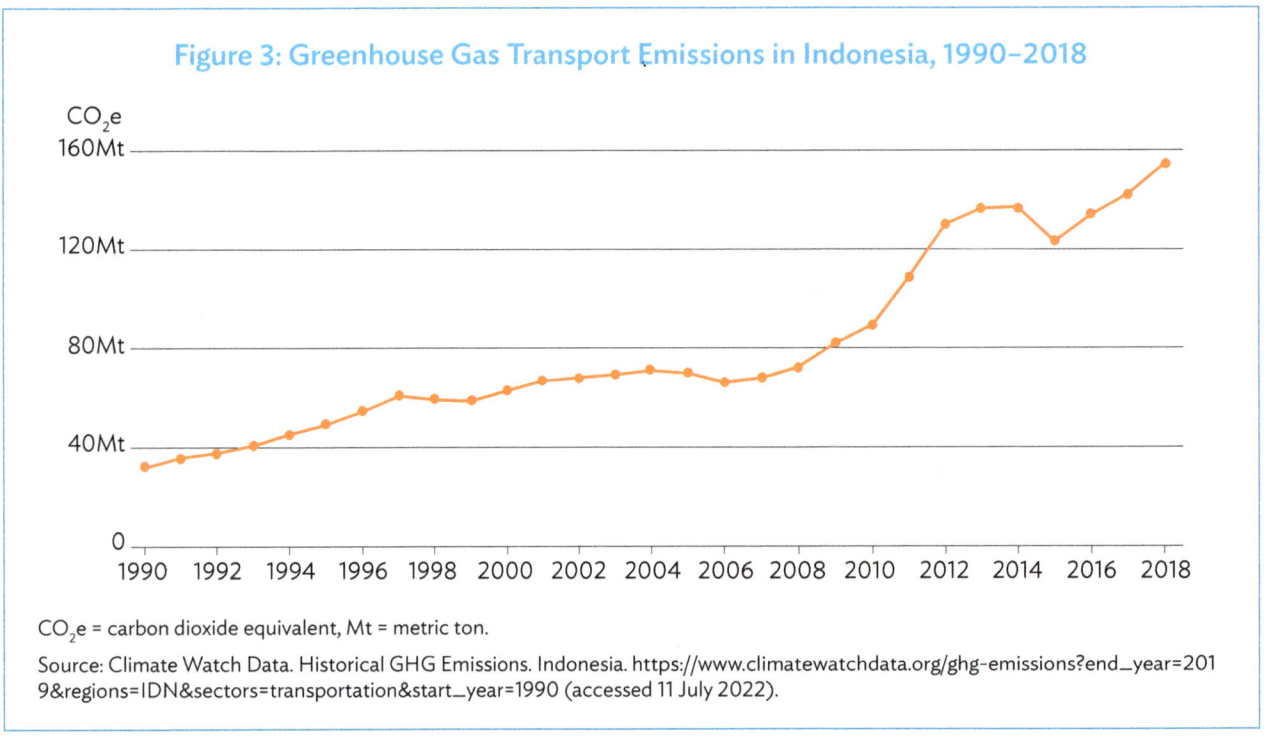

Figure 3: Greenhouse Gas Transport Emissions in Indonesia, 1990–2018

CO_2e = carbon dioxide equivalent, Mt = metric ton.
Source: Climate Watch Data. Historical GHG Emissions. Indonesia. https://www.climatewatchdata.org/ghg-emissions?end_year=2019&regions=IDN&sectors=transportation&start_year=1990 (accessed 11 July 2022).

An initial estimate of GHG emissions of two-wheelers results in around 32 $MtCO_2$ (direct emissions) or 20% of the total from transport in Indonesia.[10]

3.2 National GHG Commitments and Electric Vehicle Policies

Indonesia has committed in its nationally determined contribution (NDC) to reduce its GHG emissions unconditionally by 29% compared to a business-as-usual (BAU) scenario by 2030.[11] To achieve this target, Indonesia has focused on two sectors, i.e., LUCF and the energy sector.

E-mobility tops the political agenda in Indonesia. The Government of Indonesia's strategy on the promotion of electric vehicles aims at (i) decreasing the number of fossil-fuel-based vehicles to reduce emissions; (ii) reducing the growth of oil consumption and imports to increase energy security; and (iii) promoting innovative new technologies that ensure that Indonesia remains competitive as a vehicle manufacturer. The government also recommends the development of electric vehicles and its supporting charging infrastructure to boost electricity demand and resolve problems of oversupply at PLN.[12] Presidential Regulation No. 55 on the acceleration of battery-based electric vehicles for road transport was decreed in 2019. The regulation, which includes fiscal and non-fiscal incentives, focuses on electric two-wheelers and on electrifying public transport buses. In order to improve air quality and to create jobs, Indonesia plans to introduce a fiscal scheme that will offer tax cuts to electric vehicle battery producers and automakers, as well as preferential tariff agreements with other economies

---

[10] Calculation by Grütter Consulting.
[11] Republic of Indonesia. 2021. *2nd Nationally Determined Contribution*. The target has not changed with the updated NDC published in 2021.
[12] BAPPENAS. 2020. *Rencana Pembangunan Jangka Menengah Nasional Tahun 2020-2024*.

that have a high electric vehicle demand. The Ministry of Industry has set targets that, by 2025, 20% of all manufactured vehicles should be low carbon.[13]

3.3 Electricity Generation

The current electricity generation matrix of Indonesia is still dominated by coal (Figure 4), resulting in a high-carbon grid factor of 0.825 kilograms of carbon dioxide equivalent per kilowatt-hour ($kgCO_2e/kWh$).[14]

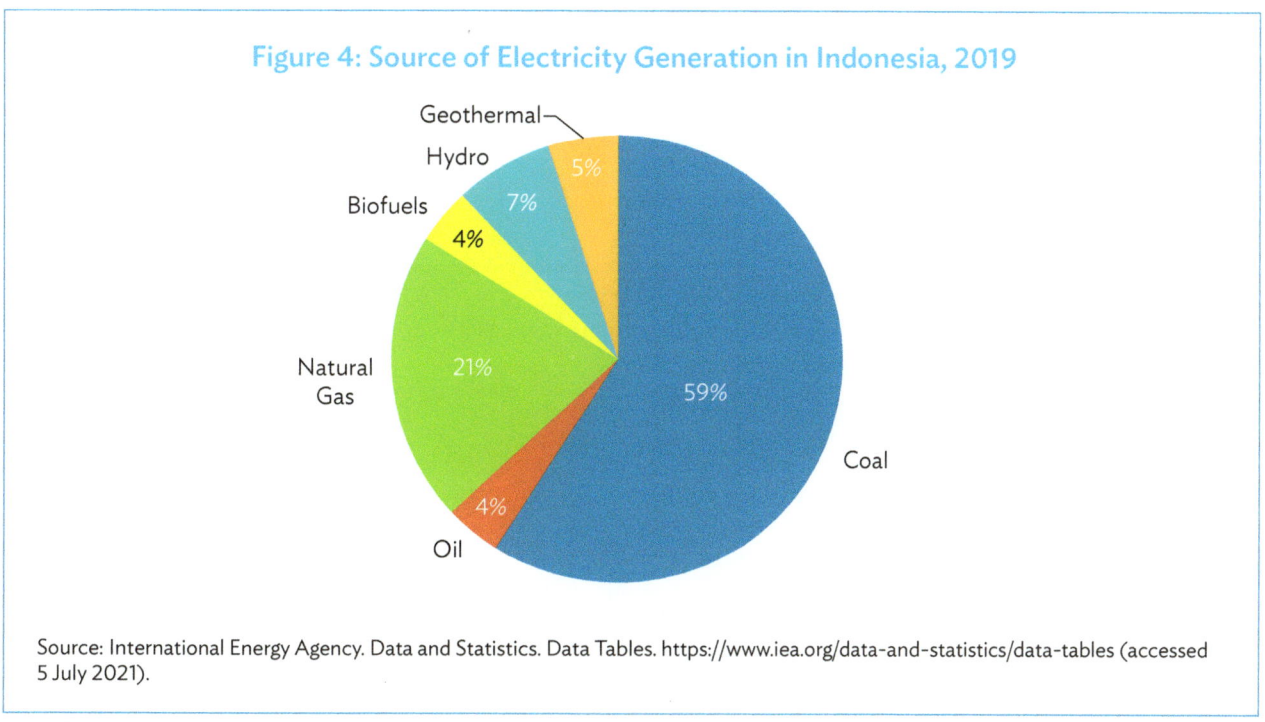

Figure 4: Source of Electricity Generation in Indonesia, 2019

Source: International Energy Agency. Data and Statistics. Data Tables. https://www.iea.org/data-and-statistics/data-tables (accessed 5 July 2021).

The grid factor has, however, been decreasing in the last 2 decades, as can be seen in Figure 5, and the renewable energy potential of the country excluding bioenergy is very high at 410 gigawatts.[15]

Based on the historic trend, the targets set in the NDC, and the renewable energy potential of Indonesia, a significant decrease of the country's electricity production carbon factor can be expected in the next decade.

---

[13] E. Gui and F. Theda. 2021. Indonesia Has Set an Ambitious Target for Electric Vehicles: What Factors Can Support the Nation's Shift to an Electric-Dominated Transport Sector? *Climateworks Centre*. 26 April. https://www.climateworksaustralia.org/news/indonesia-has-set-an-ambitious-target-for-electric-vehicles-what-factors-can-support-the-nations-shift-to-an-electric-dominated-transport-sector/.
[14] Calculation by Grutter Consulting Based on IEA/OECD data for 2018; calculated with GHG emissions of net electricity production. International Energy Agency. Data and Statistics. Data Tables. https://www.iea.org/data-and-statistics/data-tables (accessed 5 July 2021).
[15] Government of Indonesia. 2018. *Second Biennial Update Report*.

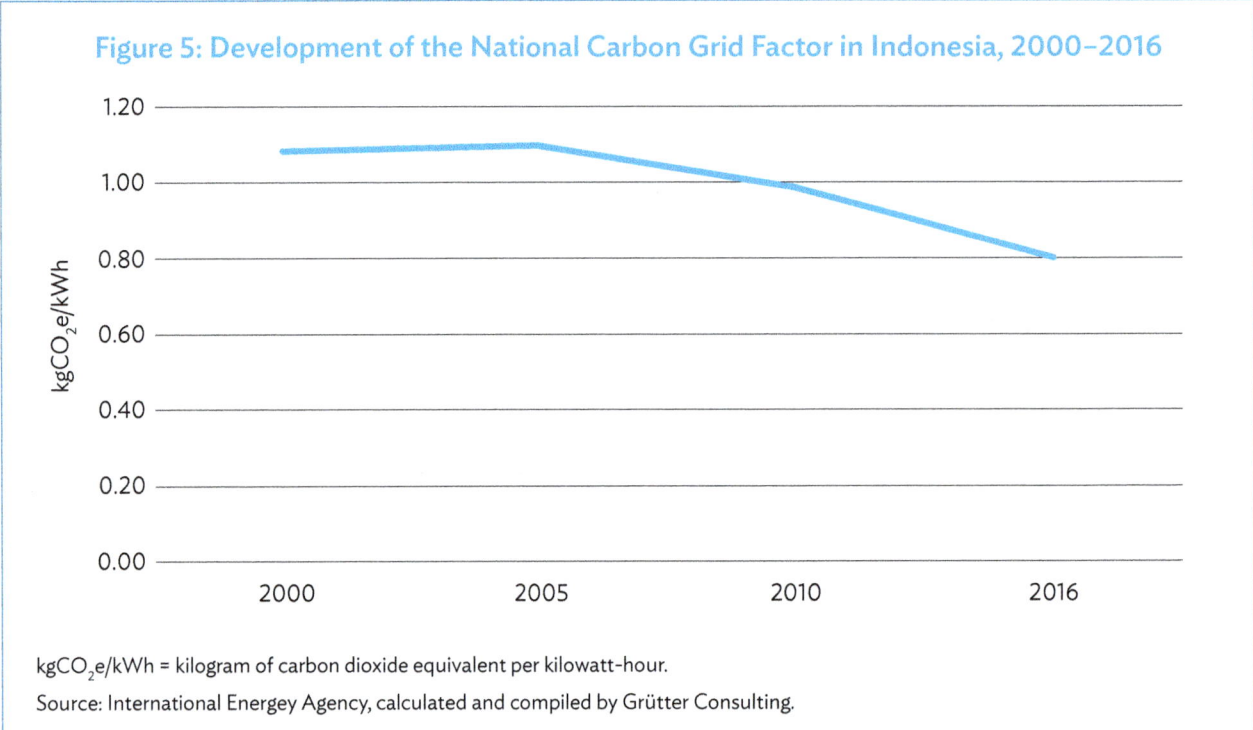

Figure 5: Development of the National Carbon Grid Factor in Indonesia, 2000–2016

$kgCO_2e/kWh$ = kilogram of carbon dioxide equivalent per kilowatt-hour.
Source: International Energey Agency, calculated and compiled by Grütter Consulting.

4. Asia's Experience with Electric Motorcycles

This chapter assesses strategies followed by other Asian Development Bank members to foster e-motorcycles and looks at their experiences. In Asia, e-motorcycles are widely used in the People's Republic of China; Taipei,China; and Viet Nam. This chapter assesses their strategies to foster e-motorcycles and looks at their experiences with charging infrastructure. Others that may be well-known for their proactive e-mobility policies—such as Iceland, the Netherlands, and Norway, as well as the state of California in the United States—have a relatively small number of motorcycles used, thus they are not considered in this chapter.

4.1 Experiences with Promotion Policies for Electric Motorcycles

Experiences in the People's Republic of China and Taipei,China

Taipei,China has been subsidizing e-motorcycles since 1996. Between 1998 and 2002, Taipei,China's Environmental Protection Agency spent $60 million on e-motorcycle subsidies, reducing purchase prices to a level comparable to gasoline-powered units. However, the program inefficiently stimulated demand because of a lack of consumer confidence in battery reliability, insufficient charging infrastructure, and e-motorcycles' lack of convenience. From 2009 to 2012, Taipei,China promoted lithium battery e-motorcycles, subsidizing some 26,000 units. Since 2013, central and local governments offered new electric two-wheeler subsidies from $240 (small scooter) to $1,200 (e-motorcycles; central plus local subsidies, including if a two-stroker is eliminated). Subsidies have been declining gradually to $1,000 in 2020 and $800 in 2021. Charging stations are also subsidized with up to 50% of construction costs, along with publicly accessible land.[16] The Ministry of Economic Affairs picked Gogoro over other e-motorcycle brands to set up Taipei,China's 1,300 battery swap stations. Battery swap sites are placed every 500 meters (m) in urban Taipei,China and turn up every 2–5 kilometers (km) in other parts of the island. Nonfinancial incentives include exclusive parking spaces, preferential parking fees, and prohibition for two-strokers in certain areas. Table 1 shows the main components of Taipei,China's e-scooter development road map from 2018 to 2022.

---

[16] B. M. Lin. 2018. Presentation on Taipei,China for Session 1: E-Vehicles and New Transport Technology. 12 September. Manila: ADB.

Table 1: Main Components of Taipei,China's E-Motorcycle Road Map 2018–2022

Area[a]	Targets[a]	Current Status[b]
Promote common components of e-motorcycle manufacturing	Common batteries (by 2018), engines (by 2019) and other components (by 2020)	Some manufacturers share Gogoro batteries, but the major competitor (KYMCO) is putting up its own battery swap stations with different battery types. The goal of common components could thus not be achieved.
Foster charging or swapping stations	Targeted number of charging stations: 2,100 by 2018, 3,500 by 2020, and 5,000 by 2022	Some 2,100 battery swap stations of Gogoro are operational in 2021 and KYMCO plans to install another 1,500 units in 2021.
Lower price of e-motorcycles	Target price below $2,300 for higher-powered and below $1,500 for lower-powered electric two-wheeler prior to 2020	The lowest cost and most popular Gogoro model in 2021 is VIVA Mix with a price tag of $2,200 but this excludes batteries and a riding and battery plan needs to be made.
Establish non-price incentives	Preferential parking spaces and lower parking costs and from 2020 prohibition for two-stroke motorcycles in some areas	Two-stroke vehicles are basically only mopeds while motorcycles are all four-stroke—thus, the impact of this incentive is very limited.

[a] B. M. Lin. 2018. Presentation on Taipei,China for Session 1: E-Vehicles and New Transport Technology. 12 September. Manila: ADB.
[b] Grütter Consulting.
Source: Authors.

The large subsidies did have a positive impact on e-motorcycle sales but have not resulted in a paradigm change of purchase practices. Gogoro sales (by far the largest electric scooter manufacturer in Taipei,China) plummeted 43% in 2020, while overall motorcycle sales increased by 3.3% in the same period and dropped another 25% in the first quarter of 2021, with the overall market growing by 13%.[17] Total market share of e-motorcycle sales grew from 3% in 2017 to 10% in 2018, to 15% in 2019, and then back to around 10% in 2020.[18] This loss of market share coincided again with decreased subsidy levels.

In the PRC, electric two-wheelers dominate the market without massive subsidies, with more than 200 million units, the majority of which are deemed to be electric scooters. Unique to the PRC is that it uses nonfinancial incentives that in fact have not been targeted toward e-scooters but have effectively favored them. Nearly every major PRC city has banned gasoline-powered motorcycles but electric bicycles (e-bikes) and scooters are frequently classified as nonmotorized transportation due to being equipped with (decorative) pedals and thus exempt from the motorcycle prohibition. In the 1990s, the PRC had also attempted to foster e-motorcycles but without much success. The rapid expansion of e-scooters came when this was the only alternative for customers if they wanted to use a two-wheeler in cities. Thus, the ultimate driver of the electric two-wheeler boom in the PRC has been the local motorcycle bans. E-scooters do create less air pollution, but have no different impact than gasoline motorcycles on congestion and safety. The loosely enforced e-scooter standards allowed them to continue operations, although some cities since 2010 started banning or restricting them.[19]

---

[17] MotorCyclesData. 2021. https://MotorCyclesData.com.
[18] J. Quartly. 2019. Electric Scooters Could be the Future of Mobility. 23 October. https://topics.amcham.com.tw/2019/10/electric-scooters-future-of-mobility/; G. Liao. 2020. KYMCO has been the best-selling brand for the first nine months of 2020. 6 October.
[19] C. J. Yang. 2010. Launching Strategy for Electric Vehicles. *Technological Forecasting and Social Change*. 77 (2010). pp. 831–834; W. Shepard.2016. Why Chinese Cities Are Banning the Biggest Adoption of Green Transportation in History. *Forbes*. 18 May. https://www.forbes.com/sites/wadeshepard/2016/05/18/as-china-chokes-on-smog-the-biggest-adoption-of-green-transportation-in-history-is-being-banned/?sh=7c4a4b5141b1.

The following conclusions can be learned:

- The PRC is dominated by slow, low-powered electric scooters or mopeds, and not motorcycles comparable to the fossil-fuel-based 100-cc units dominating the streets of Indonesia.
- The surge of electric scooters in the PRC has been due to fossil-fuel-based motorcycles not being allowed to operate in most cities. Thus, electric scooters were the only motorized option instead of a car or public transport.
- Taipei,China tried twice to foster e-motorcycles through financial incentives and succeeded in increasing the market share to around 15% of sales. However decreasing subsidies have been paired with decreasing market shares of e-motorcycles. The sustainability of support measures seems to be limited and e-motorcycles are seemingly still not competitive in terms of price and convenience to customers, despite having a dense battery swap network.

Experiences in Viet Nam

As of 2014, Viet Nam had around 43 million registered motorcycles.[20] The electric two-wheeler market peaked in 2016 and then started dropping again due to frustration of users over vehicles' low quality.

Gasoline motorcycles are four-stroke in Hanoi and Euro 2 or 3 with an engine displacement of 110 cc. Average urban fuel consumption is around 2.5 liters (l) per 100 km with an average annual mileage of 4,100 km.[21] Good quality gasoline motorcycles cost between $700–$1,400, while low-powered e-scooters are available at a lower price. However, even good quality e-scooters that have a comparable investment cost still do not have the convenience of a gasoline unit in terms of power, speed, and driving range. Also, batteries need to be replaced around every 1–2 years and are lead-acid units with a high potential for environmental damage. The majority of electric two-wheelers in Viet Nam are low-powered e-scooters used by students. E-motorcycles are not frequent.

Motorcycle use in Viet Nam. More people use conventional motorcycles than e-scooters in Hanoi (photo by Grütter Consulting).

---

[20] Viet Nam National Traffic Safety Committee. **Trang thông tin điện tử Uỷ ban An toàn Giao thông Quốc gia** (antoangiaothong.gov.vn).
[21] World Bank. 2014. *Motorcycle, Motor Scooter and Motorbike Ownership & Use in Hanoi*. Washington, DC: World Bank; original household survey data.

E-scooters have lead-acid batteries and are charged overnight. Battery swap facilities are not available. A Swiss-financed electric scooter and e-bike sharing program was of limited success and folded due to high prices and limited public interest. The system was based on a few fixed points, i.e., not free floating and thus of limited convenience for users. Also, most students (which were the target group) already owned an electric or conventional scooter.

4.2 Experiences with Charging Infrastructure for Electric Motorcycles

Electric Vehicle Batteries—Fixed and Swappable

A battery needs to be recharged when it is (almost) empty.[22] In many electric vehicles, the batteries are fixed and the charger is also on board. The number of battery packs varies with the size and the required range of the vehicle. The charging cable generally has a plug at each end, so it can be carried in the cargo space of the vehicle. The charging plug can simply be plugged into a normal wall socket (in houses, offices, commercial spaces, etc.).

If the electric vehicle has swappable batteries, no charger is needed on board (Figure 6). Batteries are charged outside the electric vehicle in a swapping station, i.e., the swapping station is at the same time a charging station. The swapping station can have a plugged grid connection or a fixed grid connection, depending on the size and power need (Figure 7).

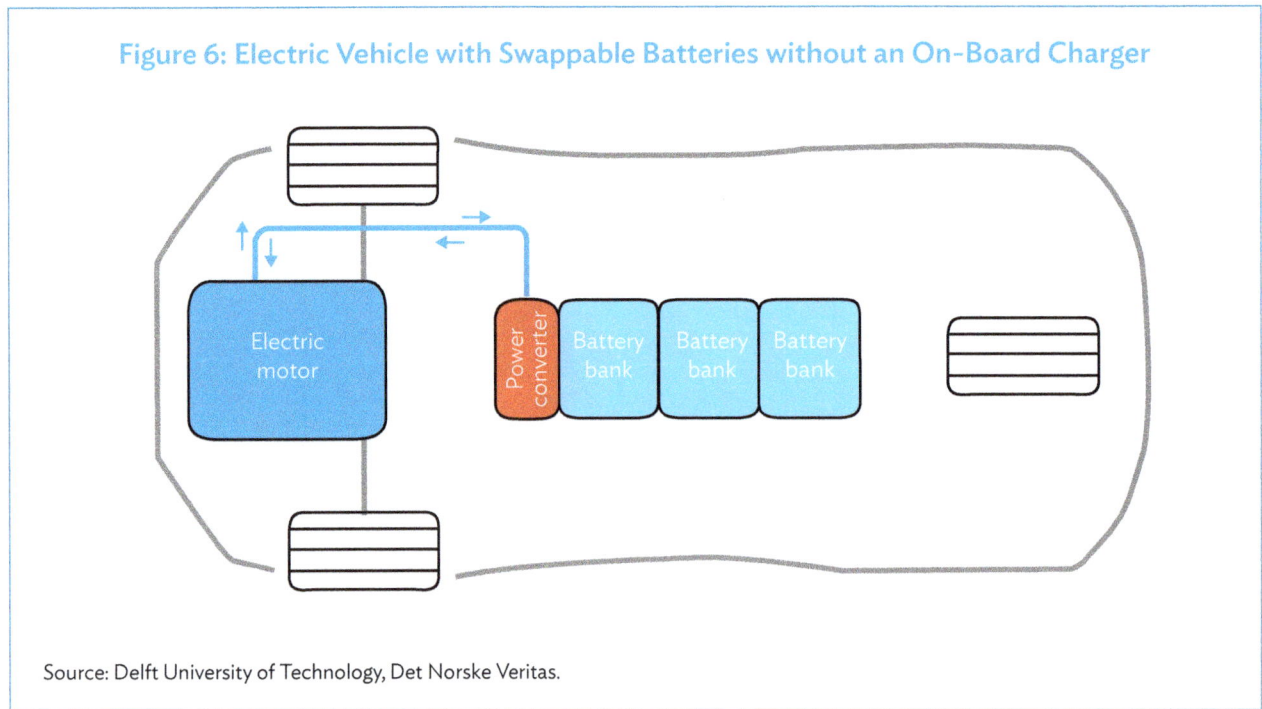

Figure 6: Electric Vehicle with Swappable Batteries without an On-Board Charger

Source: Delft University of Technology, Det Norske Veritas.

---

[22] Only lithium-ion batteries are assumed in this report, no other types of chemistries.

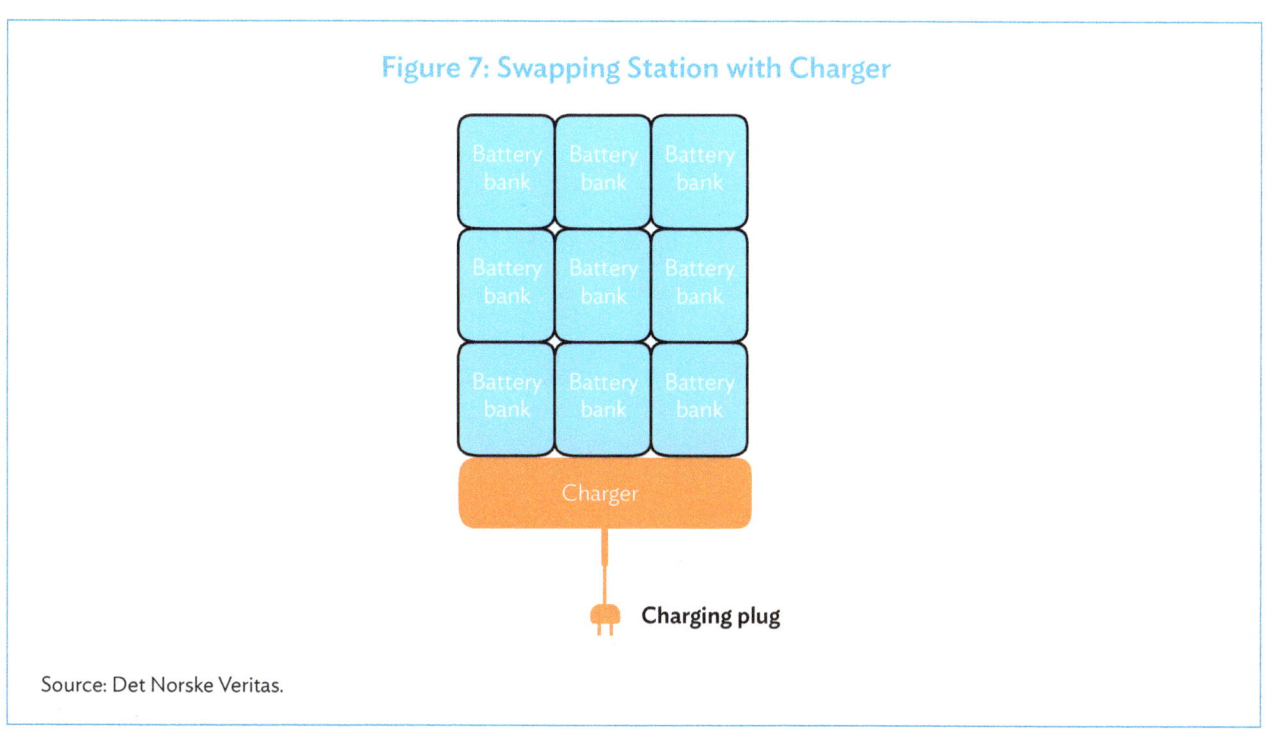

Figure 7: Swapping Station with Charger

Source: Det Norske Veritas.

A simple charging cable and plug will suffice for a two- or three-wheeler. However, for larger electric vehicles like passenger cars or trucks, a dedicated charging point is needed for power supply and safety. For these cables, plugs and charging points, various international standards of the International Electrotechnical Commission (IEC) are adhered to (the latter is working on standards for swappable batteries in two-wheelers).[23]

Technical Properties of Electric Vehicle Chargers

In this section, the hardware-related technologies of charge points are enumerated. The terms mentioned in this section are applicable to nonswappable batteries, hence the charging of the e-motorcycle (or electric vehicle) occurs onboard with the battery present in the e-motorcycle during the charging process. Charging of an e-motorcycle can be conducted either by alternating (AC) or direct (DC) current charging technology; in both approaches, the power from the grid is converted from AC to DC and is used to charge the battery that is present in the e-motorcycle. Technologies of electric vehicle charging stations can be differentiated based on the charging level, the charging mode and the charging system (Figure 8).

---

[23] The IEC is an international standards organization that prepares and publishes international standards for all electrical, electronic, and related technologies, collectively known as "electrotechnology."

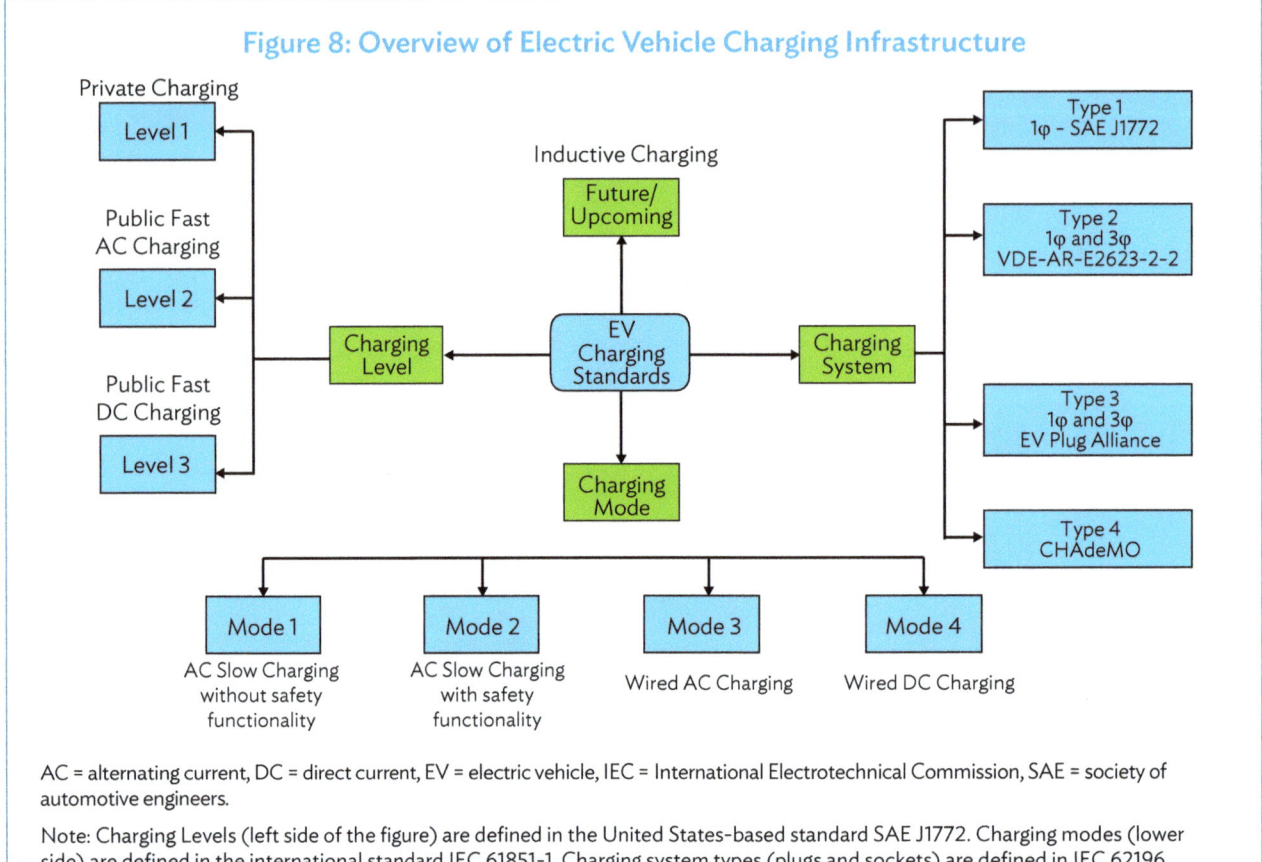

Figure 8: Overview of Electric Vehicle Charging Infrastructure

AC = alternating current, DC = direct current, EV = electric vehicle, IEC = International Electrotechnical Commission, SAE = society of automotive engineers.

Note: Charging Levels (left side of the figure) are defined in the United States-based standard SAE J1772. Charging modes (lower side) are defined in the international standard IEC 61851-1. Charging system types (plugs and sockets) are defined in IEC 62196, referring to other standards.

Source: Det Norske Veritas.

Charging Levels, SAE J1772

AC charging of an e-motorcycle is executed utilizing the AC/DC power converter that is present on board. AC charging can also be listed based on charging levels. AC Level 1 refers to a 120-volt single phase AC charging capability of maximum 16 A. Level 1 charging can hence be carried out by a line cord charger that can be plugged into the e-motorcycle and a wall socket at home. Level 2 charging refers to a 240-volt single phase AC charging capability of maximum 80 A. Level 2 charging is hence carried out by a dedicated e-motorcycle charger from which a cord can be plugged into the e-motorcycle.

Charging Modes, IEC 61851-1

The IEC standard 61851-1:2017 "Electric Vehicle Conductive Charging System - Part 1: General Requirements" defines AC and DC charging modes for all electric vehicle supply equipment for charging electric road vehicles, with a rated supply voltage up to 1,000 volts (V) AC or up to 1,500 V DC and a rated output voltage up to 1,000 V AC or up to 1,500 V DC. The AC charging modes are listed as Mode 1, Mode 2, and Mode 3; the DC charging mode is Mode 4. In summary: Mode 1 and Mode 2 are suitable for charging an emotorcycle or an e-scooter. Mode 3 charging would require special adaptations to the e-motorcycle connector or plug. Mode 4 DC charging is unsuitable for two or three-wheelers.

Mode 1 (AC)

This mode entails slow AC charging via a regular electrical socket (e.g., in the house or office). There is no communication between the vehicle and the charging point. It is therefore required to provide an earth wire to the electric vehicle and have an external means of protection against faults. In many places, this form of charging is considered unsafe and is not allowed due to the lack of communication and protection devices. However, in the case of two/three-wheelers, Mode 1 charging could be considered due to the limited battery capacity (and therefore a lower safety risk; Figure 9).

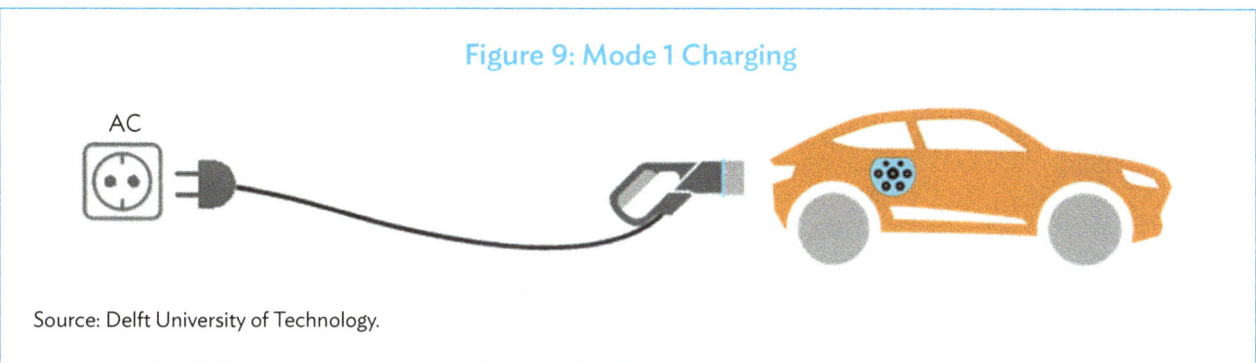

Figure 9: Mode 1 Charging

Source: Delft University of Technology.

Mode 2 (AC)

This mode provides for slow AC charging from a regular electricity socket. In addition, the charging cable is equipped with an In-Cable Control and Protection Device, that is responsible for control, communication and protection (including residual current protection). This is the preferred charging mode for two or three-wheelers (Figure 10).

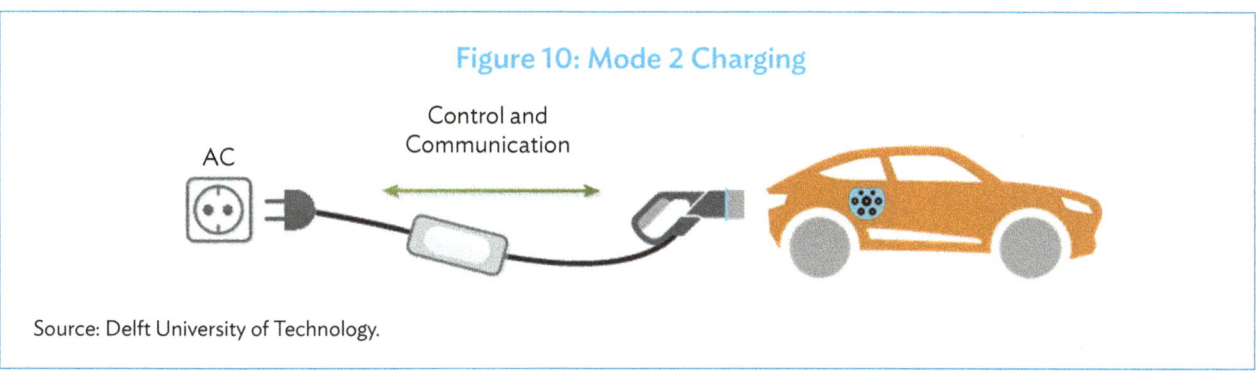

Figure 10: Mode 2 Charging

Source: Delft University of Technology.

Mode 3 (AC)

This mode entails both slow and semi-fast charging via a dedicated electrical socket (a wall box or a charge pole) for electric vehicle/e-motorcycle charging. The charger (or the charging point) has an electric vehicle specific socket, generally corresponding to Type 1 or Type 2 (see below). A charging cable permanently fixed to the charger, or with an electric vehicle plug on both sides, is used to connect the electric vehicle to the charger. The charging station is responsible for the control, communication, and protection of the charging process (including residual current protection). This mode is commonly used for public charging stations for four-wheelers (passenger cars and small trucks/vans; see Figure 11).

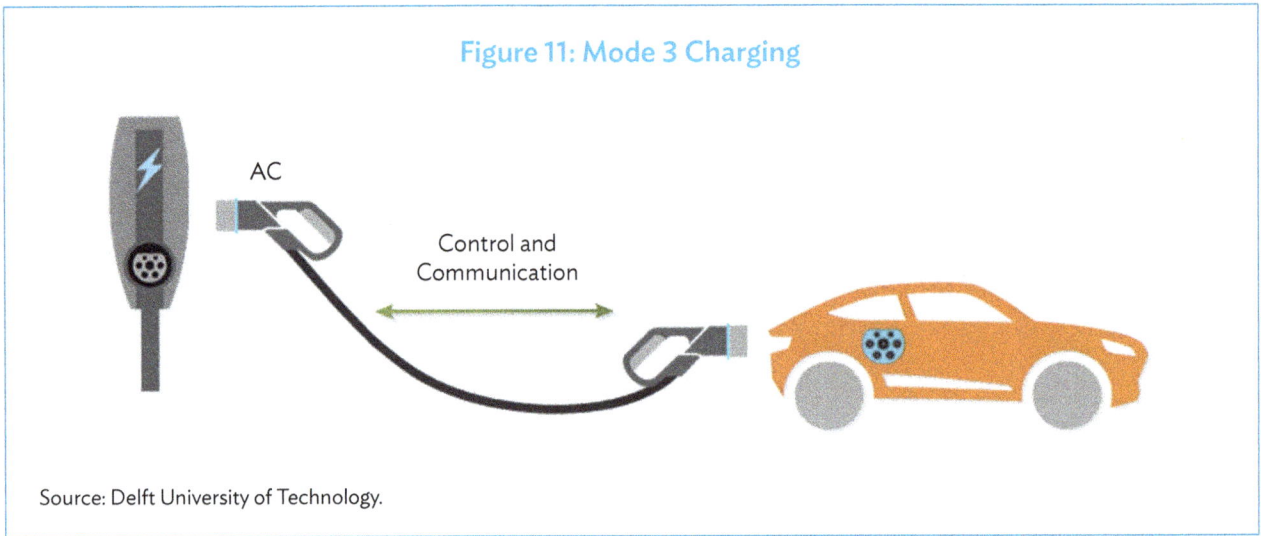

Figure 11: Mode 3 Charging

Source: Delft University of Technology.

Mode 4 (DC)

DC enables charging power levels beyond 50 kilowatts (kW) for electric vehicles. DC charging is defined under Mode 4 according to IEC 61851-1. Mode 4 uses a dedicated electrical socket for electric vehicle charging. The charger has a permanently fixed cable with an electric vehicle plug. Mode 4 is specifically used for DC, which is recommended for fast charging of larger electric vehicles; it is not suitable for two- or three-wheelers because their batteries are relatively small and cannot handle the power. In the case of DC, the AC/DC converter is located within the charging station. The control, communication, and protection functions are built into the charging station (Figure 12).

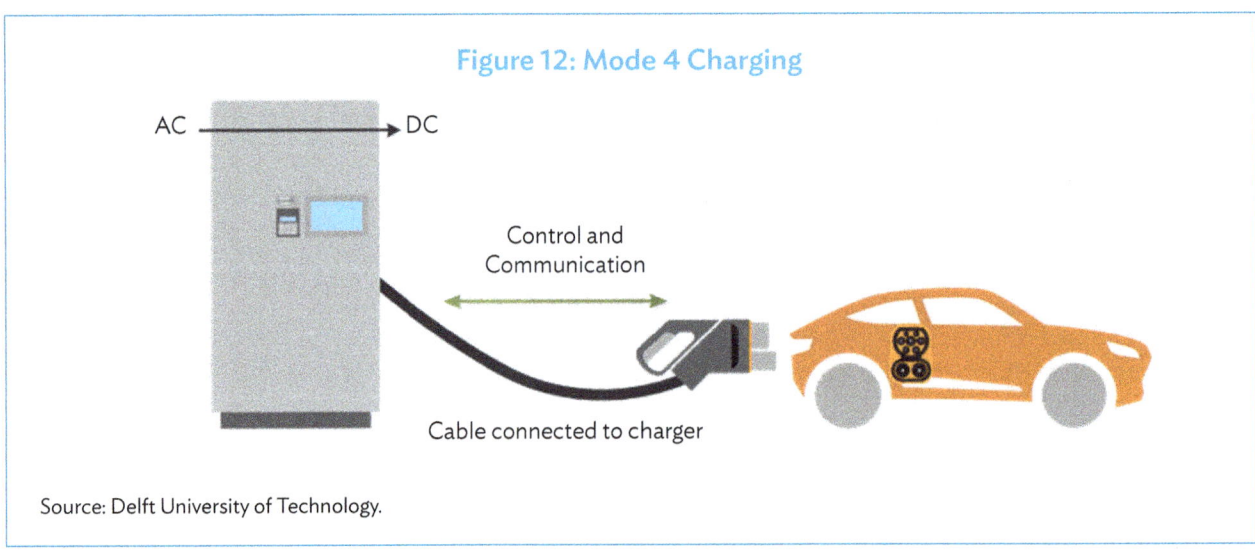

Figure 12: Mode 4 Charging

Source: Delft University of Technology.

Charging Types: Connectors (Plugs and Sockets)

The types of AC charging connectors for Mode 3 are listed as Type 1 and Type 2 and are used globally (Figure 13). Mode 1 and Mode 2 charging cables and plugs are connected to regular wall sockets in the office, commercial, or residential building.

Type 1 refers to a single-phase charger that is primarily used in the US, which is defined according to the standard SAE J1772-2017 (equal to IEC 62196 Type 1). The Type 1 plug contains three power pins that are phase (L1), Neutral (N) and Earth pin (E) for single-phase charging.

Type 2, referred commonly as Mennekes, is a single- and three-phase charger that is primarily used in Europe, which is defined according to the standard IEC 62196 Type 2. The Type 2 plug contains three or five power pins, which are one- or three-phase pins (L1, L2, and L3), Neutral (N), and Earth pin (E).

For DC charging, other types of connectors are available, such as CCS (Europe, US), ChaDeMo (mainly in Japan), Tesla (worldwide for Tesla cars), and GB/T (PRC).

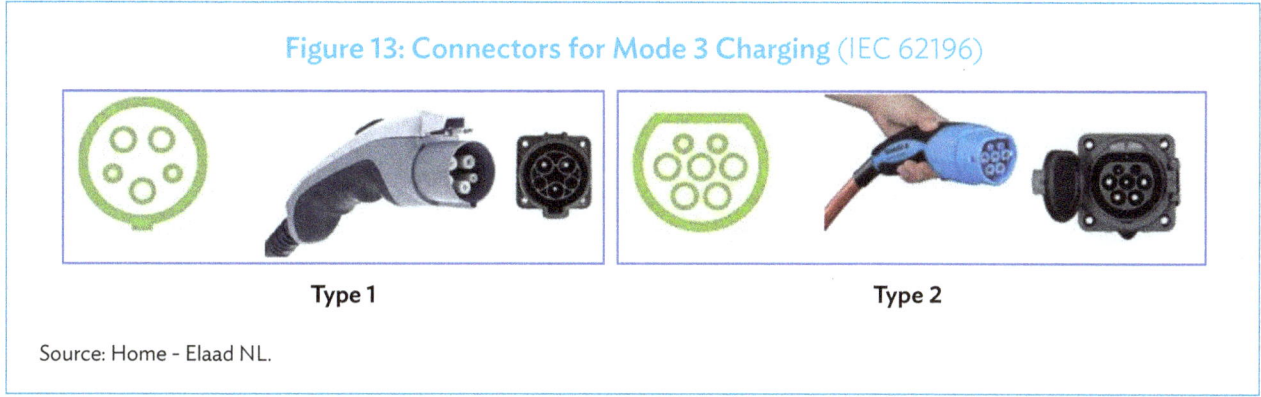

Figure 13: Connectors for Mode 3 Charging (IEC 62196)

Type 1   Type 2

Source: Home - Elaad NL.

Technical Properties of Battery Swap Stations

Battery swapping for cars or buses is complex and expensive and asks for a sophisticated regional battery logistics organization. However, swapping is potentially a viable option for two and threewheelers. This means that the (almost) empty battery is taken off the vehicle and recharged inside the house or building, using Mode 1 or Mode 2 charging. After recharging, the battery can be put back onto the vehicle for the next ride. Alternatively, at removal of the empty battery, it can be swapped for a full battery and the ride can continue almost immediately. Of course, this practice depends on the ease of removing the battery from the vehicle and on the weight of the battery. This is a general practice in the PRC, the US, and Europe for electric bicycles.

At present, the Level 1 portable charger is most commonly used for e-motorcycle charging, since separate charger installation is not required. Level 1 charging takes from 1 to a few hours to fully charge an e-motorcycle depending on the model of the vehicle and the available grid power.

Battery swapping stations provide a viable solution to provide faster and/or frequent recharges. Battery swapping also helps in reducing space and weight constraints since there is no necessity for an onboard charger on the e-motorcycle. Models that have swappable or extractable batteries, such as KYMCO and Gogoro, are currently the early adopters of this strategy. Battery swapping provides portability since the batteries can be taken for charging in a dedicated swapping station or in personal places. The driver of the e-motorcycle can swap batteries and continue to operate without needing to take breaks for recharging. This charging strategy is hence interesting for delivery service operators and for fleet e-motorcycles.

Gogoro, founded in 2011, introduced e-motorcycles with battery infrastructure in Taipei,China with around 2,100 local swapping station locations across convenience stores, supermarkets, and parking lots.[24] KYMCO provides a network of battery swap stations along with the ambition to standardize universal removable and swappable batteries.[25] Battery vending machines are deployed where batteries can be swapped.

Standards

Lack of standardization is one issue that inhibits public swapping stations, because batteries from different brands will have different dimensions and different connectors. This means that swapping systems, to be successful, require a large number of same-brand electric vehicle motorcycles or fleet operations, wherein all electric vehicles have the same type of batteries, and swapping stations that are owned, leased, or contracted by the fleet operator are placed at locations where most of the electric vehicles will pass during their daily routes, e.g. at the base station of the fleet company or at popular sites. Gogoro charging stations are, for example, available around every 500 m in urban Taipei,China and every 2 to 5 km in other parts of the island.

Presently, international standardization is ongoing at the IEC regarding charging for two- and three-wheelers at a voltage of 120 V max. This is mainly focusing on electrical safety, not on standardizing dimensions of batteries of swap stations. The new standard, IEC 61851-3, includes requirements for conductive charging <120 volt direct current, battery swap systems, and communications between the electric vehicle and the charger, and between the battery and the charger inside the swap/recharge station. Appendix 2 has an overview of this standard under development.

Technical Properties

Table 2 shows the technical properties of a typical swappable electric vehicle battery and battery swap station.

The maximum charging power of a swappable battery is in the range of 1 to 2 kW. The actual charging power will vary and can be controlled by the battery or the swap station, or it can be limited by the house or building connection. At maximum charging power, the charging time is around 1 hour. If less power is available, the charging will take longer.

The battery needs a battery management system (BMS) that is an integral part of the battery pack. The BMS must safeguard the battery (monitor voltage, current, power, and temperature) and issue warnings and stop operations if something is wrong. Furthermore, the BMS must calculate the actual energy content of the battery; this is the state of charge (SoC). The SoC is proportional to the remaining driving range (distance). The BMS will also record and keep track of the use and the health status of the battery.

---

[24] Gogoro. https://www.gogoro.com/gogoro-network/.
[25] *Kymco.* 2021. Ionex Premiere Conference. 18 March. https://www.kymco.com/news/ionex-premier-conference.

Table 2: Technical Properties of a Typical Swappable Electric Vehicle Battery and a Typical Swap Station

Battery metric	Value	Remark
Voltage	24 V or 48 V	<60 V for electrical safety
Energy capacity	1–2 kWh	Typical range
Charging power (max)	1–2 kW	Typical range
Weight	10–15 kg	Typical range
Dimensions (LxWxH)	350 x 200 x 150 mm	Typical values
Swap station metric	Value	Remark
Number of batteries	10–30	Typical range
Charging power (max)	10–30 kW	At 1 kW per battery
Grid connection power	15–40 kW	Additional power, e.g., for cooling

kg = kilogram, kW = kilowatt, kWh = kilowatt-hour, mm = millimeter, V = volt.
Source: Gogoro, Sun Mobility, Det Norske Veritas analysis.

To inform the driver about the battery status and the SoC, the battery needs to have a communication system. Furthermore, the battery also needs to communicate with the swap/recharge station. Communication can be arranged through wires and pins in the battery connectors, or though wireless communication. Information can be shared through displays on the vehicle and the swap station, or there can be a smartphone app.

A monitoring system would be desired to keep track of all batteries, electric vehicles, and swap station operations, preferably in a coordinated way. Therefore, a monitoring and back-office system would be needed.
The complexity of the back-office system depends on the monitoring functions needed in the fleet operation.

One battery is sufficient for a light two-wheeler, e.g., a small scooter. Larger two-wheelers can be equipped with two or three or even more swappable batteries. For standardization of swappable batteries, it is important that the batteries have standardized physical dimensions, voltage level, physical connectors, and communication protocols. For the near future, this can be arranged by fleet-based operation in a collaboration between a few electric vehicle builders, battery suppliers, swap station suppliers and/or operators, and electric vehicle fleet owners and/or operators (the latter could be, e.g., a delivery company or a ride-hailing company). However, in the future, a more generalized standardization may emerge (e.g., at a national level) that would enable interoperability of electric vehicles, batteries, and swap stations of different brands and vendors.

Environmental and Safety Aspects

It might be interesting to place battery swap stations near fuel stations, because they are located on traffic routes in a dense network, and drivers are used to going there. Care must be taken that the national regulations for co-location of electric vehicle charge and/or swap stations and fuel stations are followed. As a common rule, the charge points shall be installed outside the extent of hazardous areas at the fuel service stations (mainly areas designated as explosive atmospheres, e.g., around the fuel hoses of the pumps). It is often required to conduct a detailed risk assessment about the safety, installation, handling, and operation of the charging station at fuel stations, but also at other locations. This is even more important, because public charging and battery swapping is new to the general public, so safety and user acceptance are very important.

Experience with Swapping Systems

Taipei,China

Gogoro is the market leader for e-motorcycles in Taipei,China. While the customer owns the Gogoro motorcycle, the batteries are owned by the company and the client needs to subscribe to a membership to gain access to a swapping network with battery reservation performed through an app. The subscription includes the batteries and the swapping service. If your battery does not work anymore, you can just replace it with a fresh one in a swap station and Gogoro will take care of the repair. The energy charged into the battery is billed separately. Gogoro uses algorithms to optimize where to distribute battery inventory and when to charge its batteries. Thus, it can also take advantage of charging when prices are low and avoids overstressing the grid. The company now sees itself becoming more of an energy utility, offering city-wide battery storage and feeding back into the power grid if needed, rather than a motorcycle manufacturer.[26] Currently some 2,100 battery swap stations of Gogoro are available in Taipei,China.[27] This results in an average of one swap station per 17 square kilometers (km^2). The number of Gogoro e-motorcycles in Taipei,China is around 375,000, i.e., there is a swap station for every 180 e-motorcycles. KYMCO plans to install another 1,500 units in 2021.

---

[26] K. Hao. 2021. The Future of Transportation May Be About Sharing Batteries, Not Vehicles. *Quartz*. 25 September. https://qz.com/1084282/the-future-of-transportation-may-be-about-sharing-batteries-not-vehicles/.
[27] *Gogoro*. 2020. 2020–A Year of Positive Change. 31 December. https://www.gogoro.com/news/2020-year-in-review/.

5. Electric Two-Wheeler User Categories

Figure 14 shows different segments and profiles of motorcycle users.

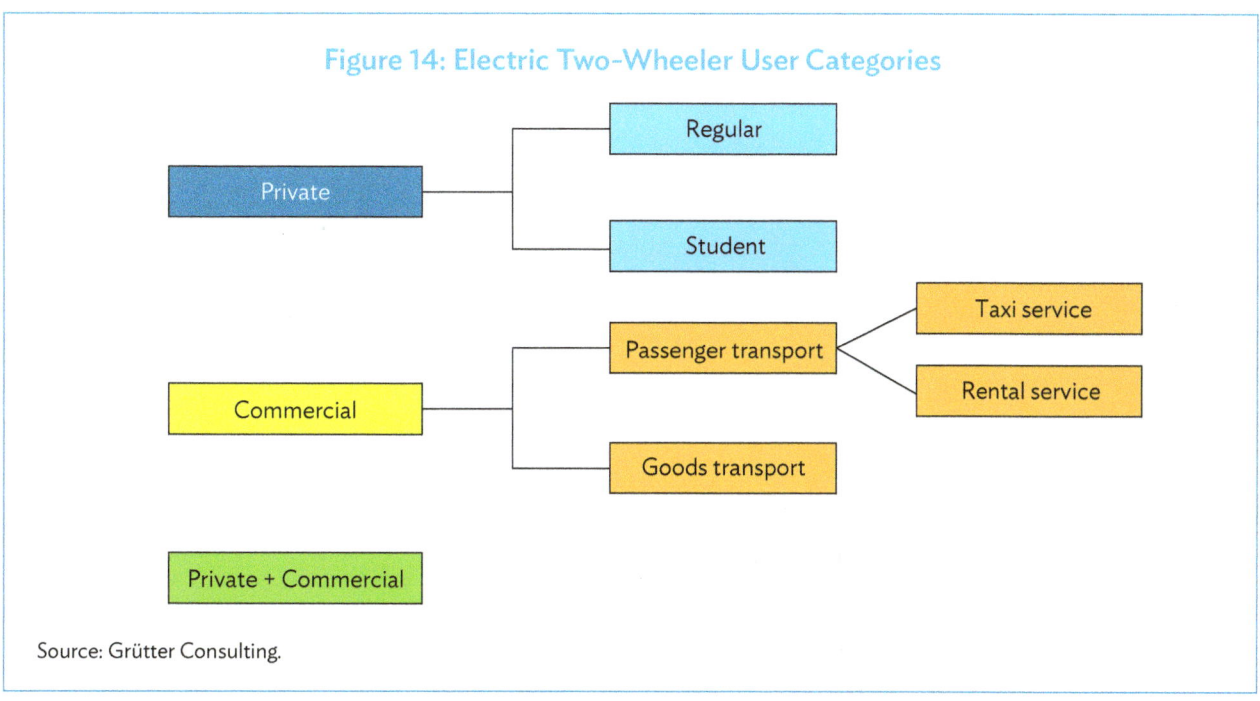

Source: Grütter Consulting.

The different users have a distinct profile, use their vehicles in a different manner, and have different vehicle specification demands. This results in different types of electric two-wheelers and also in different charging strategies.

Private use. Private users can be differentiated in regular or standard electric two-wheeler users and students. Regular owners use their vehicle for daily trips to work, shopping, visiting friends, or other activities. In urban areas, the electric two-wheelers, which are basically used for urban trips, can also be used for excursions, which implies other trip distances and speed demands. The average trip length is 9–13 km in the urban area of Jakarta.[28] For motorcycle commutes, the average trip length is 19 km one way, i.e., 38 km per day.[29] Noteworthy is that 21%

---

[28] Lower value for higher income population probably and higher trip distance for lower income population (JICA, 2019, Annex 02: JABODETABEK Urban Transportation Master Plan).

[29] BPS. 2019. Statistik Komuter Jabodetabek 2019 (JABODETABEK Commuter Statistics 2019). https://www.bps.go.id/publication/2019/12/04/eab87d14d99459f4016bb057/statistik-komuter-jabodetabek-2019.html (accessed 5 July 2021).

of external trips out of the urban zone of Jakarta are by motorcycle, i.e., while they are predominantly used for short urban trips, a considerable number of trips are also made inter-urban with longer distances.[30]

Students are an important segment of the motorcycle user population. This is especially relevant for electric two-wheelers. Low-powered and low-speed electric scooters are very popular among students as they do not require a license and can often be driven without a helmet.

Commercial use. Commercial users can be divided into ride-hailing services for passengers, rental services, and goods transport. Passenger ride-hailing services are different from motorcycle rental services, which are important in, for example, tourism sites. Goods transport includes courier services, food, grocery, and other deliveries. On average, commercial users drive their motorcycles 80–100 km per day.[31]

Commercial and private use. The large majority of motorcycles used for passenger ride-hailing services or for goods delivery are owned by the driver and thus are also used for private purposes. The purchase decision is with the private person and the motorcycle must be convenient for work as well as for private usage. Also, daily mileage will not only be during work hours but also to commute to and from work. Payment of vehicle operators includes (partially) the cost of purchasing, maintaining, and operating the motorcycle. If the company provides the motorcycle on an exclusive basis, the driver will require a private motorcycle to get to and from the workplace except if the company allows the driver to use the company-owned unit for private purposes. A system with company-owned motorcycles is thus potentially less attractive for the driver, as well as for the company (higher payment for the motorcycle purchase due to having to pay the full cost of the motorcycle and not sharing it with the driver).

---

[30] JICA, 2019, Annex 02: JABODETABEK Urban Transportation Master Plan.
[31] Grab, Data, 2021. Jakarta.

6. Motorcycle Classification and Comparison

6.1 Private Users

For students, low-powered e-scooters are an interesting alternative to gasoline mopeds, bicycles, or public transport. That said, the emission impact of such e-scooters can be negative if they replace public transport and bicycle trips.

Standard motorcycles as purchased in Indonesia have 110 to 150 cc with a maximum power of 6.5 to 12 kW (9 to 16 horsepower). Table 3 lists electric two-wheelers as sold in Indonesia and their power and maximum speed.

Table 3: Sample of Electric Two-Wheelers Sold in Indonesia

Brand	Rated Real Engine Power (W)	Maximum Speed (km/h)
Niu EUB-01 Sport	250	25
Selis Hornet	350	30
Sepeda Listrik	350	30
Viar Akasha	500	35
Viar Q1	800	60
United T1800	1,800	70
Gesits	2,000	70
Niu NGT	3,500	70

km/h = kilometer per hour, W = watt.

Note: Electric two-wheeler manufacturers often state real and peak power (e.g., Gesits real power being 2,000 and peak power 5,000 W); in the perfect scenario, which is a straight, long, flat road with no obstacles on it, and ideal temperatures, the vehicle will be able to generate the most power it possibly can. This is known as its peak motor power. This is uncommon, and most motors usually start to overheat. The power that the electric two-wheeler produces most of the time, in actual real-world scenarios, with driving in traffic, stopping frequently, turning, and avoiding obstacles, and going up and down hills, will be its real motor power.

Source: Grütter Consulting, based on market survey.

In terms of power, none of the electric two-wheelers offered are in the range of a fossil-fuel-based motorcycle. With peak power, they can get close, but they cannot be considered to be fully comparable in terms of convenience and power to fossil-fuel-based units. Gogoro (not active in Indonesia), as well as some other manufacturers, do have 5–7 kW e-motorcycles, which can be considered as compatible. While a 2,000-watt engine might be sufficient for urban purposes and delivery companies, private users might demand more power, comparable to their gasoline version, which will allow them to easily drive along with two persons also outside the city at higher speeds.

The average driving range of the electric two-wheelers listed is 50 km. The average commuter trip length in Jakarta is 38 km. This means that a 50-kilometer range for a large share of commuters will be insufficient without recharging due to

- realization of not only commuter trips but also additional trips;
- decreasing state of health of batteries, with which the range will drop by 10%–20% within a year; and
- many commuters having longer than average commuter trip distances.

Thus, either charging facilities at work or school (so-called destination chargers) will be critical to reduce range anxiety issues or purchasers of electric two-wheelers will have to opt for a two-battery pack version with a higher price tag.

Table 4 compares the main features and cost components of electric and gasoline motorcycles (not scooters) for Indonesia for a private user.

Table 4: Main Features and Cost Components of Gasoline and Electric Motorcycles

Parameter	Value	Source
General Parameters		
Exchange rate	Rp14,300 = $1	May 2021; https://www1.oanda.com/currency/converter/.
Annual mileage	13,680 km	Daily mileage of 38 km[a] +20% for 300 days
Annual compound interest rate for motorcycles (real)	29%	Nominal rate minus inflation; based on compound annual rate[b]
Share of financing	75%	Down payments can also be only 10% but then the interest rate tends to be higher and reverse (some e-motorcycle manufacturers claim that down payments for e-motorcycles are higher than the ones for gasoline units, presumably due to risk of low resale price perceived to be higher of e-motorcycles).
Loan tenor	2 years	BFI; some dealers provide up to 36 months.[b]
Electricity price home charging	Rp1,445/kWh	Residential rate, non-subsidized[c]
Gasoline price	Rp7,850/liter	May 2021 based on "Pertalite", the cheapest gasoline normally bought by motorcycle operators[d]
Inflation rate	2%	For 2020[e]
Gasoline Motorcycle		
CAPEX gasoline motorcycle	Rp17,000,000	Honda Beat 110cc (top selling motorcycle in Indonesia)
Gasoline consumption	2.5 l/km	average value monitored, e.g., in Viet Nam

continued on next page

Table 4: *continued*

Parameter	Value	Source
Annual maintenance cost	Rp600,000	First year (free service/manpower): 4,000 km tune up, lubricant Rp45,500; 8,000 km tune up, lubricant, spark plug, diff Rp86,000; 12,000 km tune up, lubricant Rp45,500; Second year: 16,000 km tune up, lubricant, spark plug, diff lubricant, filter, front brake Rp292,500; 20,000 km tune up, lubricant, rear brake Rp220,500; 24,000 km tune up, lubricant, spark plug, diff lubricant, v-belt, roller, cvt grease, piece slide, braking fluid; IESR, 2020.[f]
Lifespan of motorcycle	5 years	same as electric; BPPT uses an 80,000 km mileage lifetime (around 6 years) for their comparison.
Electric Motorcycle		
CAPEX e-motorcycle	Rp 40,000,000	average 2,000–3,500W e-motorcycles (comparable power to gasoline motorcycle)
CAPEX battery	Rp5,700,000	1.5 kW battery
Projected battery cost reduction in 2.5 years	25%	United States Department of Energy
Electricity consumption	0.030 kWh/km	average value
Annual maintenance cost	Rp370,000	Institute for Essential Service Reform, 2020
Lifespan of motorcycle	5 years	same assumed as gasoline
Average lifespan of battery	2.5 years	500–1,000 cycles
Capacity of battery	1.5 kWh	standard for this motorcycle power
Driving range with 1 battery	50 km	NIU and Gesits

CAPEX = capital expenditure, cc = cubic centimeter, JABODETABEK = DKI Jakarta, Bogor, Depok, Tangerang and Bekasi, km = kilometer, kW= kilowatt, kWh = kilowatt-hour, l = liter, Rp = Indonesian rupiah.

[a] Badan Pusat Statistik (Statistics Indonesia). 2019. *Statistik Komuter Jabodetabek 2019* (JABODETABEK Commuter Statistics 2019). https://www.bps.go.id/publication/2019/12/04/eab87d14d99459f4016bb057/statistik-komuter-jabodetabek-2019.html (accessed 5 July 2021).
[b] Peta Situs BFI Finance (BFI Finance Sitemap). https://www.bfi.co.id/en/product/product/vehicle-motorcycle.
[c] *World Today News.* 2021. This Is the PLN Electricity Tariff for the April-June 2021 Period. 8 March. https://world-today-news.com/this-is-the-pln-electricity-tariff-for-the-april-june-2021-period/; State Electricity Company (PLN). 2021. Penyesuaian Tarif Tenaga Listrik (Tariff Adjustment) July to September 2021. https://web.pln.co.id/statics/uploads/2021/06/tf_juli_sep_2021.pdf.
[d] Pertamina. 2021. Daftar Harga BBK TMT 01 April 2021 (Price List). 1 April. https://www.pertamina.com/id/news-room/announcement/daftar-harga-bbk-tmt-01-april-2021.
[e] Statista. Indonesia: Inflation Rate From 1986 to 2026. https://www.statista.com/statistics/320156/inflation-rate-in-indonesia/ (accessed 15 June 2021).
[f] IESR, 2020. The Role of Electric Vehicles in Decarbonizing Indonesia's Road Transport Sector.

Source: Grütter Consulting.

Table 5 realizes a financial comparison of gasoline and electric motorcycles based on the total cost of ownership (TCO).

A more or less comparable e-motorcycle is around 57% more expensive and requires a 2.5x higher initial investment, which also means 2.5x more equity investment. Per-kilometer costs of gasoline motorcycles are very low, which also means that for an e-motorcycle to be attractive it would have to provide the same convenience at a comparable investment cost since operational savings are not very relevant and, in absolute terms, are very low.

Table 5: Cost Comparison Electric and Gasoline Motorcycle Indonesia, 2021
(Rp)

Item	Gasoline	Electric
CAPEX	17,000,000	40,000,000
Battery replacement	0	4,275,000
Annual maintenance cost	600,000	370,000
Annual energy cost	2,684,700	593,028
Annual finance cost	2,101,103	4,943,771
TCO Rp/km	**550**	**862**
Annualized cost	7,525,000	11,796,000
Life cycle cost	37,600,000	59,000,000
Incremental cost		**57%**

CAPEX = capital expenditure, km = kilometer, Rp = Indonesian rupiah, TCO = total cost of ownership.
Source: Grütter Consulting.

Table 6: Cost Components of High-Powered Electric Scooters for Urban Usage

Parameter	Value	Source
CAPEX e-scooter (Rp)	24,000,000	average Gesits 2,000 W, United T1800 and Viar Q1 800 W
CAPEX battery (Rp)	5,000,000	1.2 kW battery
Electricity consumption (kWh/km)	0.025	average value
Annual maintenance cost (Rp)	370,000	Institute for Essential Service Reform, 2020
Lifespan scooter (Year)	5	same assumed as gasoline
Average lifespan battery (Year)	2.50	500–1,000 cycles; assumed one cycle per day
Capacity of battery (kWh)	1.2	standard for this vehicle power
Range with one battery (km)	50	Gesits, United, Viar
Projected reduction of battery cost in 2.5 years	25%	United States Department of Energy

CAPEX = capital expenditure, km = kilometer, kW= kilowatt, kWh = kilowatt-hour, l = liter, Rp = Indonesian rupiah, W = watt.
Source: Grütter Consulting based on market survey.

While having a high-powered motorcycle can be in line with the consumer preference, the necessity of this for urban trips is questioned. Urban trips can be made just as quickly and conveniently with a high-powered electric scooter as with a low-powered e-motorcycle instead of a higher-powered e-motorcycle. Table 6 shows the standard features and costs of a higher-powered electric scooter, i.e., versions that can drive 70–80 km/h without problems.

Table 7 compares the financial costs of such a lower-powered e-motorcycle (equivalent to a high-powered e-scooter) against a fossil-fuel-based motorcycle. The difference to the former comparison is that the e-motorcycle is of significantly lower power resulting in lower purchase costs. It is important to reiterate that this type of e-motorcycle, in terms of power and speed, is not comparable to a fossil-fuel-based motorcycle. However, it has sufficient power to comply with urban requirements and can thus, in terms of convenience, be considered comparable to a fossil-fuel-based motorcycle (not necessarily, however, in terms of preference).

Table 7: Cost Comparison of High-Powered Electric Scooters and Gasoline Motorcycles in Indonesia, 2021
(Rp)

Item	Gasoline	Electric
CAPEX	17,000,000	24,000,000
Battery replacement	0	3,750,000
Maintenance cost, annual	600,000	370,000
energy cost annual	2,684,700	494,190
finance cost annual	2,101,103	2,966,263
TCO Rp/km	**550**	**556**
Annualized cost	7,525,000	7,601,000
Life cycle cost	37,600,000	38,000,000
Incremental cost		1%

CAPEX = capital expenditure, km = kilometer, Rp = Indonesian rupiah, TCO = total cost of ownership.
Source: Grütter Consulting.

A high-powered electric scooter (or low-powered e-motorcycle) with sufficient power and speed for an urban setting (maximum speed of 70 km/h with peak speed potentially more) has the same total cost of ownership as a gasoline motorcycle. The initial investment is still 40% higher, which can be a deterrent but annual operational costs excluding financing are 80% lower. The profitability of the incremental investment is 10%. The incremental investment is recovered (including finance costs based on loans for 2 years) at the end of the fifth year (in the third year, the owner needs to purchase a new battery, thereby pulling the differential cash flow again into the negative). Thus, from a financial perspective, the two options can be considered comparable. However, vehicle purchase has little in common with a rational financial calculation. Table 8 exemplifies why e-motorcycles are not attractive for private users and will not take off under current conditions and why higher-powered electric scooters, albeit rationally attractive, have not been the preferred choice of customers in Indonesia, as well as many other parts of the world with high shares of motorcycles.

The comparable e-motorcycle is too costly while still having range issues and not having a comparable convenience value. Even significant subsidies will not eliminate these problems and will not be sustainable. The lower-powered e-motorcycle, which would cater to the demands of urban trips and reflect a rational customer choice, is not in line with the aspirations of customers concerning power and speed and has additionally driving range issues. Again, this problem will not be resolved with financial support. Neither technology trends nor financial support will resolve in the short- to medium-term (next 5 years) the power-cum-cost and range issues of e-motorcycles. However, based on a purely rational purchase choice, lower-powered e-motorcycles would be financially attractive and sufficient for urban trips. From a societal point of view, e-motorcycles are beneficial due to reduced air and noise pollution. Therefore, it could be justified that the government introduces regulations that pit the emotional benefits of high power and speed against reduced environmental pollution and improved health. This would even be financially beneficial to customers (not consumer surplus or welfare benefits as the latter include emotional benefits). This could be done in a straightforward manner by only allowing circulation of e-motorcycles in urban areas of the city. This measure would need to be announced with a lead-time of a minimum 2 years to allow people to renovate their motorcycles.

Table 8: Are E-Motorcycles Attractive for Clients?

Parameter	Comparison of high-powered e-motorcycle with gasoline motorcycle	Comparison of low-powered e-motorcycle (high-powered e-scooter) with gasoline motorcycle
Power, speed	👎	👎👎
Range	👎👎	👎👎
Investment	👎👎	👎
Operating cost	👍👍	👍👍
Lifetime cost	👎	neutral
Overall	👎	👎

👎: gasoline version is preferred by customers and has advantages compared to electric versions.

👍: electric version is preferred by customers and has advantages compared to gasoline versions.

Source: Grütter Consulting.

6.2 Commercial Users

Commercial clients use the same gasoline motorcycles as private clients, but with more mileage. Yet, it is assumed that they could also use low-powered electric motorcycles as they are more rational and performance-oriented compared to individuals. However, they would also purchase the motorcycle with two batteries replacing one at their premises (or at swapping sites; Tables 9 and 10).

Table 9: Cost Components of Commercial Electric Motorcycles for Urban Usage

Parameter	Value	Source
CAPEX e-motorcycle (Rp)	29,000,000	average 800–2,000 W e-motorcycles
CAPEX battery (two units) (Rp)	10,000,000	1.2 kW battery; cost for two units
Electricity consumption (kWh/km)	0.025	average value
Annual maintenance cost (Rp)	740,000	Institute for essential Service Reform, 2020 (double mileage compared to private e-motorcycle)
Lifespan motorcycle (Years)	4	same assumed as gasoline
Average lifespan of battery (Years)	2	500–1,000 cycles; assumed one cycle per day 330 days
Capacity of battery (kWh)	1.2	standard for this motorcycle power
Range with two batteries (km)	100	Gesits, United, Viar
Projected reduction of battery cost in 2.5 years	25%	United States Department of Energy

CAPEX = capital expenditure, km = kilometer, kW = kilowatt, kWh = kilowatt-hour, l = liter, Rp = Indonesian rupiah, W = watt.

Source: Grütter Consulting based on market survey.

The financial model thus includes two battery sets.

Table 10: Cost Comparison between Electric and Gasoline Motorcycles for Commercial Usage, 2021 (Rp)

Item	Gasoline	Electric
CAPEX	17,000,000	29,000,000
Battery replacement	0	7,500,000
Annual maintenance cost	1,200,000	1,480,000
Annual energy cost	4,710,000	127,000
Annual finance cost	1,050,551	1,637,624
TCO Rp/km	**467**	**515**
Annualized cost	11,210,551	12,369,624
Life cycle cost	44,842,205	49,478,497
Incremental cost		**10%**

CAPEX = capital expenditure, km = kilometer, Rp = Indonesian rupiah, TCO = total cost of ownership.

Note: based on 24,000 km per annum; two batteries replaced after 2 years; other costs per kilometer idem to private motorcycles.

Source: Grütter Consulting.

TCOs are comparable with a fossil-fuel-based or an e-motorcycle. Commercial users will also be able to get a discount on the motorcycle as well as the battery. The main issue with commercial motorcycles is that they are in general not owned by the delivery company but by the drivers. This means that the motorcycle is also used to commute to work as well as for private usage. This entails following difficulties:

- Private owners will have a preference for the gasoline motorcycle for private usage due to power.
- Due to commuting mileage, one additional spare battery would be required for daily operations, thus increasing costs.
- Drivers currently receive a compensation that partially pays for the acquisition of the motorcycle. If the company supplies the e-motorcycle and it needs to be charged and left at the premises of the company, they will still need their private motorcycle to commute to work, which can reduce their net income as they would not receive the benefit of partial payment of the asset. If the e-motorcycle is not left at the company premises for charging, this barrier does not exist, but an additional battery will be required.
- For the company owning the motorcycle, this results in a higher cost due to the need to purchase the e-motorcycle while they only pay part of the investment cost in the private motorcycle. The alternative is that the company rents the e-motorcycle from the driver as with fossil-fuel-based units and obliges the driver to purchase an electric unit.

Therefore, some barriers exist that prevent the market from switching toward e-motorcycles for commercial applications on its own, although system costs are comparable.

6.3 Summary Electric Two-Wheeler Usage Type

The typical or standard electric two-wheelers and their charging infrastructure as used for projections and for modelling purposes are shown in Figure 15 and Table 11.

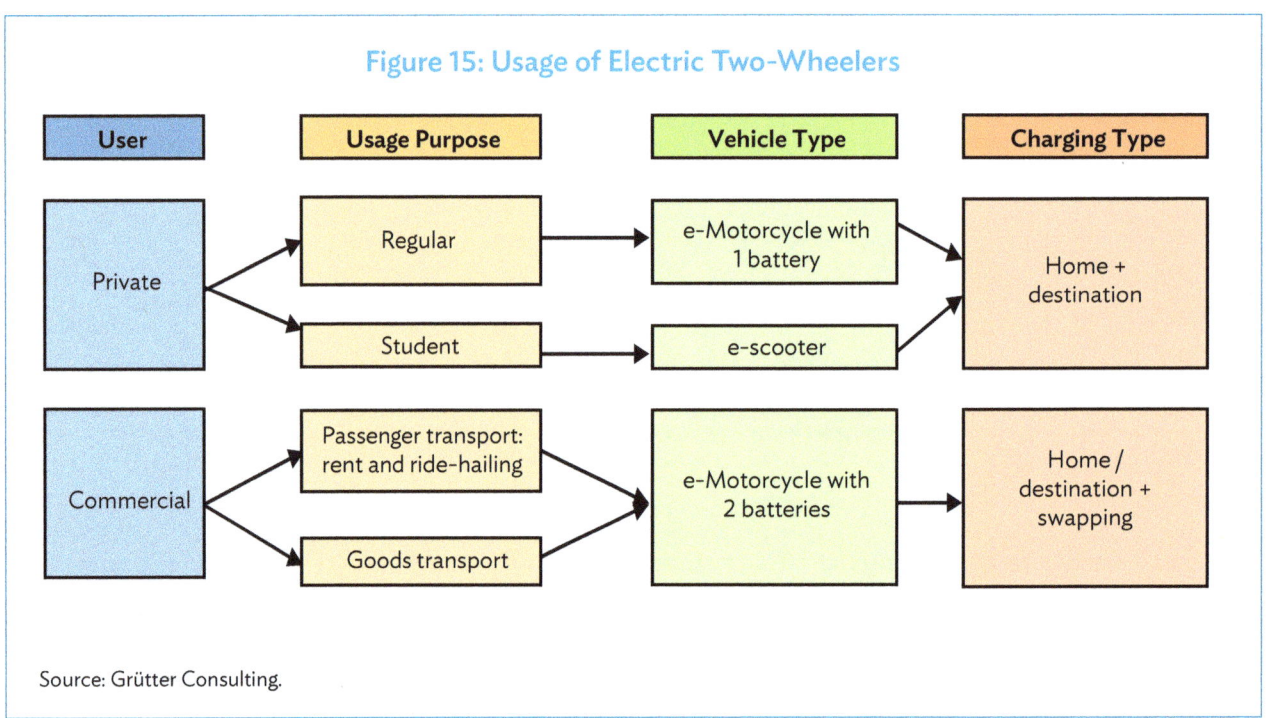

Figure 15: Usage of Electric Two-Wheelers

Source: Grütter Consulting.

Table 11: E-Scooter Characteristics

Parameter	Value
Average engine power	250–800 W capable of speeds of 25–35 km/h
Battery capacity	0.7 kWh
CAPEX e-scooter including battery	Rp7 million
Battery cost	Rp3 million
Range with one battery	40 km
Electricity usage	0.017 kWh/km
Main charging system	Home charging and destination charging

CAPEX = capital expenditure, km = kilometer, km/h = kilometer per hour, kWh = kilowatt-hour, Rp = Indonesian rupiah, W = watt.

Source: Grütter Consulting.

E-scooters are not further considered in projections or modelling as they typically replace bicycles and public transportation.

Table 12 summarizes the main features of the targeted e-motorcycles. As mentioned, they are low- to medium-powered e-motorcycles, which have less power and a lower maximum speed than a conventional gasoline unit but are more than adequate for urban usage and also for short inter-urban trips.

Table 12: E-Motorcycle Characteristics

Parameter	Private usage	Commercial usage
Average engine power	1,800–2,500 W	1,800–2,500 W
Maximum speed	70–80 km/h	70–80 km/h
Driving range	50 km (1 battery)	100 km (two batteries)
Battery capacity	1.2–1.5 kWh (one battery)	2.4–3 kWh (with two batteries)
CAPEX e-scooter	Rp24 million (with one battery)	Rp29 million (with two batteries)
Battery cost per unit	Rp5 million	Rp5 million
Electricity usage	0.025 kWh/km	0.025 kWh/km
Average daily trip length	45 km	80 km
Annual average mileage	13,700 km	24,000 km

CAPEX = capital expenditure, km = kilometer, km/h = kilometer per hour, kWh = kilowatt-hour, Rp = Indonesian rupiah, W = watt.
Source: Grütter Consulting.

The same type of e-motorcycles can be used for private or commercial usage with the difference being that the e-motorcycles for commercial use will generally be equipped with two batteries to increase range and flexibility.

Private e-motorcycles will be charged at home and the destination. Battery swapping is neither a necessity for private users nor a big advantage, except perhaps for long-distance rides. For commercial users, battery swapping has an advantage as daily mileage is higher and battery swapping reduces the recharging time. While uniform battery technologies would facilitate swapping and reduce costs, this is not a necessity as smaller swap stations can be used or with different battery types. It is not deemed realistic that manufacturers will agree on a specific battery type given that it is a distinctive component of an e-motorcycle. Uniform battery types could also hamper competition and thus avoid innovation and further development of this technology.

7. Conversion of Gasoline Motorcycles and Battery Standardization

7.1 Conversion of Motorcycles

Indonesia is interested in converting used petrol motorcycles to electric units and has issued Regulation No. 65/2020 regarding conversion of internal combustion engine (ICE) motorcycles to e-motorcycles.

Trials have been conducted in Indonesia to convert used gasoline motorcycles to electric units. The conversion would include a 2,000 W engine, the battery pack, a main controller, and a speed regulator. The conversion cost is estimated at Rp10.5–11 million, excluding the cost of the old gasoline motorcycle and certification costs and profits of the conversion company (MEMR pilot conversion project). The project estimates are based on using 10-year-old gasoline motorcycles. If the assumption is made (as in the cost estimate above) that the old motorcycle has no resale value, this implies that the individual components such as brakes, wheels, chassis, lights, etc., are all without value anymore. To make conversion costs comparable, the value of the old motorcycle plus a profit from the conversion company needs to be considered. The resultant cost of a converted but still not new e-motorcycle would then be around Rp16 million.[32]

The client receives an old motorcycle with outdated chassis, brakes, lights, etc., and new electric components without an original manufacturer guarantee that costs as much as a new gasoline motorcycle. A purpose-built e-motorcycle is designed to incorporate a battery, wiring, and the hub, thus maximizing the "e" side of the e-motorcycle in contrast to retrofitted gasoline motorcycles. Putting electric components on an old motorcycle results in a costly old motorcycle. For a 50% additional investment (RP24 million), the client could get a same-powered new e-motorcycle with brand-new components and a manufacturer warranty. For a similar price, the client could purchase a 2- to 3-year used e-motorcycle or a new gasoline motorcycle. It makes absolutely no financial sense and is not attractive for a customer to get an old motorcycle with many old components that will need replacement but with a costly new drive-train and without a guarantee from a manufacturer. Conversions, offered initially in Viet Nam for example, have not proven to be popular. The market for conversions might be limited and attractive for special motorcycles but not for standard units. The same is true for all other electric road vehicles; initially, some conversions were made but as soon as manufacturers started mass-producing electric units, the market for such backyard ventures disappeared.

Mass conversion of existing vehicles is useful for compressed natural gas or liquefied propane gas vehicles, but for electric vehicles this is not considered to be a useful strategy as the electric vehicle components easily make up more than 50% of the total vehicle cost and thus an old and low-value vehicle would be upgraded with a very expensive equipment, without being at the end a new unit.

---

[32] Based on a 5-year-old gasoline motorcycle with a remnant value of 20% of the original investment of Rp17 million plus 10% profit margin for a converter.

7.2 Battery Standardization

Indonesia has plans to standardize batteries for two-wheeler usage. Standardized batteries have the advantage that they allow for easy interchange and for a higher density of swapping stations as all motorcycles would have the same battery and thus stations can get a larger market. This sounds initially attractive and Taipei,China has included standardization of batteries in its tasks and road map. This target could never be achieved and batteries have not been standardized. Taipei,China also heavily subsidized just one supplier (Gogoro) with its battery-swap stations; nonetheless the market has come up with another brand offering its own charging stations (KYMCO). Standardization of batteries had also been tried early on in the PRC, when battery swapping was made with buses and passenger cars; however, the PRC also dropped this approach.

For battery standardization to reach its target of having uniform units, it must include not only voltage levels, battery dimensions, and shape, but also core properties of the battery such as chemistry, C-rate, energy density, lifespan, capacity, etc. If these elements are not identical, the client will not receive an identical product back by swapping but potentially a battery with lower energy density and range or less capacity, resulting in changing potentially a high-value product with a low-value one.

Battery standardization problems are related to the dynamics of market forces. The battery is a core element of an e-motorcycle and a main competitive distinction. It is also a major cost component. Standardization reduces competition between e-motorcycle and battery manufacturers as, e.g., higher power density or reduction of size and weight will not be honored in the market. Reducing competition in a highly dynamic market will reduce the innovative potential and will result in less dynamics toward decreasing prices. Standardization can thus result in a reduced uptake of e-motorcycles in the medium term as it results in reduced competition, less innovation, and less price pressure on manufacturers. There is also no demand for battery swapping from private users of e-motorcycles. They can purchase an e-motorcycle with one or two batteries, which is sufficient for their daily ranges and will charge basically at home or at their destination. Battery swapping is required more for commercial clients that drive long distances daily and want to be able to recharge or swap batteries within minutes. However, commercial customers can establish a cooperation agreement with a manufacturer to standardize their fleet and thus have a sufficient motorcycle density with identical batteries to warrant the set-up of battery swap stations. As the analysis in the following chapters for Bali and JABODETABEK also shows, the required number of identical e-motorcycles for efficient battery swapping is not very high and can be achieved quickly. Also, battery swapping and recharging facilities are for various battery types and standards, i.e., one swapping station can accommodate up to three battery types and the client can exchange theirs with the same type of battery.

8. Electric Motorcycle Projections

Based on the Indonesian State Police, there were 113 million motorcycles in Indonesia in 2019. Compared to the statistics of 2018, the number of motorcycles has been reduced by 14 million for 2018.[33] However, this number also presumably includes many motorcycles that are out of use or only in marginal use, as the annual sales numbers of 6 to 6.5 million units are of the same magnitude as the annual increase of registered motorcycles, while some motorcycles that are very old or suffer accidents would be retired from traffic.

To establish alternative energy vehicle penetration scenarios, the estimated annual vehicle sales rate is taken. Based on a market assessment, the share of clients that are potentially willing to purchase an electric unit is estimated. The resultant electric fleet is integrated with the total fleet to calculate vehicle penetration ratios.

For projection purposes, motorcycle sales prior to COVID-19 are taken. In 2019, these were 6.5 million units.[34] Projections for 2025 point to 9.5 million units.[35]

8.1 Official Scenarios

The Ministry of Industry (MoI) Ministerial Regulation 27/2020 provides a tentative target on the number of electric two- and three-wheelers to be manufactured in Indonesia (Table 13).

Table 13: Tentative Target of Electric Two-Wheeler Production and Sales in Indonesia

	Variable	2020	2025	2030	2035
Production	Total (units)	7,500,000	8,800,000	9,800,000	10,750,000
	electric vehicle %	10	20	25	30
	electric vehicle Total (units)	750,000	1,760,000	2,450,000	3,225,000
Domestic Sales	Total (units)	6,750,000	7,700,000	8,400,000	9,000,000
Export	Total (units)	750,000	1,100,000	1,400,000	1,750,000

Source: Government of Indonesia, Ministry of Industry. 2020. Ministerial Regulation 27/2020.

---

[33] In 2018, 120.1 million motorcycles were originally reported, and this number was reduced to 106.7 million units; Badan Pusat Stastik. Statistics Indonesia 2018 and 2019. Jakarta.
[34] Association of Indonesia Motorcycle Industry (AISI). Statistic Distribution. https://www.aisi.or.id/statistic/ (accessed 2021).
[35] Statista Market Forecast. www.statista.com accessed 2021.

The **National Energy Masterplan** (RUEN) has a BAU scenario of 2.1 million e-motorcycles operating by 2025. The optimistic scenario has 100 million e-motorcycles by 2025; this, however, is unlikely given that between 2021 and 2025, the total sales market for motorcycles in Indonesia is only estimated at around 41 million units, i.e., a large number of existing motorcycles would have to be converted to electric units, which makes only limited financial sense.

From the **energy sector**, the electric vehicle deployment target is linked with efforts to curb fuel oil imports and to utilize high-generation reserve margins, especially for the Java-Bali grid. Prior to the acceleration program, the national energy masterplan released by the National Energy Council (DEN) put a minimum target of 2,200 electric four-wheelers and 2,100,000 electric two-wheelers in operation by 2025. This is regarded as the BAU scenario by the government. With the acceleration program, the target was increased as reflected in the draft of the national Grand Strategy for Energy (GSE) document, which is yet to be released by DEN. In 2025, the number of operational units is expected to reach 374,000 four-wheelers and 11,800,000 two-wheelers (Table 14).

Table 14: Electric Vehicle Deployment Target Based on the Draft Grand Strategy for Energy

Electric Vehicle Target	2025	2030	2035
Four-Wheeler	374,000	1,700,000	2,100,000
Two-Wheeler	11,800,000	13,000,000	28,000,000

Source: Data provided by by the Government of Indonesia, Ministry of Energy and Mineral Resources.

In the recent public program, MEMR also tried to gather the electric vehicle unit deployment planning from various government bodies, SOEs, and private companies as illustrated in Table 15.

Table 15: Electric Vehicle Deployment Target Based on the Public Launching Commitment

Electric Vehicle Target	2025
Four-Wheelers	34,000
Two-Wheelers	750,000

Source: Government of Indonesia, Ministry of Energy and Mineral Resources. 2021. Rekapitulasi Data Jumlah KBLBB di Indonesia, 2021–2025 (English Translation). Presentation. 11 January.

By the end of 2021, 219 public electric vehicle charging stations were available throughout Indonesia.[36]

---

[36] Government of Indonesia, MEMR. 2022. PLN Engages Private Sector To Install More Charging Stations. 4 January. https://www.esdm.go.id/en/media-center/news-archives/pln-gandeng-pihak-swasta-perbanyak-spklu-dengan-skema-bagi-hasil (accessed 21 February 2022).

8.2 Scenario Modelling

From a market perspective, e-motorcycles will be purchased if they offer a higher value than a conventional unit. Three scenarios have been created by Grütter Consulting for this purpose:

- **Business-as-usual.** This means no government interventions. Under this scenario, only low-powered electric scooters are purchased, which are used at least partially in lieu of public transport and bicycles and are not registered vehicles. Under the BAU scenario, the share of e-motorcycles is marginal as fossil-fuel-based units have lower costs and are more convenient.
- **Financial incentives.** This scenario would be in accordance with the path followed by Taipei,China: the incremental cost of an e-motorcycle that is comparable to a fossil-fuel-based version is subsidized (currently that would entail a subsidy of around Rp20 million per motorcycle). Swapping systems would also be subsidized to around 50%. It is estimated that this would result in a comparable market share for e-motorcycles as in Taipei,China, i.e., in the order of 10%–20%. Gasoline-powered motorcycles would remain to be more convenient.
- **Regulation.** A third scenario is based on having regulatory measures not allowing the circulation of fossil-fuel-based motorcycles in (certain) urban areas and/or not allowing people and freight carriers to operate with fossil-fuel-based motorcycles. Such measures would allow for a massive and rapid move toward e-motorcycles.

Figure 16 shows the number of e-motorcycles under each scenario compared with annual motorcycle sales. This includes only e-motorcycles and not electric scooters.

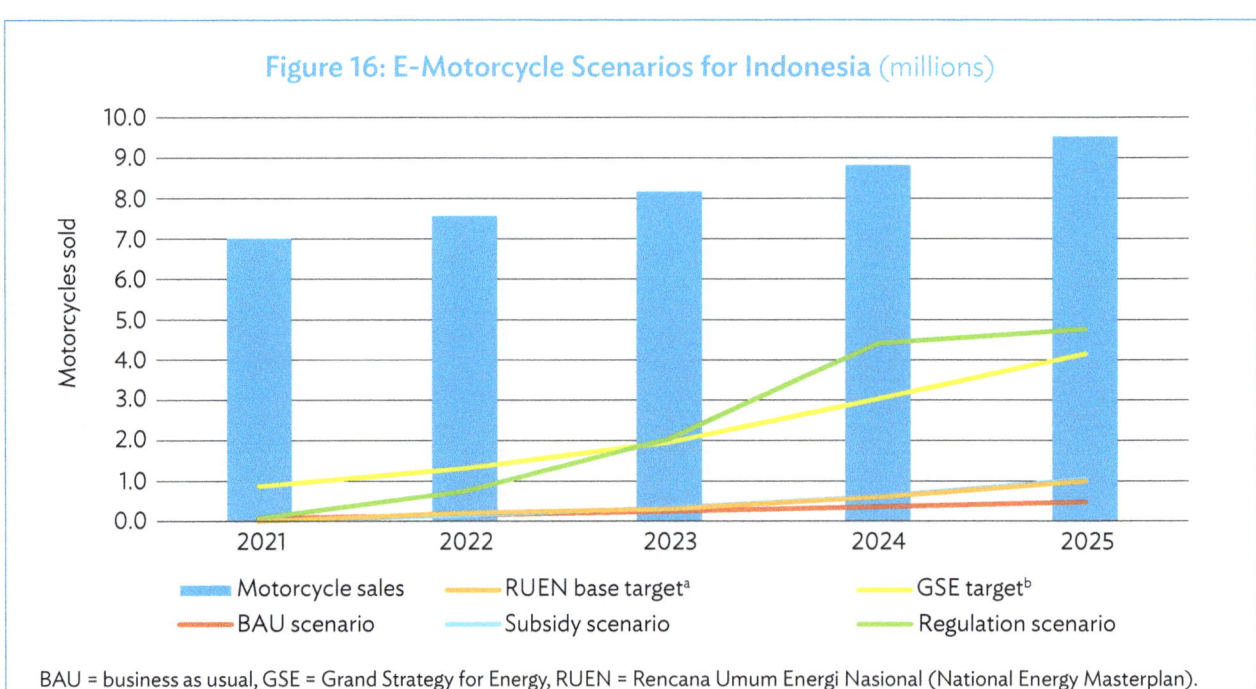

Figure 16: E-Motorcycle Scenarios for Indonesia (millions)

BAU = business as usual, GSE = Grand Strategy for Energy, RUEN = Rencana Umum Energi Nasional (National Energy Masterplan).
[a] This results in around 2.1 million e-motorcycles by 2025.
[b] This results in around 11.8 million e-motorcycles by 2025.
Source: Grütter Consulting.

The following points can be noted:

- Under a BAU scenario, e-motorcycles will play a marginal role with an expected 0.5 million units sold in 2025 representing 5% of sales and 0.04% of the total motorcycle fleet.
- The RUEN BAU/DEN target of 2.1 million e-motorcycles is comparable to a scenario with high financial incentives, i.e., to materialize this target, the government would need to considerably subsidize the e-motorcycle market. This could result in sales of 1 million e-motorcycles by 2025, representing 11% of sales and 2% of the total motorcycle fleet.
- The GSE target of around 12 million e-motorcycles could be achieved with a strategy that makes use of e-motorcycles compulsory for commercial and/or urban operations. This could result in sales of 4–5 million e-motorcycles by 2025, representing 45%–50% of sales and 11% of the total motorcycle fleet.

8.3 Impact of Decreasing Electric Motorcycle Prices

E-motorcycles are expected to become less expensive due to decreasing battery component costs and increased competition. Based on the car market, price tag parity of higher-powered e-motorcycles with comparable power levels to gasoline motorcycles is expected by 2030.[37] This results in average expected price decreases of 9% from 2022 to 2030. Figure 17 shows the expected price decrease of higher-powered e-motorcycles in Indonesia, as well as the resultant TCOs for gasoline and e-motorcycles over time.

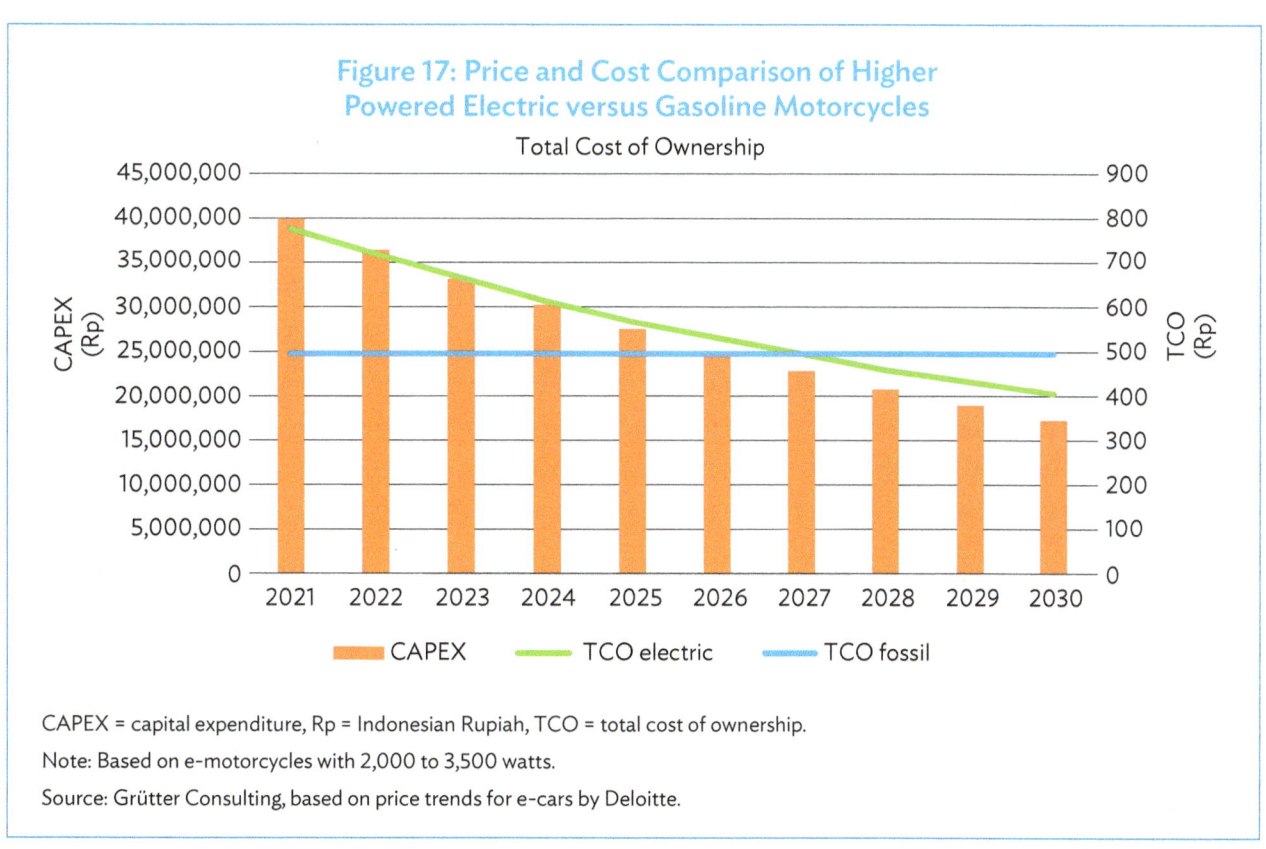

Figure 17: Price and Cost Comparison of Higher Powered Electric versus Gasoline Motorcycles

CAPEX = capital expenditure, Rp = Indonesian Rupiah, TCO = total cost of ownership.
Note: Based on e-motorcycles with 2,000 to 3,500 watts.
Source: Grütter Consulting, based on price trends for e-cars by Deloitte.

---

[37] Deloitte. 2020. *Electric Vehicles - Setting a Course for 2030.*

Sticker price parity of an electric and a gasoline motorcycle would be achieved by 2030. By 2027, the life cycle costs of comparably powered e-motorcycles would be equivalent to gasoline units. Life cycle costs, however, are not considered a common criterion for private vehicle purchases, with sticker price being far more convincing and even this is not sufficient to make large shifts in the motorcycle market, as the experience in Taipei,China has shown. The BAU uptake is thus modelled primarily around the e-scooter uptake and not an e-motorcycle uptake prior to 2030.

8.4 Impact of a Carbon Tax

The impact of a potential carbon tax of Rp30,000 per ton of CO_2 on the demand for e-motorcycles was modelled and the main results are shown in Table 16.

Table 16: Core Elements and Impacts of a Carbon Tax on Fuels

Parameter	Value	Comment
Carbon price	Rp30,000 /tCO$_2$	Proposed carbon price by Ministry of Finance[a]
Impact of carbon tax per liter of gasoline	Rp68 /l	Calculated based on CO_2 emissions per liter of gasoline (tank-to-wheel)
Projected increase in gasoline price	1%	Relative to price in May 2021
Cost increase per km of fossil-fuel-based motorcycle	Rp2 /km	Based on average fuel consumption of motorcycles
Annual cost impact for fossil-fuel-based motorcycle operator	Rp23,000	Based on average annual mileage
TCO gasoline motorcycle excl. carbon tax	Rp550 /km	
TCO gasoline motorcycle incl. carbon tax	Rp552 /km	

km = kilometer, l = liter, Rp = Indonesian rupiah, TCO = total cost of operation, tCO$_2$ = ton of carbon dioxide.

[a] R. Simatupang, J. Pineda, and T. Murdjijanto. 2021. On Indonesia's New Carbon Tax and Its Effectiveness at Reducing Greenhouse Gas Emissions. *Devtech*. 24 November. https://devtechsys.com/insights/2021/11/24/on-indonesias-new-carbon-tax-and-its-effectiveness-at-reducing-greenhouse-gas-emissions/ (accessed 15 December 2021).

Source: Calculations by Grütter Consulting.

The price tag difference between a gasoline and a similar powered e-motorcycle is Rp23 million. Additional savings due to a carbon tax of Rp30 per kilogram of CO_2 of the e-motorcycle for a 5-year period non-discounted are around Rp0.1 million. The TCO of a same-powered e-motorcycle is Rp862/km and the TCO of a fossil-fuel-based one with or without carbon tax is significantly lower, with the carbon tax making an extremely marginal difference. Calculation results thus show that the carbon tax will not have any measurable impact on e-motorcycle sales. Increases in fuel prices due to a carbon tax also result not only in potential changes of the vehicle stock toward energy saving units but also to fuel price usage decrease, e.g., through less driving, usage of nonmotorized and public transport, and more fuel-efficient driving. Fuel prices are not elastic, with short-term average elasticities of around –0.3 and long-term ones of around –0.6, i.e., a 1% increase of fuel prices results in a decrease of 0.3% to 0.6% of fuel consumption.[38]

---

[38] H. B. Huntington, J. J. Barrios, and V. Arora. 2019. Review of Key International Demand Elasticities for Major Industrializing Economies. Energy Policy. 133 (October). 110878. https://doi.org/10.1016/j.enpol.2019.110878.

The impact of a carbon tax of Rp30,000 on the e-motorcycle market is therefore considered to be negligible. However, if revenues from the carbon tax are invested into a specific promotion of e-motorcycles, the impact could be far higher. Switzerland, for example, established more than a decade ago a very minor carbon levy on fossil-fuel-based fuels ($0.01 per liter of diesel and gasoline). This had no direct impact on fuel consumption. However, the proceedings of this levy were used for a climate fund that co-funded domestic offset projects, e.g., investments in e-mobility. These projects then received funding that could be on the order of +$150/t$CO_2$, thereby avoiding having a significant impact on uptake of e-mobility. In short, the existence of a low-carbon tax on transportation fuels is not deemed to have a notable impact on the deployment of e-motorcycles, especially in light of low price elasticities and standard market fluctuations of liquid fossil fuel prices, which go far beyond the proposed carbon tax. However, if such proceeds would be used to cofinance individual offset projects, e.g., in the realm of e-mobility, then the impact could be significant.

8.5 Conclusions on Business-As-Usual Development

Without massive financial subsidies or restrictions on fossil-fuel-based motorcycle usage, the BAU scenario is the most probable one. The market itself, with some minor interventions like the carbon tax, will not result in a massive deployment of e-motorcycles by 2030. For a significant deployment of e-motorcycles that goes beyond e-scooters, either massive government subsidies or government regulations concerning usage of fossil-fuel-based motorcycles are required.

8.6 Subsidy Scenario

An estimate of the required subsidies to achieve the DEN target (2.1 million e-motorcycles operating in 2025) results in a price tag of around $1.1 billion (Rp$1.6*10^{13}$) of which the large part would be for subsidies to motorcycles and a smaller part for subsidies of charging stations (Table 17).

Table 17: Estimated Subsidy Requirement to Achieve Target of 2.1 Million E-Motorcycles by 2025

Parameter	Value	Source/Explanation
Targeted e-motorcycles	2.1 million	DEN masterplan target for 2025
Number of swapping stations	10,500	200 motorcycles per swap station based on data of Taipei,China (e-motorcycle registration data and official data of number of swapping stations)
Average subsidy level per e-motorcycle	Rp7.5 million $520	Initially Rp10 million, reduced gradually to Rp5 million; subsidy level based on covering at minimum 50% of incremental cost of comparable power electric scooter to gasoline unit based on experience in Taipei,China
Average subsidy level per swapping station	Rp35 million $2,500	Based on cost per swapping station of $5,000 excluding land with 50% subsidy level based on Taipei,China
Total subsidy	Rp$1.6*10^{13}$ $1,100 million	Subsidy motorcycle plus subsidy for 25% of all swapping stations

Source: Grütter Consulting.

Figure 18 compares the required subsidy level and a projected revenue level of the proposed carbon tax (only using gasoline). Not even using 100% of the carbon tax on gasoline (to be potentially levied) would be sufficient for the subsidy levels required. Currently, no gasoline subsidy is made by the government based on the enactment of the Presidential Regulation 191/2014, which removed the subsidy for RON 88 gasoline.[39]

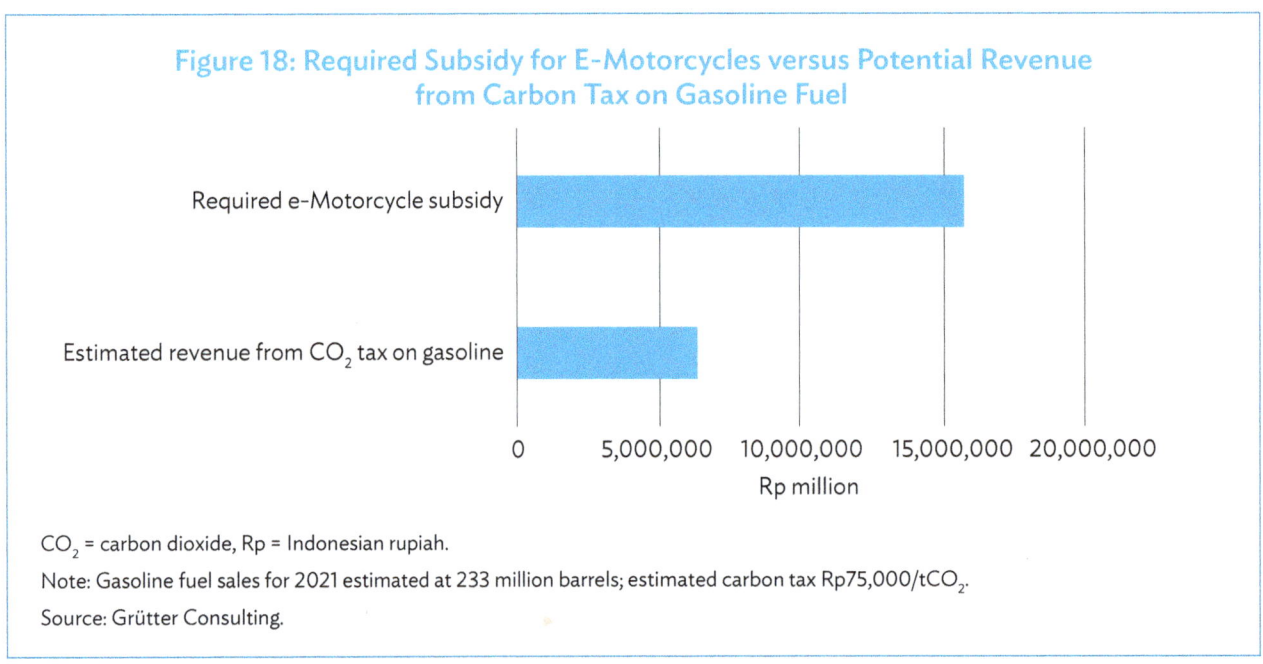

Figure 18: Required Subsidy for E-Motorcycles versus Potential Revenue from Carbon Tax on Gasoline Fuel

CO_2 = carbon dioxide, Rp = Indonesian rupiah.
Note: Gasoline fuel sales for 2021 estimated at 233 million barrels; estimated carbon tax Rp75,000/tCO_2.
Source: Grütter Consulting.

This subsidy would be the equivalent of around $530 per e-motorcycle, including the proportion on swapping stations. The economic value of emission reductions is, however, only around $280, i.e., not justified from an economic viewpoint (Table 18).

Table 18: Subsidy Level versus Economic Benefits of Emission Reductions per E-Motorcycle

Parameter	Value	Source/Explanation
Estimated average subsidy level per electric motorcycle	Rp7.5 million/ $530	Grütter Consulting
Economic Benefits of reduced greenhouse gas emissions	Rp1.8 million/ $130	Based on lifespan mileage of around 65,000 km and emission factors well-to-wheel for electric and gasoline motorcycles; social cost of carbon of $40/t
Economic benefits of reduced local air pollutants	Rp2.2 million/ $160	Based on lifespan mileage of 65,000 km and combustion emission factors for NO_x and $PM_{2.5}$; economic costs of pollutants based on IMF data[a] for Indonesia
Total economic benefits of reduced emissions	Rp4.1 million $280	

IMF = International Monetary Fund, km = kilometer, NOx = nitrogen oxides, PM2.5 = particulate matter 2.5, Rp = Indonesian rupiah, t = ton.

[a] I. W. H. Parry et al. 2014. *Getting Energy Prices Right: From Principle to Practice.* IMF. https://www.imf.org/en/Publications/Books/Issues/2016/12/31/Getting-Energy-Prices-Right-From-Principle-to-Practice-41345.
Source: Grütter Consulting.

[39] Government of Indonesia, MEMR, and Ministry of Finance. 2019. *Indonesia's Effort to Phase Out and Rationalise Fossil-Fuel Subsidies: A Self Report on the G20 Peer Review of Inefficient Fossil-Fuel-Based Fuel Subsidies that Encourage Wasteful Consumption in Indonesia.* https://www.oecd.org/fossil-fuels/publicationsandfurtherreading/Indonesia%20G20%20Self-Report%20IFFS.pdf.

8.7 Regulatory Scenario

The regulatory scenario would prescribe that motorcycles need to be electric to enter specific zones or areas. The regulatory scenario requires no subsidies. Swapping stations can be established without subsidies as they can charge sufficiently for their services due to having a captive demand. Lower-powered e-motorcycles would be chosen by the people and commercial agents as they can fulfill the urban demands. They would not have the opportunity of using higher-powered gasoline units. Therefore, they would also not entail a financial loss, as these e-motorcycles have comparable total financial costs to gasoline versions.

Tables 19 and 20 illustrate the projected number of e-motorcycles for Indonesia and specifically for Bali and JABODETABEK under a scenario of regulatory interventions for usage of e-motorcycles.

Table 19: Projected Population
(million persons)

Area	2022	2023	2024	2025	2026	2027	2028	2029	2030
Indonesia	137.9	139.1	140.4	141.6	142.7	143.9	145.0	146.1	147.2
JABODETABEK	37.6	38.9	40.1	41.5	41.6	41.7	41.9	42.0	42.1
Bali	4.5	4.6	4.6	4.7	4.7	4.8	4.8	4.9	4.9

JABODETABEK = DKI Jakarta, Bogor, Depok, Tangerang and Bekasi.
Source: Statistics Indonesia (BPS). Japan International Cooperation Agency. 2019. JABODETABEK Urban Transportation Policy Integration Project Phase 2 in the Republic of Indonesia.

Table 20: Projected Number of E-Motorcycles with Regulatory Interventions
(million operational units)

Area	2022	2023	2024	2025	2026	2027	2028	2029	2030
Indonesia	0.80	2.90	7.30	12.00	18.20	26.00	35.00	45.00	56.00
JABODETABEK	0.12	0.40	1.02	1.69	2.56	3.65	4.91	6.28	7.85
Bali	0.03	0.09	0.24	0.40	0.60	0.86	1.16	1.48	1.85

JABODETABEK = DKI Jakarta, Bogor, Depok, Tangerang and Bekasi.
Source: Grütter Consulting.

It is assumed that 90% of e-motorcycles are private units while the rest are commercial units. The projected environmental and economic impacts of this strategy are discussed in Chapter 13.

8.8 Comparison of Electric Motorcycle Deployment of Scenarios in JABODETABEK and Bali

Tables 21 and 22 compare the projected deployment of e-motorcycles with the different scenarios in JABODETABEK and Bali. Scenario 1 requires financial subsidies and scenario 2 requires regulatory steps limiting the usage of fossil-fuel-based motorcycles in the area. In the absence of subsidies or regulations, the BAU scenario is the probable outcome.

Table 21: Projected Number of E-Motorcycles in JABODETABEK with Different Scenarios ('000)

Scenario	2022	2023	2024	2025	2026	2027	2028	2029	2030
Total motorcycles	17,848	18,205	18,387	18,387	18,387	18,387	18,387	18,387	18,387
BAU e-motorcycles	3	4	6	7	8	10	11	13	14
Scenario 1: RUEN / DEN with subsidies	21	67	154	301	517	829	1,250	1,887	2,869
Scenario 2 e-motorcycles: GSE with regulations	116	403	1,022	1,690	2,556	3,648	4,911	6,276	7,847

BAU = business as usual, DEN = National Energy Council, GSE = Grand Strategy for Energy, JABODETABEK = DKI Jakarta, Bogor, Depok, Tangerang and Bekasi, RUEN = National Energy Plan.
Source: Grütter Consulting.

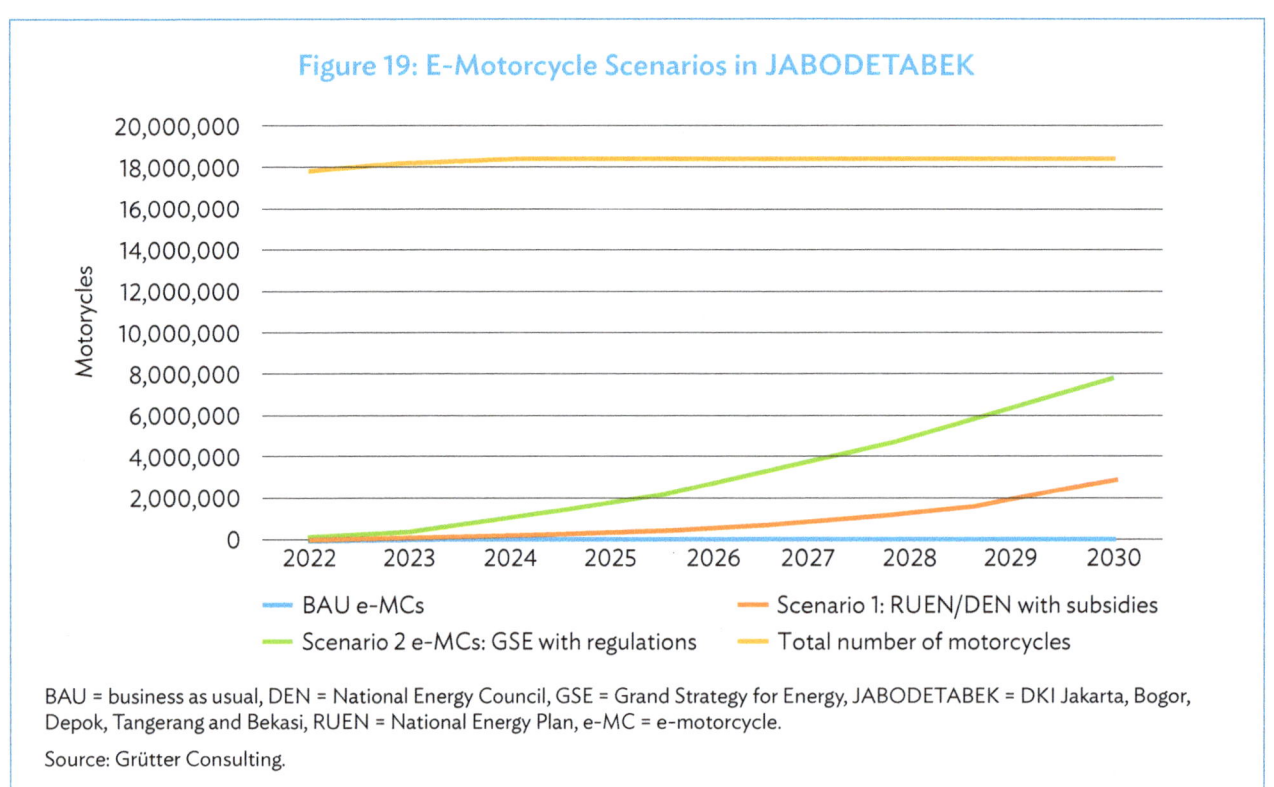

Figure 19: E-Motorcycle Scenarios in JABODETABEK

BAU = business as usual, DEN = National Energy Council, GSE = Grand Strategy for Energy, JABODETABEK = DKI Jakarta, Bogor, Depok, Tangerang and Bekasi, RUEN = National Energy Plan, e-MC = e-motorcycle.
Source: Grütter Consulting.

Table 22: Projected Number of E-Motorcycles in Bali with Different Scenarios
('000)

Scenario	2022	2023	2024	2025	2026	2027	2028	2029	2030
Total motorcycles	4,209	4,293	4,336	4,336	4,336	4,336	4,336	4,336	4,336
BAU e-motorcycles	1	1	1	2	2	2	3	3	3
Scenario 1: RUEN / DEN with subsidies	5	16	36	71	122	196	295	445	677
Scenario 2 e-motorcycles: GSE with regulations	27	95	241	399	603	860	1,158	1,480	1,851

BAU = business as usual, DEN = National Energy Council, GSE = Grand Strategy for Energy, RUEN = National Energy Plan.
Source: Grütter Consulting.

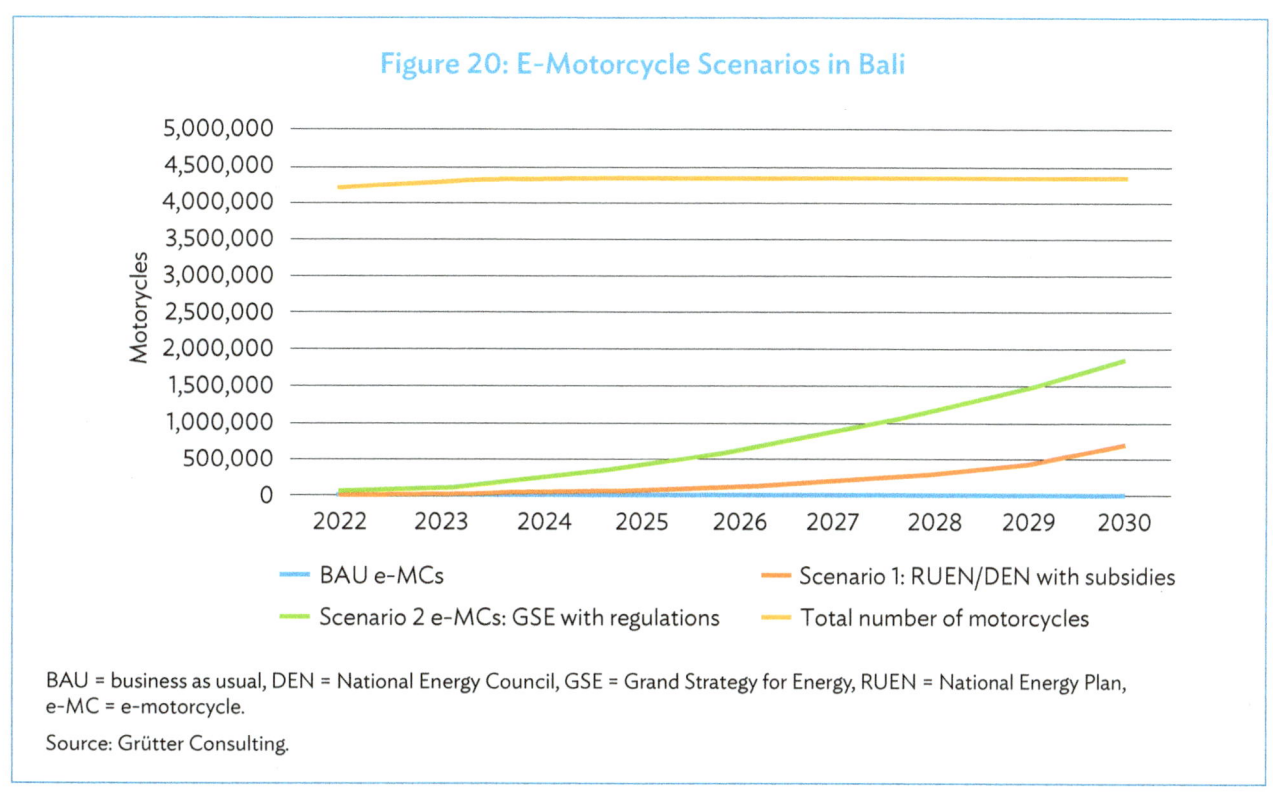

Figure 20: E-Motorcycle Scenarios in Bali

BAU = business as usual, DEN = National Energy Council, GSE = Grand Strategy for Energy, RUEN = National Energy Plan, e-MC = e-motorcycle.
Source: Grütter Consulting.

8.9 Viewpoint of Manufacturers

EzyFast

PT EzyFast Energi Pratama Indonesia (EzyFast) is a battery swap service provider for e-motorcycles operating in the Jakarta area. EzyFast has a certain target for their battery swap facility (a grid of 3x3 to 4x4 km²) for Jakarta. Once this target is achieved, they plan to expand their service to Surabaya and Bali. At the moment, the EzyFast battery swap stations are still in the pilot stage. However, they claim that they are prepared to commercialize it using a business-to-business scheme. The battery swap station provided by EzyFast has 12 slots or dockings, which is quite large compared to other companies. The electric power consumed per cabinet is ±4,500 kW. The parts are imported from the PRC and assembled in Indonesia. EzyFast plans to produce in the medium term their own cabinet in Indonesia to achieve a higher domestic content level, in collaboration with the Indovickers company.

Battery health and maintenance is EzyFast's responsibility. Every battery has a battery management system (BMS), which is integrated with the EzyFast application using internet-of-things technology to maintain its condition. EzyFast has a collaboration with several e-motorcycle manufacturers, e.g., Viar and Gesits. Customers can purchase a Viar e-motorcycle without the battery and opt for the battery service provided by EzyFast. To enable this, EzyFast modifies their battery to fit the holder in the e-motorcycle. With Gesits, the battery is compatible. The battery swap locations planned by EzyFast are at the site of PLN's substations. Tariffs have not yet been established but a monthly subscription with unlimited battery swapping is estimated at Rp350,000 (this would be around the equivalent of gasoline costs for 1,800 km). Per swapped battery, the cost would be around Rp8,000, which amounts to a cost of Rp160/km (gasoline cost is around Rp200/km).

Source: EzyFast.

Indonesia Battery Corporation

The Indonesia Battery Corporation (IBC) is a national battery holding company with the shareholder composition of Antam, Mining Industry Indonesia (MIND ID), Pertamina, and PLN, each having 25% ownership. It was legally established on 21 April 2021. IBC's mission is establishing an electric vehicle battery ecosystem, and supporting Indonesia as a production hub for battery and electric vehicle production in Southeast Asia. IBC is looking at the entire value chain for the electric vehicle battery ecosystem development from the raw material to battery recycling facilities.

IBC projections of e-motorcycles are based on PLN projections (Chapter 8). The IBC target is to manage the precursor, cathode, and cell (nickel-based) plants by 2025 (Figure 21).

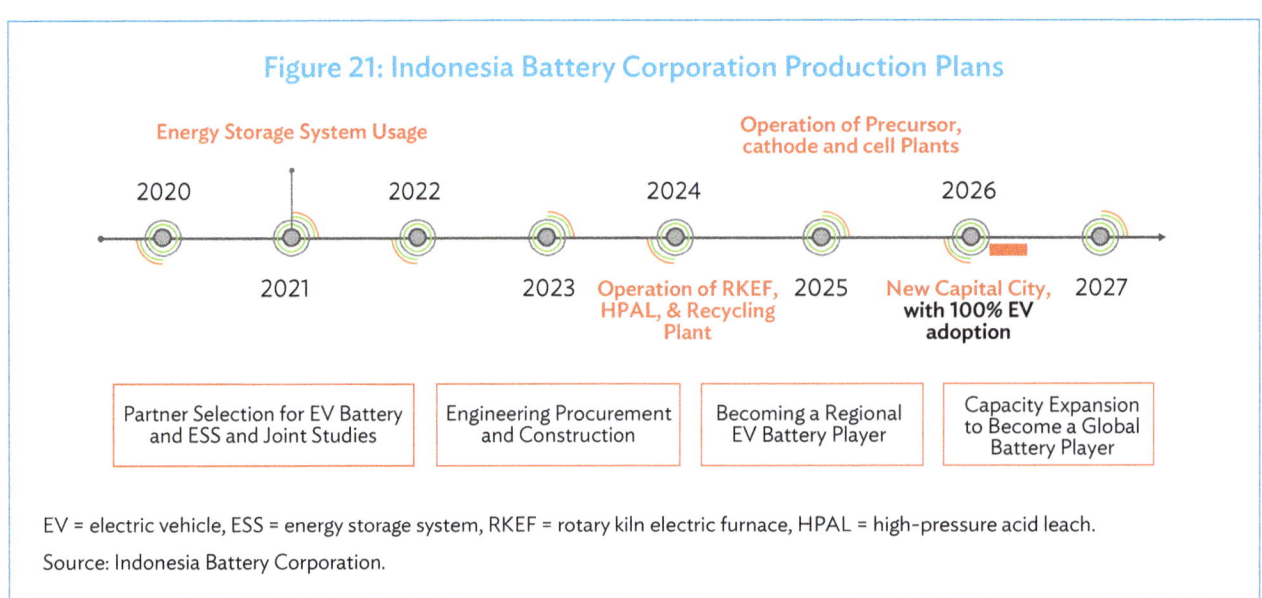

EV = electric vehicle, ESS = energy storage system, RKEF = rotary kiln electric furnace, HPAL = high-pressure acid leach.
Source: Indonesia Battery Corporation.

Next to the upstream manufacturing business, as a short-term business plan, IBC is exploring the downstream battery ecosystem business opportunity including battery pack production, charging infrastructure, and battery recycling.

PT WIKA Industri Manufaktur–Gesits

PT WIKA Industri Manufaktur (WIMA) is a joint venture between PT Wijaya Karya Industri & Konstruksi (WIKON, a state-owned company) and PT Gesits Technologies Indo (GTI). WIMA's business line revolves on electric two-wheeler research and development, manufacturing, and after-sales service. Their first and most well-known product is called Gesits. WIMA has one factory for assembling Gesits, located in Cileungsi, Bogor, Indonesia. Their current production capacity is 200 units per shift, with a maximum capacity of up to 500 units per two-shift per day. As of June 2021, their sales target was 48,000 units per year.[40]

Viar/Vrent

Viar is a motorcycle manufacturer, including electric ones. In June 2017, they introduced Viar Q1, their first e-motorcycle. Viar Motor Indonesia split their electric two-wheeler products into two segments, electric motorcycles (e-motorcycle; 800 W unit) and electric scooter or e-bike (400 W unit). The main sales barrier is the lower power when compared with the ICE. Also, much higher down payments are asked for electric units compared to gasoline motorcycles, probably due to risks concerning the resale price of used e-motorcycles. The current production capacity for all their electric vehicle products is 200 units per day (73,000 per year). Currently, this capacity is split into 60% for e-motorcycles and 40% for e-scooters. If needed, they can allocate all 200 for e-motorcycles only. Viar is quite confident of its long-term market prospect but more careful with its short-term expansion plan. Viar relies more on home and destination charging and not on battery swapping, but they are open to any collaboration with battery swap developers and have an agreement with EzyFast.

Viar believes that standardization of specific battery types will be a barrier for technology improvement and innovation, i.e., while standardization removes a certain barrier of battery swap, it can create other long-term problems of lack of innovation and a decline in cost.

Viar also has a subsidiary for renting electric two-wheelers, called Vrent, operating both as a business-to-business and business-to-consumer business in JABODETABEK, but mainly in Jakarta with currently 500 e-motorcycles and e-scooters. Users have to meet a number of requirements to ride the e-motorcycle, i.e., must be at least 17 years old, have a driving license (in Indonesia called "SIM C"), not exceed the maximum capacity load of the e-motorcycle (250 kg), use a helmet while riding, and obey the traffic rules. The e-motorcycle has an official vehicle registration number released by the Indonesian National Police. E-motorcycles can be rented for 15 minutes (Rp2,500) up to 1 day (Rp50,000). Monthly schemes were introduced during the COVID-19 pandemic, at Rp650,000 for e-scooters and Rp800,000 for the higher-powered version.

---

[40] G. Satria. 2021. Target Penjualan Gesits 2021, Ikuti Kapasitas Produksi (Gesits Sales Target 2021, Follow Production Capacity). *Kompas*. 6 April. https://otomotif.kompas.com/read/2021/04/06/171100215/target-penjualan-gesits-2021-ikuti-kapasitas-produksi.

Swap Energi

Swap Energi has three business lines related to electric two-wheelers and battery usage:

- As a battery swap service provider for electric two-wheelers, they currently operate in JABODETABEK, but mainly in Jakarta, their docking station has three battery slots with a 1,000 W power rating.
- As an energy provider, they use battery swap technologies, however this business line is still in the planning stage and is a part of their expansion plan.
- They are also an electric two-wheeler manufacturer under the brand Smoot (1,500 W unit).

Swap Energi battery is currently only compatible with Smoot, an electric two-wheeler brand under the same company as a part of its ecosystem. Every purchase of a Smoot e-motorcycle has already included one swap battery inside. Expanding the compatibility to other manufacturers is part of their expansion plan. Every battery has an ID number and is integrated with the Swap App using internet-of-things technology to maintain its condition. It also has a BMS to avoid battery damage from overcharging and overheating.

Swap Energi offers different subscription packages: Rp20,000 per 100 km (valid for 30 days), Rp45,000 per 250 km (valid for 60 days), and Rp80,000 per 500 km (valid for 60 days). This means that the tariff per km with battery swap scheme is Rp160–200 (this is less than the gasoline cost per kilometer for a typical motorcycle, which amounts to around Rp200; however, the e-motorcycle is, at 1,500 W, not identical to a gasoline motorcycle in terms of power and speed).

Swap Energi's expansion plans for docking stations are listed in Table 23. The e-motorcycle production capacity is planned to be expanded from 3,000 units in 2021 to 50,000 units in 2025 and 400,000 units by 2030.

Table 23: Docking Station Plans Swap Energi

Docking Stations	2021	2025	2030
JABODETABEK, Bandung	500	4,000	10,000
Bali, Surabaya, Jogjakarta	0	2,500	8,000
Indonesia	500	6,500	18,000

Source: Swap Energi.

Astra Honda Motor

Astra Honda Motor is a market leader in the motorcycle industry in Indonesia. As of 2020, Astra Honda Motor sold ± 3 million units of ICE motorcycles. Astra Honda Motor currently has the PCX Hybrid electric vehicle (1,400 W) and the Honda PCX electric vehicle (4,200 W). The Honda PCX electric vehicle is not yet commercially available. Currently, Astra Honda Motor does not have a specific road map for e-motorcycles in their production line as they are more in a wait-and-see position. Astra Honda Motor can currently manufacture 3,000 Honda PCX Hybrid electric vehicles per year.

9. Electric Motorcycle Charging Systems for Indonesia

In Chapter 6, motorcycle usage was divided into private usage (e-motorcycle users and students with electric scooters) and commercial usage; the latter can be divided into passenger and goods transport. Within passenger transport, ride-hailing (i.e., taxi) services constitute an important part of the national system. Scooter rental services are important in tourism sites such as Bali. Goods transport includes courier services, food, grocery, and other deliveries.

Battery swapping is not standardized yet. This can cause issues if different types of batteries are not compatible with different swap stations. Swapping infrastructure could be standardized on a national level; like the known AA-size "penlight" cell, this standard size could be produced by many manufacturing companies. This could be an opportunity for the Government of Indonesia, since the swapping concept is at its nascent stage. Taipei,China followed a different route: they picked Gogoro over other electric scooter brands to collaborate on battery swap stations, thereby promoting a private brand as the de facto standard of battery swapping in the country. However, this did not work since KYMCO is currently putting up different swapping stations not compatible with the Gogoro units. Drawbacks regarding standardization are that the competition around battery performance could be hampered. Without standardization, local fleet operations can team up with a swap infrastructure company. Because service companies have a limited geographical service area, the swapping infrastructure can focus on this area and expand from there. Lack of standardization is therefore not considered to be a major impediment to e-motorcycle and swapping station deployment.

9.1 Battery Swapping Infrastructure

This section presents scenarios for the deployment of swapping stations that match the electric vehicle projections of Table 20 based on a regulatory scenario. It is assumed that 90% of all e-motorcycles are for private usage and 10% are for commercial usage. Commercial e-motorcycles are assumed to have at least two batteries on board and private ones, on average, have only one. Commercial users would then swap batteries once or twice a day while also charging at home or at the nighttime destination. It is assumed that private users, in general, charge the battery at home or use destination charging, i.e., the usage of swapping stations of private users would be limited. At swapping stations, it is assumed that the user immediately receives a fully charged equivalent battery, i.e., the battery received needs to be identical to the battery turned over. This allows the driver to continue their journey and also avoids having to return to the station to recover the charged battery.

Inside the swap station, the recharging time is assumed to be 1 hour or less, so each dock in the station can give a full battery every hour. This means that the maximum number of batteries that can be serviced equals the number of batteries inside the swap station multiplied by the number of hours per day the station is operational (e.g., 16 hours from 6 a.m. to 10 p.m.). It is further assumed that swapping stations have a minimum of 10 docking stations, i.e., they could serve around 100 batteries per day (Table 24). Swapping stations with 20 slots would serve around 200 batteries per day, which is a comparable number to Taipei,China.

Table 24: General Assumptions for Swapping and Charging Infrastructure

Parameter	Commercial Usage	Private Usage
Number of batteries per e-motorcycle	2	1
Distance driven daily (km)	80	46
Specific energy usage (kWh/km)	0.025	0.025
Battery useable capacity (kWh/battery)	1	1
Battery swaps per day per motorcycle (swaps/day/motorcycle)	1.5	0[a]
Charging power per battery (kW)	1	
Slots/docks at swap station	10	
Station number of operating hours (hour)	16	
Average recharge time per battery (hour)	1	
Station capacity (slots x operating hours)	160	
Projected station utilization	60%	
Projected number of battery swaps per station per day	96	
Calculated e-motorcycles attended per day[b] (e-motorcycles)	64	

km = kilometer, kW = kilowatt, kWh = kilowatt-hour.
[a] Private users are assumed to charge in general at home or use destination charging.
[b] Average value assuming same motorcycle swaps 2x battery.
Source: Grütter Consulting and Det norske veritas.

With these assumptions, the number of swap stations needed for a certain number of electric vehicles in an area can be calculated. Furthermore, the distance between swap stations must not be too large for general users. Initially, it makes sense to focus on fleet operations in a limited area to have the electric vehicles with swappable batteries circle around the swap station(s) that would be located more or less in the center of the fleet delivery area. When many swap stations are available, it makes sense to have a typical distance between swap stations of around 5–6 km resulting in around 9 km² of capture area per swapping station.[41] This would mean that a rider can start looking for a swap station when the motorcycle's battery is at 10%–20%.[42]

At a certain level of electric vehicle and corresponding swap station deployment, the theoretical average distance between swap stations could become relatively small (e.g., less than 3 km). In that case, it would be logical to group swap stations together in one location with a larger number of docks. However, if batteries are not standardized—which resembles the most probable case—multiple swapping stations with different battery types can be located at the same site. For modelling purposes, a scenario with "standardized" battery sets and one with non-standardized battery sets is assumed. For the latter, it is assumed that three different battery types for swapping are offered.

---

[41] With 6 km between each station, the capture area is roughly 9 km².
[42] This swapping area coincides with that defined by EzyFast.

Swapping Infrastructure in JABODETABEK

Table 25 shows general features relevant for the swapping infrastructure in JABODETABEK.

Table 25: Overview JABODETABEK

Parameter	2022	2025	2030
JABODETABEK land area[a]	7,000 km² of which DKI Jakarta 660 km²		
Projected inhabitants	38 million	41 million	42 million
Total number of motorcycles, of which 10% are commercial	18 million	18 million	18 million
Number of e-motorcycles • BAU scenario • Scenario 1: RUEN / DEN with subsidies • Scenario 2: GSE with regulations	3,000 21,000 116,000	7,000 300,000 1,690,000	14,000 2,870,000 7,850,000

BAU = business as usual, DEN = National Energy Council, GSE = Grand Strategy for Energy, RUEN = National Energy Plan.

[a] I. F. Robbany, A. Gharghi, K-P. Traub. 2019. Land Use Change Detection and Urban Sprawl Monitoring in Metropolitan Area of Jakarta (JABODETABEK) from 2001 to 2015. KnE Engineering. 10.18502/keg.v4i3.5862.

Source: Grütter Consulting; for number of e-motorcycles per scenario, see Table 20.

Table 26 shows the required number of swapping stations and the service area they would have to attend to. The service area is inversely correlated to the number of e-motorcycles, i.e., the more e-motorcycles circulate, the smaller the service area that each swapping station must cover.

Table 26: Scenarios for 2025 in JABODETABEK

Parameter	BAU	Scenario 1: RUEN–DEN/Subsidies	Scenario 2: Scenario GSE/Regulations
Number of e-motorcycles	7,000	300,000	1,690,000
Total number of battery swaps per day	1,050	45,000	254,000
Number of swap stations	11	470	2,640
Service area per swap station "standardized"	640 km²	15 km²	2.7 km²
Service area per swap station "non-standardized"	1,914 km²	45 km²	8 km²

BAU = business as usual, DEN = National Energy Council, GSE = Grand Strategy for Energy, JABODETABEK = DKI Jakarta, Bogor, Depok, Tangerang and Bekasi, km² = square kilometer, RUEN = National Energy Plan.

Note: Non-standardized assuming three battery types; based on stations with 10 slots

Source: Grütter Consulting.

Eventually, the number of service stations will be less but with more slots. From the data on Table 26, the following conclusions can be drawn:

- Initially the swapping stations will require a focus on a certain geographic area. If initially the focus is on Central Jakarta the service area by 2025 would be less than 2 km² for the two scenarios assuming standardized batteries and less than 5 km² assuming non-standardized batteries.
- With non-standardized batteries, only scenario 2 results in a sufficient density of swapping stations by 2025.

Initially, the focus could thus be on DKI Jakarta getting from the start a sufficient density of swapping stations and then expanding to the entire urban zone. Table 27 and Figure 22 detail the annual increase of swapping stations for scenario 2 (regulatory scenario).

Table 27: Projected Number of Swapping Stations in JABODETABEK under Scenario 2

Parameter	2022	2023	2024	2025	2026	2027	2028	2029	2030
Total e-motorcycles (thousand)	116	403	1,022	1,690	2,556	3,648	4,911	6,276	7,847
Swapping stations standardized	181	629	700	700	700	700	700	700	700
Area per swap station standardized (km²)	39	11	<10	<10	<10	<10	<10	<10	<10
Swapping stations non standardized	181	629	1,596	2,100	2,100	2,100	2,100	2,100	2,100
Area per swap station non-standardized (km²)	116	33	13	<10	<10	<10	<10	<10	<10

JABODETABEK = DKI Jakarta, Bogor, Depok, Tangerang and Bekasi, km² = square kilometer.

Note: This is based on stations with 10 slots; minimum service area 10 km², i.e., if the area drops below this threshold value, the number of slots is increased per swapping station and not the number of swapping stations.

Source: Grütter Consulting.

The high initial number of e-motorcycles would be sufficient to establish a relatively dense network of swap stations in DKI Jakarta but not all over JABODETABEK. Without battery standardization, by 2025, the density would be sufficient for the entire region. From there on, it would be expected that the number of swap stations would not continue to grow much more, i.e., the growth would be more in the number of slots, as this would be more profitable than expanding the number of stations.

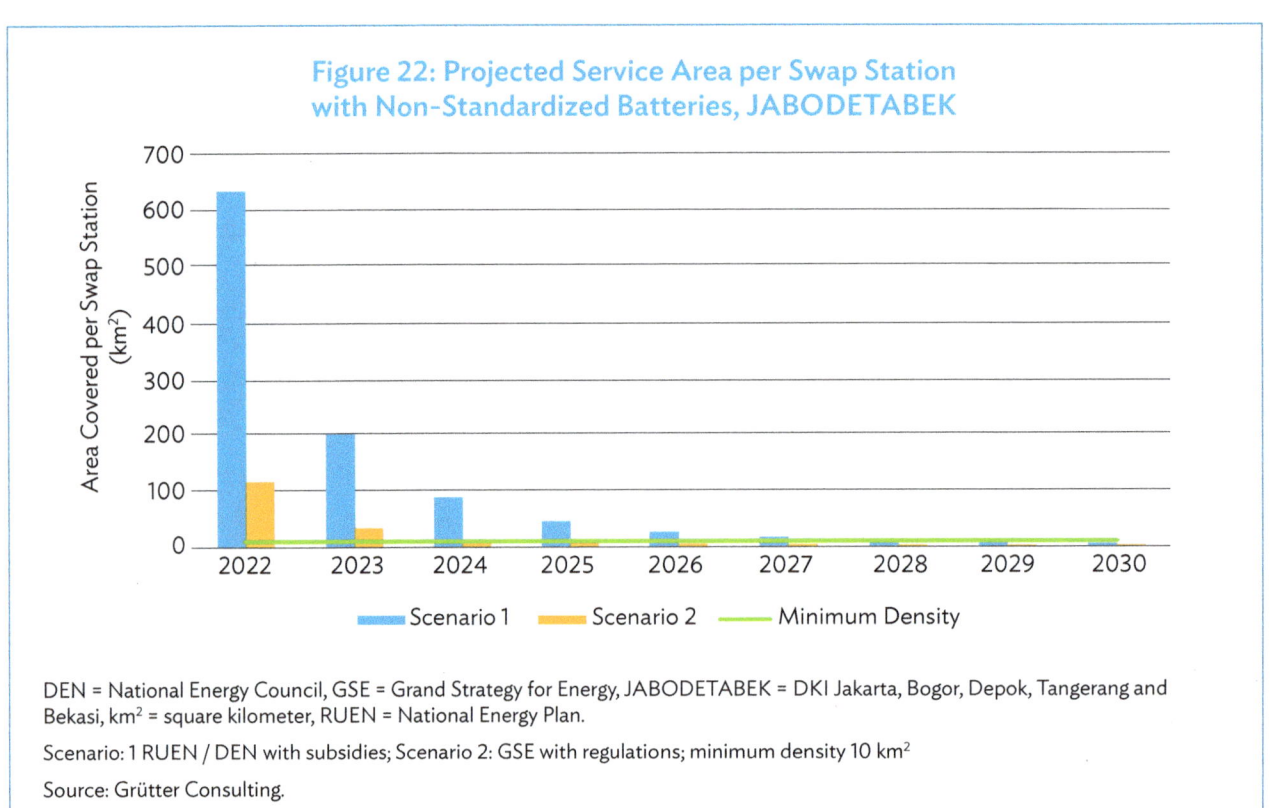

Figure 22: Projected Service Area per Swap Station with Non-Standardized Batteries, JABODETABEK

DEN = National Energy Council, GSE = Grand Strategy for Energy, JABODETABEK = DKI Jakarta, Bogor, Depok, Tangerang and Bekasi, km² = square kilometer, RUEN = National Energy Plan.

Scenario: 1 RUEN / DEN with subsidies; Scenario 2: GSE with regulations; minimum density 10 km²

Source: Grütter Consulting.

The number of required swap stations under a model of standardized batteries is significantly smaller and would reach the required density quicker. However, the probability of achieving such a standardization is limited as market players prefer to push their technologies and standardization would require same type batteries, which also influences the design of the motorcycle.

Under scenario 1, with financial incentives, the number of e-motorcycles would be much lower, resulting in a sufficient density of swapping stations by around 2026–2028 assuming standardized and non-standardized batteries, which, in effect, means that charging stations need to be subsidized under that scenario (compare with Figure 25). Scenario 2, with regulations, has a clear advantage in terms of density of swapping stations but, more importantly, does not require a politically and economically difficult standardization of battery types.

Swapping Infrastructure in Bali

Table 28 shows general features relevant for the swapping infrastructure in Bali.

Table 28: Overview of Bali

Parameter	2022	2025	2030
Bali land area[a]	5,800 km², of which Kota Denpasar 124 km²		
Projected inhabitants	4.5 million	4.7 million	4.9 million
Tourists on island during peak time	0.1 million	0.1 million	0.1 million
Total number of motorcycles, of which 10% are commercial and 25,000 for rent	4.2 million	4.3 million	4.3 million
Number of e-motorcycle • BAU scenario • Scenario 1: RUEN / DEN with subsidies • Scenario 2: GSE with regulations	1,000 5,000 27,000	2,000 70,000 400,000	3,000 680,000 1,850,000

BAU = business as usual, DEN = National Energy Council, GSE = Grand Strategy for Energy, km² = square kilometer, RUEN = National Energy Plan.
[a] *Encyclopaedia Brittanica.* "Bali." https://www.britannica.com/place/Bali-island-and-province-Indonesia (accessed 21 February 2022).
Source: Grütter Consulting; for the number of e-motorcycles per scenario, see Table 21.

Table 29 shows the required number of swapping stations and their service area they would have to attend to.

Table 29: Scenarios for 2025 in Bali

Parameter	BAU	Scenario 1: RUEN - DEN / subsidies	Scenario 2: Scenario GSE / regulations
Number of e-motorcycles	2,000	70,000	400,000
Total number of battery swaps per day	250	11,000	60,000
Number of swap stations	3	110	620
Service area per swap station "standardized"	2,240 km²	52 km²	9 km²
Service area per swap station "non-standardized"	entire Bali	160 km²	28 km²

BAU = business as usual, DEN = National Energy Council, GSE = Grand Strategy for Energy, km² = square kilometer, RUEN = National Energy Plan.
Source: Grütter Consulting and Det Norske Veritas.

From the data on Table 29, the following conclusions can be drawn:

- Initially, the swapping stations will require a focus on a certain geographic area. If initially the focus is on Kota Denpasar, the service area by 2025 would be less than 2 km² for the two scenarios assuming standardized batteries, and less than 10 km² assuming non-standardized batteries.
- With non-standardized batteries only, scenario 2 can result in a sufficient density of swapping stations in the medium term.

Initially, the focus could thus be on Kota Denpasar getting a sufficient density of swapping stations from the start and then expanding to the entire island. Table 30 and Figure 23 detail the annual increase of swapping stations for scenario 2 (regulatory scenario).

Table 30: Projected Number of Swapping Stations in Bali under Scenario 2

Parameter	2022	2023	2024	2025	2026	2027	2028	2029	2030
Total e-motorcycles (thousands)	27	95	241	399	603	860	1,158	1,480	1,851
Swapping stations standardized	43	148	376	580	580	580	580	580	580
Area per swap station standardized (km²)	136	39	15	<10	<10	<10	<10	<10	<10
Swapping stations non standardized	43	148	376	623	942	1,344	1,740	1,740	1,740
Area per swap station non-standardized (km²)	407	117	46	28	18	13	<10	<10	<10

km² = square kilometer.

Note: This is based on stations with 10 slots; minimum service area 10km², i.e., if the area drops below this threshold value, the number of slots is increased per swapping station and not the number of swapping stations.

Source: Grütter Consulting.

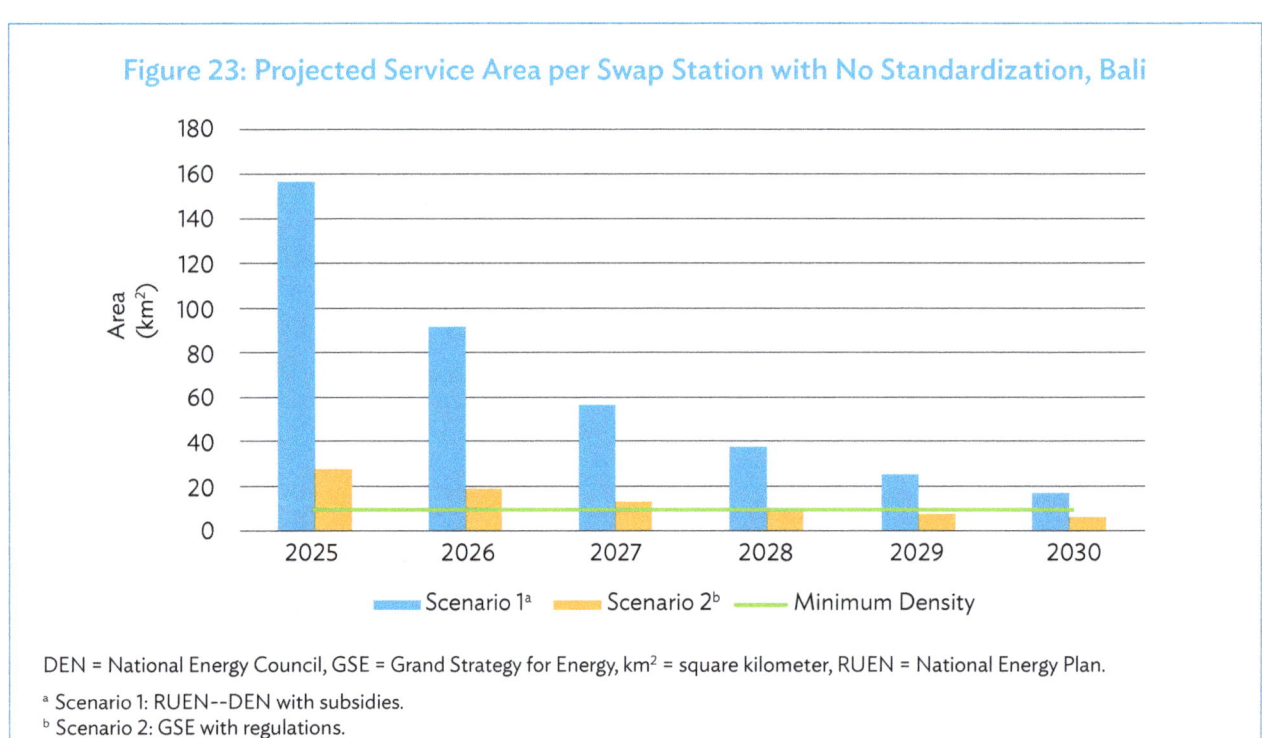

Figure 23: Projected Service Area per Swap Station with No Standardization, Bali

DEN = National Energy Council, GSE = Grand Strategy for Energy, km² = square kilometer, RUEN = National Energy Plan.

[a] Scenario 1: RUEN--DEN with subsidies.
[b] Scenario 2: GSE with regulations.

Source: Grütter Consulting.

The initial number of e-motorcycles would not establish a relatively dense network of swap stations sufficient for the requirements. However, the focus could be initially on Kota Denpasar. This means that, at the start, focus should be given to the main towns, and to the touristic areas to have sufficient stations in these places. This would also match two important touristic uses of the wheelers: ride-hailing and rental. Without battery standardization, an island-wide sufficient density could be reached around 2028. Under scenario 1, with financial incentives, the number of e-motorcycles would be much lower resulting in a sufficient density of swapping stations only after 2030 (compare with Figure 23). The graph only shows the stations as per 2025 onwards. Prior to 2025, no sufficient density can be achieved with either scenario without focusing on certain regions of Bali.

Scenario 2 with regulations allowing for a quick increase of e-motorcycles thus has a clear advantage in terms of density of swapping stations but, more importantly, does not require a politically and economically difficult standardization of battery types.

Expected Usage Pattern of a Swapping Station

It is assumed that most of the battery swapping will take place during the day, e.g., between 6 a.m. and 10 p.m. The average charging time of the batteries inside the swap station is assumed to be 1 hour, so every dock of the station can make one swap per hour. If all 10 docks are continuously used for 16 hours, 160 swaps can be made per day. Assuming a utilization of 60%, this is almost 100 swaps. This would also mean a consistently high charging power close to the maximum of 10 docks times 1 kW, i.e., 10 kW. A typical charging profile of one larger swap station with 20 docks could look like the pattern in Figure 24.

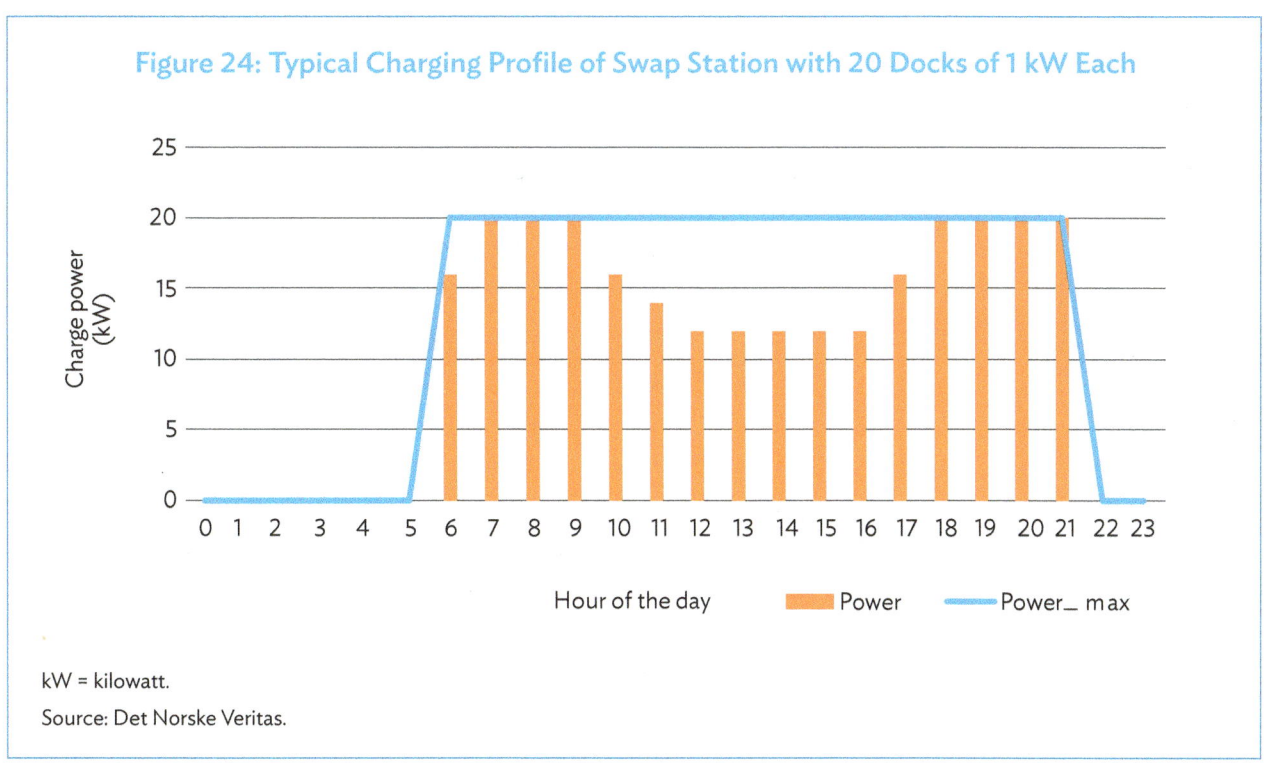

Figure 24: Typical Charging Profile of Swap Station with 20 Docks of 1 kW Each

kW = kilowatt.
Source: Det Norske Veritas.

Safety Aspects

A swapping station needs to be a safe installation on different aspects:

- **Mechanical.** The integrity of the swap station should be checked regularly, which can be done by the owner or operator of the site where it is located, with users reporting damage by an app or by phone.
- **Electrical.** Electrical safety must be maintained by a service team at least once per year. The station design should include protection against over-current, short-circuit, and electric shock.
- **Thermal.** Overheating of a battery or charger may lead to fire. Also, a temperature below 40 °C is best for battery longevity. Therefore, cooling of the batteries in the swap station is recommended. It is also advised to have a fire extinguisher (CO_2 or water) at the swap station.
- **Safety.** A first-aid kit would be handy for personal injuries.

Business Models

The peer companies investigated, like Gogoro and Sun Mobility, use a subscription model for the battery and the swapping service. Furthermore, the electricity for the battery recharge must be paid separately, e.g., through credits on the subscription card (uploaded by the rider). As a big advantage to electric vehicle riders or owners, they do not need to buy the electric vehicle batteries. Moreover, the risk of a failed battery is borne by the swap operator: if something is wrong with the battery, the rider can just swap it for a healthy one. If this is not the case, then the swapping company will have to charge a base swapping fee, including electricity cost. A typical swap cost for a motorcycle battery is around Rp8,000.[43] Around Rp1,000 is due to the electricity cost and Rp7,000 due to the swapping cost. For owners of motorcycles, it is clear that home charging is more profitable than battery swapping. Private users will only use battery swapping when they ride for longer distances. For most owners, this will still be a better option than purchasing an additional battery (investment of Rp4–5 million). For commercial users, two batteries in general will be purchased. They will have agreements with battery swap stations or even their own battery swapping sites. Also, substantial charging can be done at the premises of the service company, especially if the latter is related to courier or postal services with sites where parcels are picked up once or twice per day.

Swapping stations can be automated like the stations of Gogoro or, at a lower investment cost, be located within a small shop as an additional business. This reduces overhead costs considerably.

9.2 Battery Charging Infrastructure

This section presents scenarios for the deployment of charging stations or chargers that match the electric vehicle projections. For two-wheelers, both home and destination charging are considered. If there are many electric two-wheelers in the future, parking areas with many chargers will be needed. In this report, a maximum of 1,000 chargers per parking area is assumed. Of course, charging locations with fewer chargers will also exist.

---

[43] Based on EzyFast with Rp800 per 10% discharge of battery; Swap Energi charges Rp160–200 per kilometer, which amounts to Rp80,000–10,000 pre-swapped, based on a 50-kilometer range of a battery.

For the scenario analysis, charging locations of various sizes are assumed. The maximum power of each charger is assumed to be 1 kW, so the maximum charging power at a certain location is equal to the number of chargers multiplied by 1 kW. In many cases, the charging power may be an issue for the local grid connection. Therefore, it is assumed that all chargers can reduce the power in case of grid constraints (smart charging), and that all chargers at a location can share the available grid power (smart charging or load balancing). It is assumed that charging control is part of the charge point (Mode 3 charging), or built in the electric vehicle cable, i.e., an in-cable control box (Mode 2 charging; Table 31).

Table 31: Potential Size of Charging Locations

Charging location (examples)	Number of Chargers	Maximum Charging Power (kW)
Home	1, 2, 5	1, 2, 5
Small parking area (office, workplace)	10	10
Medium parking area (business area)	100	100
Large parking area (shopping mall, university)	1,000	1,000

Source: Det Norske Veritas.

It is assumed that an electric vehicle will start charging when it is connected to the charger. The smart charger will then control the power level. Typical charging power profiles during a day are shown in Figures 25, 26, and 27. Important aspects are therefore

- Home charging will primarily occur in the evening or at night (Figure 25).
- Small-sized area charging will mainly occur in the daytime (Figure 26).
- Medium- and large-sized area charging will occur during the entire day (Figure 27).

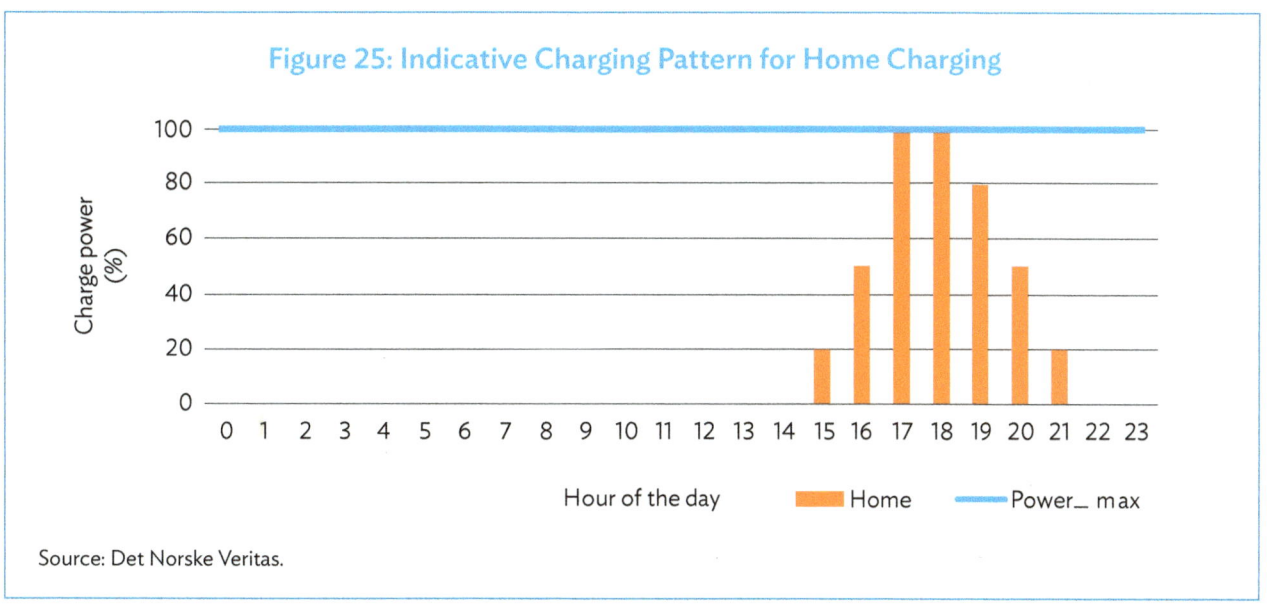

Figure 25: Indicative Charging Pattern for Home Charging

Source: Det Norske Veritas.

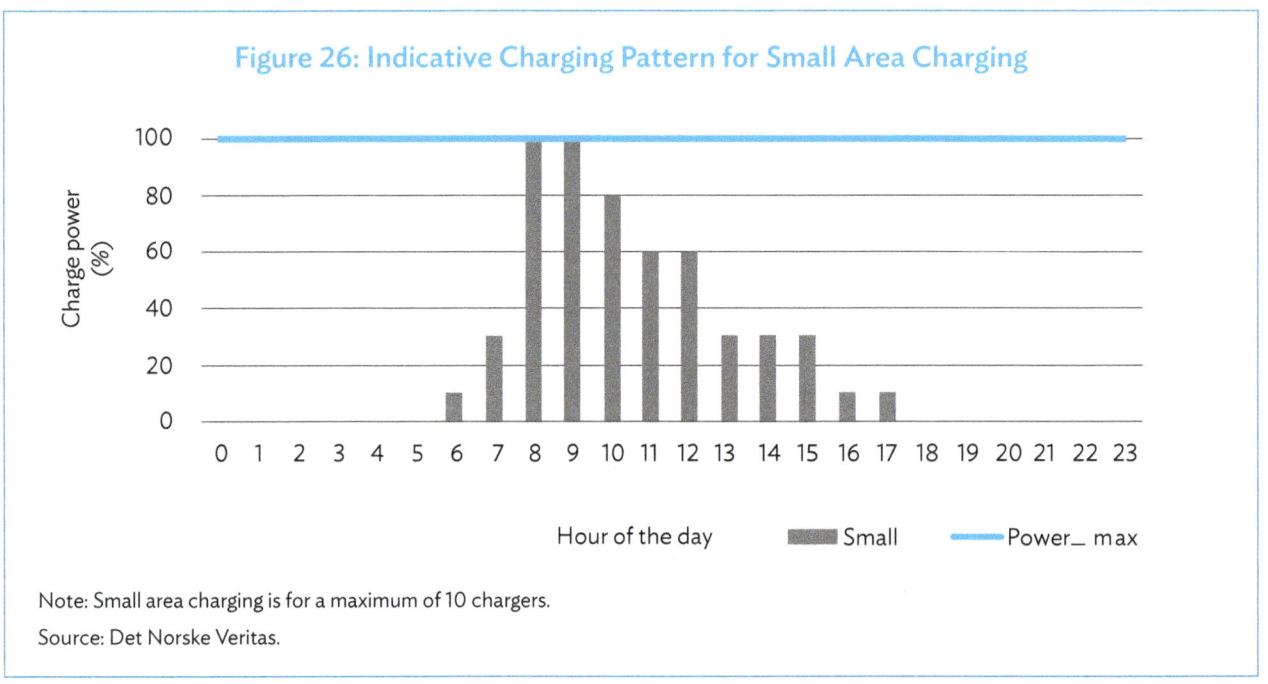

Figure 26: Indicative Charging Pattern for Small Area Charging

Note: Small area charging is for a maximum of 10 chargers.
Source: Det Norske Veritas.

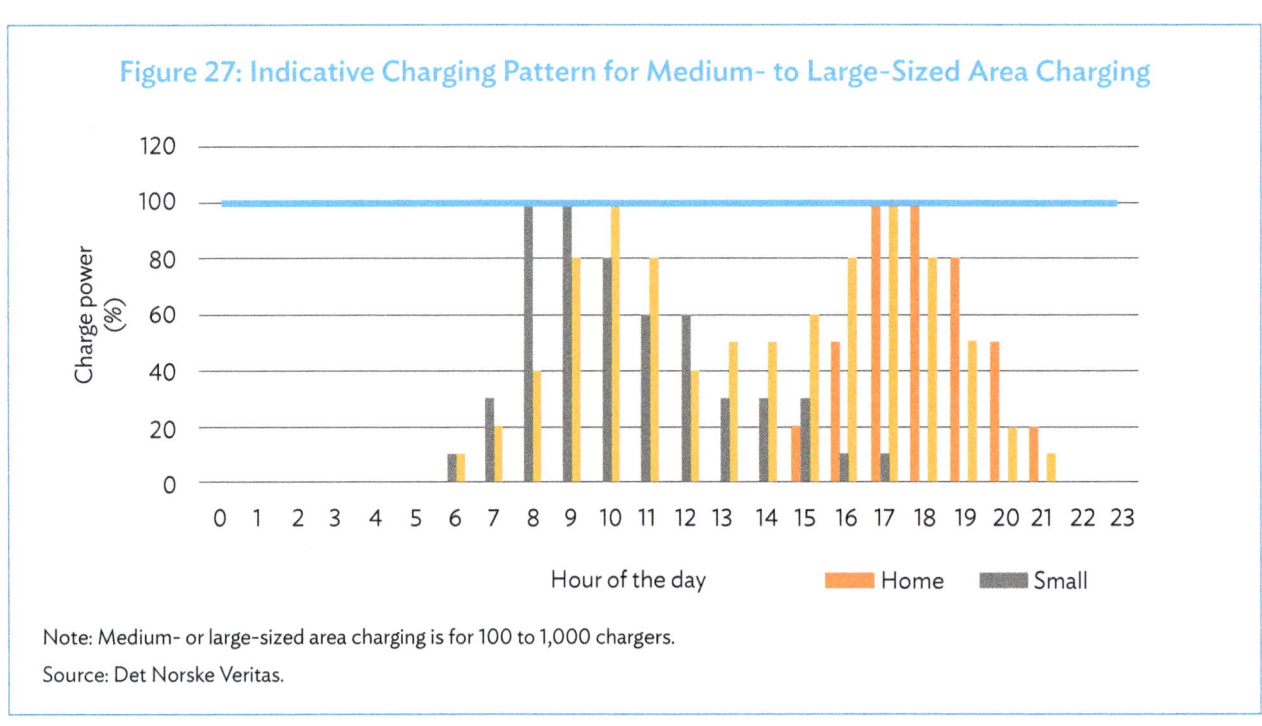

Figure 27: Indicative Charging Pattern for Medium- to Large-Sized Area Charging

Note: Medium- or large-sized area charging is for 100 to 1,000 chargers.
Source: Det Norske Veritas.

The capacity of the electric vehicle battery is set at 1 kWh. Generally, the electric vehicle will be charged partly at home and partly at the destination. This means that a charging session at full power will last less than 1 hour. With reduced power, the charging session may take several hours. Reduced-power charging is a good strategy for home charging, where the grid connection power may be limited. In that case, the charging can take all night, as long as the e-motorcycle is fully charged in the morning. At the destination, it may not be necessary that the electric vehicle is fully charged, as long as there is enough charge for the next ride. Of course, when not enough chargers are available, this can become a problem, so the number of chargers must be sufficient to serve all electric vehicles, but there is no need to have one charger for each. With low numbers of electric vehicles, the number of chargers is relatively high; with high numbers of electric vehicles, the number of chargers can be much lower.

The geographical distribution of charger locations is different than the spread of swap stations. Electric vehicle charging is done while working or doing other business. Stations need not be distributed in a fine mesh. On the other hand, it is important that sufficient chargers are available at a certain location, especially at popular sites.

Regarding the chargers needed, in the first year with a small number of electric vehicles, the number would be almost equal to that. In later years, the number of chargers is estimated to be approximately one-tenth the number of electric vehicles.[44] In a massive deployment of electric vehicle chargers, vehicles will be grouped in the stations. These stations could have 10, 100, or even 1,000 chargers at a single location, as previously explained.

The overall projected numbers of chargers for two-wheelers in JABODETABEK and Bali in 2025 are shown in Table 32.

Safety aspects for a charger location are the same as for swapping stations.

Table 32: Number of Chargers in JABODETABEK and Bali in 2025 for E-Motorcycle Scenarios

JABODETABEK	BAU	Scenario 1: RUEN - DEN / subsidies	Scenario 2: Scenario GSE / regulations
Number of e-motorcycle	7,000	300,000	1,690,000
Number of e-motorcycle private usage (90%)	6,300	270,000	1,520,000
Number of chargers	630	27,000	152,000
Bali	**BAU**	**RUEN**	**GSE**
Number of e-motorcycle	1,700	700,000	400,000
Number of e-motorcycle private usage (90%)	1,500	490,000	360,000
Number of chargers (#e-motorcycle/10)	150	49,000	36,000

BAU = business as usual, DEN = National Energy Council, GSE = Grand Strategy for Energy, JABODETABEK = DKI Jakarta, Bogor, Depok, Tangerang and Bekasi, RUEN = National Energy Plan.
Source: Grütter Consulting, Det Norske Veritas.

---

[44] Estimate by DNV; this was also mentioned in discussions with PLN.

10. Grid Impacts

This chapter provides an overview of the impact of charging e-motorcycles on the power system, including generation, transmission networks, distribution networks, and network connections (Figure 28).

The chapter will be structured around four typical charging locations:

- **Large charging sites.** These are sites with 1,000 chargers with a typical connection power of 1,000 kW.
- **Medium-sized charging sites.** These can be located in shops or shopping malls with 50–100 chargers with a typical connection power of 50–100 kW.
- **Swapping stations.** These are stand-alone stations with 10–30 battery chargers with a typical connection power of 15–40 kW.
- **Home charging.** Typically one or more two-wheelers charged from home connections.

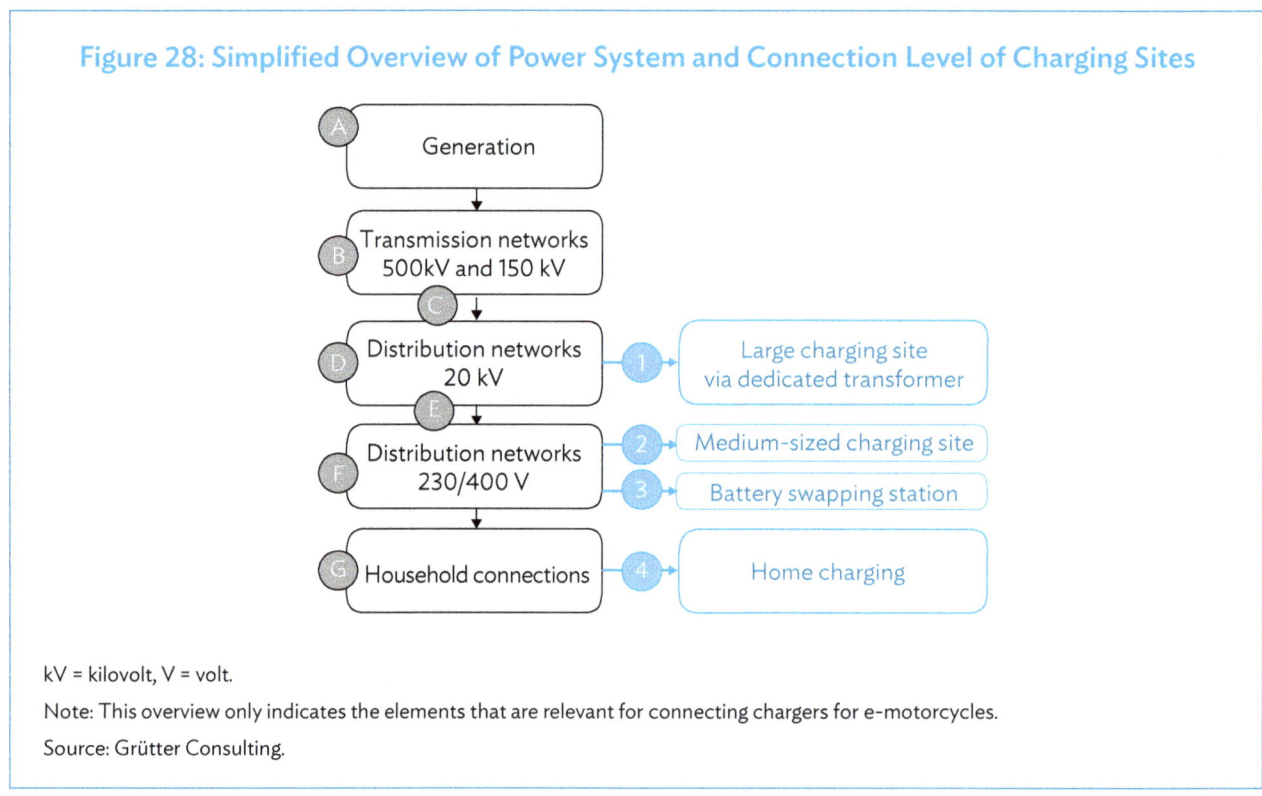

Figure 28: Simplified Overview of Power System and Connection Level of Charging Sites

kV = kilovolt, V = volt.
Note: This overview only indicates the elements that are relevant for connecting chargers for e-motorcycles.
Source: Grütter Consulting.

The left-hand side of Figure 31 shows a simplified overview of the power system in Indonesia and, more specifically, in the subsystem of Java and Bali. The generation of electricity (A) is dominated by centrally located large power plants that generate most of the power in Java and Bali. The centrally generated electricity is transported by 500-kilovolt and 150-kilovolt transmission networks (B) to the load areas, including JABODETABEK and Bali.[45] In 150/20-kilovolt substations (C), the electricity is transformed to 20 kilovolts (kV) and accordingly distributed via underground 20-kilovolt distribution networks (e.g., in the center of Jakarta) or overhead 20-kilovolt distribution networks (e.g., in outskirts of Jakarta and Bali) (D) to 20-kilovolt/400-volt transformers that transform the electricity to 400 V (E).[46] Then, 400-volt underground cables or overhead lines (F) distribute the power accordingly to the household customers (G). Section 11.1 describes the impact of the charging e-motorcycles on the different parts of the network.

The right-hand side of Figure 31 indicates at which level the four types of charging locations will be connected to the power system. Large charging sites (1) will typically connect via one or more dedicated transformers connected to the 20-kilovolt feeders. Medium-sized charging sites and battery swapping stations (2 and 3) will be connected directly to the low voltage grid (400 V). Home chargers (4) may connect to a normal power point behind the household power connection. Section 0 discusses these connections.

10.1 Impact of Charging Electric Motorcycles on the Power System

Because of the largely central generation in the power system on Java and Bali, charging of e-motorcycles will typically increase the load on all parts of the power system. After first discussing the impact on electricity demand, the sections below will therefore discuss the impact on electricity generation plant, transmission networks, and distribution networks.

Electricity Supply

Table 33 shows e-motorcycles' projected electricity demand from scenario 2.

Table 33: Projected Electricity Usage of E-Motorcycles with Regulatory Interventions (GWh)

Area	2022	2023	2024	2025	2026	2027	2028	2029	2030
Indonesia	304	1,054	2,676	4,427	6,696	9,555	12,864	16,437	20,553
JABODETABEK	43	148	376	622	940	1,342	1,806	2,308	2,886
Bali	10	35	89	147	222	316	426	544	681

GWh = gigawatt-hour, JABODETABEK = DKI Jakarta, Bogor, Depok, Tangerang and Bekasi.
Source: Grütter Consulting.

---

[45] There is currently no 500-kilovolt transmission network to Bali. Bali is only connected by 150-kilovolt transmission lines. A 500-kilovolt line between Java and Bali is being planned.
[46] In this document, low-voltage networks are referred to as 400-volt networks, which is the nominal phase-to-phase voltage in Indonesia. This 400-volt phase-to-phase voltage aligns with the 230-volt (phase-to-neutral) voltage that is applied in (single phase) household connections.

According to PLN's long-term demand forecasts for 2022 to 2028, the electricity sales in Indonesia increase 6%–7% per year. Figure 29 compares this increase with the additional electricity sales caused by charging e-motorcycles in Indonesia according to scenario 2 with regulatory interventions. The figure shows that the impact on the total sales increase is relatively small. However, by the end of the decade, more than 4% of the electricity sold by PLN in Indonesia may be used for e-motorcycle charging.

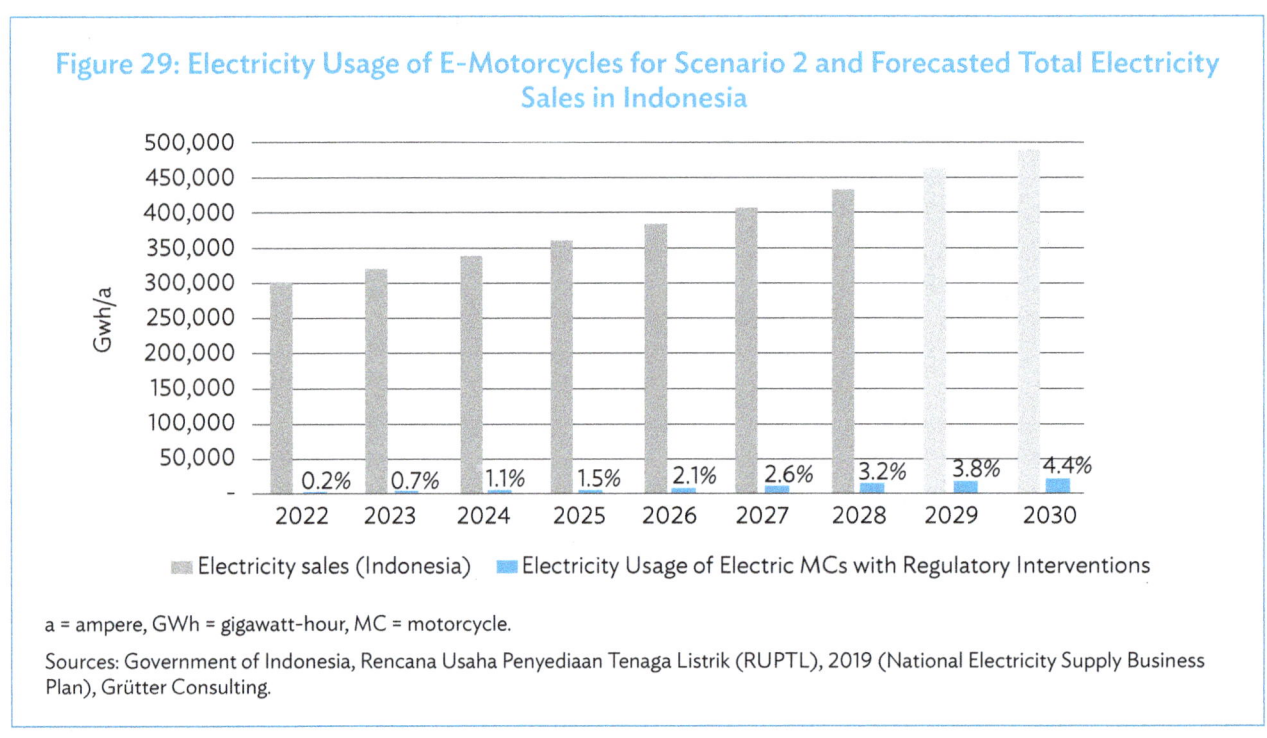

Figure 29: Electricity Usage of E-Motorcycles for Scenario 2 and Forecasted Total Electricity Sales in Indonesia

a = ampere, GWh = gigawatt-hour, MC = motorcycle.
Sources: Government of Indonesia, Rencana Usaha Penyediaan Tenaga Listrik (RUPTL), 2019 (National Electricity Supply Business Plan), Grütter Consulting.

Generation Capacity

Figure 30 compares the projected generation capacity in the Bali and Java power system (blue lines) and the forecasted peak demand (red line). The figure shows that the expected increase of the peak demand until at least 2025 is similar to the increase of generation capacity.

Reserve Margin and Peak Power

Figure 31 shows the reserve margin, which is the difference between the total installed generation capacity and the peak demand. The reserve margin provides an easy-to-understand indicator that shows the adequacy of power generation capacity.[47] Setting the target for a reserve margin depends on many issues such as generation type and is different for each power system. The figure shows that, at least until 2026, the reserve margin is quite high. This is due to an overestimated load increase in the previous decade being followed up by a large generation development program.

---

[47] It is noted that reserve margin is a simplified parameter that does not cover complexity such as availability of water for hydro plants or differences between plants.

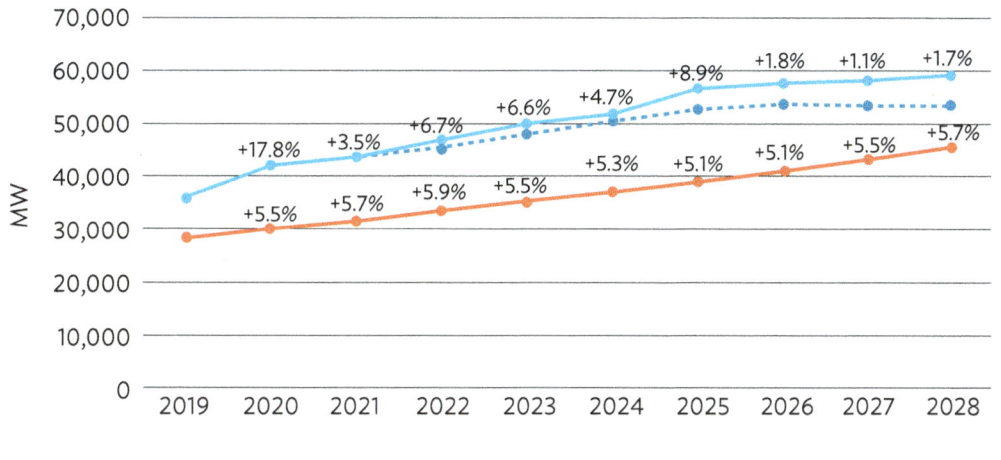

Figure 30: Net Peak Demand Projections Compared with Generation in the Power System of Bali and Java

MW = megawatt.
Source: Government of Indonesia, Rencana Usaha Penyediaan Tenaga Listrik (RUPTL), 2019 (National Electricity Supply Business Plan).

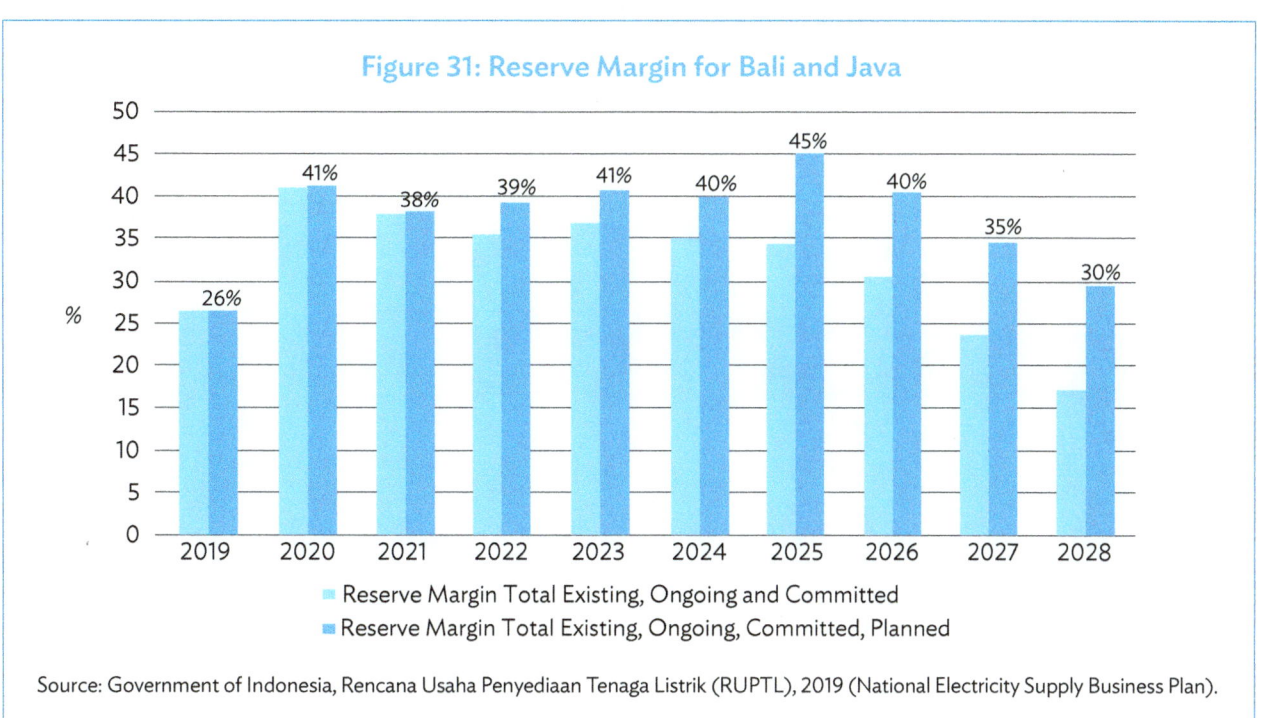

Figure 31: Reserve Margin for Bali and Java

Source: Government of Indonesia, Rencana Usaha Penyediaan Tenaga Listrik (RUPTL), 2019 (National Electricity Supply Business Plan).

Although the generation capacity in the Java/Bali system should be sufficient to facilitate the small impact of demand by e-motorcycles until 2025, the reserve margins drop after 2025. To prevent reserve margins being below the target, in 2027–2028, additional generation plants may need to come online. Charging an electric vehicle can reduce its impact on the need for additional generation capacity by limiting its contribution to the load peak. Hence, if possible, charging should take place outside the hours that the electricity demand is at its peak, which, in Jakarta, is around noon and during the evening in Bali. PLN's initiatives in "smart charging" (Box 1) for four-wheelers are therefore of large importance for reducing the necessity of new generation plants or replacing plants in (especially) the next decade. The same may apply for e-motorcycles. In section 11.3, smart charging is discussed for the different charging sites.

Transmission Networks

Transmission networks transport electricity in bulk from the large generation plants to the load centers. Transmission networks are characterized by long overhead power lines and large substations. Planning and realization of these power lines and substations typically take 5 to 10 years. Consequently, transmission systems should be planned well in advance and based on a long-term demand and generation forecast (Map 1).

Map 1: Java-Bali Electricity Transmission Map

Note: blue line = existing 500 kV transmission, and dashed line = planned transmission.

Source: M. R. Abdullah. 2020. Averting Another 8 Hours of Dark Ages. Purnomo Yusgiantoro Center. 15 June. https://www.purnomoyusgiantorocenter.org/averting-another-8-hours-of-dark-ages/.

JABODETABEK and Bali are connected to the transmission network of the Java/Bali power system. This transmission network consists of overhead lines measuring hundreds of kilometers. JABODETABEK is connected with both 500-kilovolt and 150-kilovolt lines. In the central Jakarta area, underground 150-kilovolt cables transport the electricity in bulk to the dense load centers. Bali is only connected with 150-kilovolt lines, although a 500-kilovolt connection is penciled in PLN's plans.

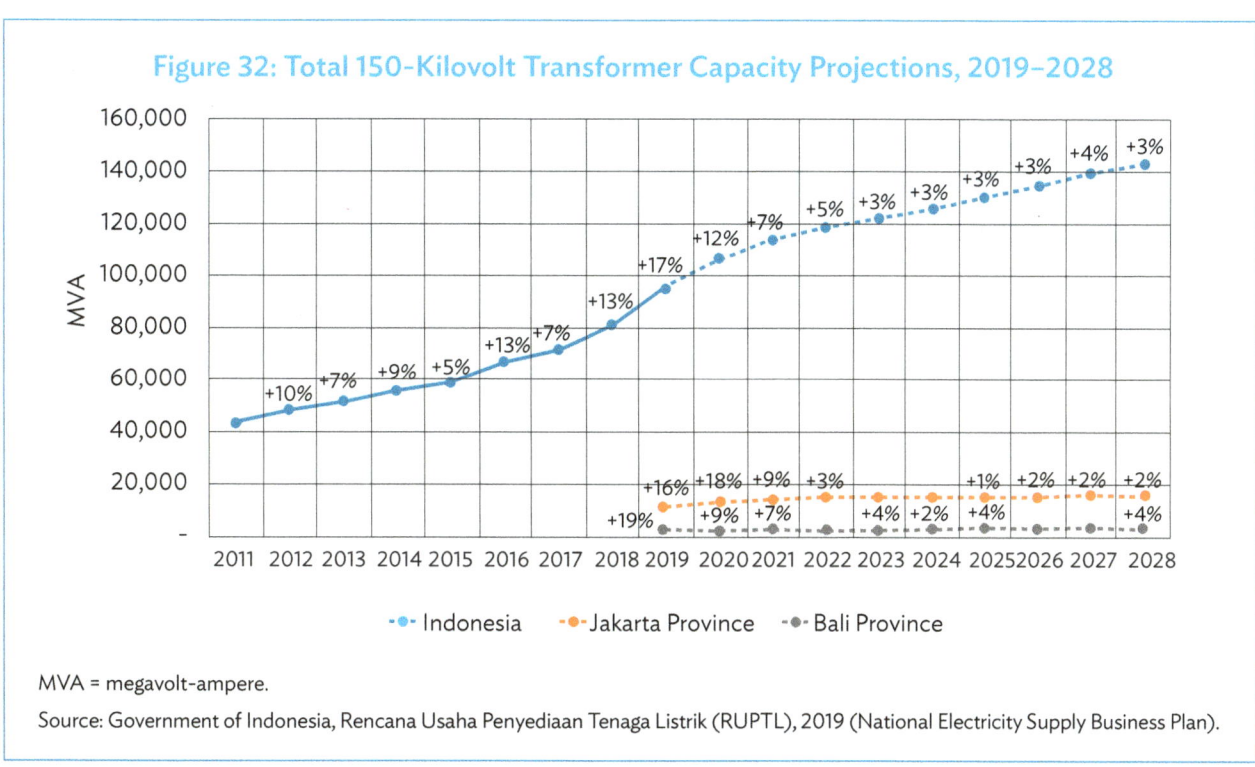

MVA = megavolt-ampere.
Source: Government of Indonesia, Rencana Usaha Penyediaan Tenaga Listrik (RUPTL), 2019 (National Electricity Supply Business Plan).

Simultaneous with increasing generation capacity, PLN is reinforcing the transmission network that connects the generation plant with the distribution networks in JABODETABEK and Bali. In 2019, PLN realized investments that increase the total Indonesian substation capacity by 17,674 megavolt-amperes and completed 6,222 km of transmission lines.[48] The investment value in the Indonesian transmission systems in 2019 was Rp39 trillion ($2.7 billion). Figure 33 shows the realized and planned capacity of 150-kilovolt transformers that connect the transmission system with the distribution system. Although the capacity increase in recent years seems to exceed the increase in generation capacity, in the coming years, the planned transformer capacity increase is lower than the load increase.

As the additional increase by e-motorcycle load is limited, it may be considered just a small addition to the total load. However, here the same applies as for generation, which means that if electric vehicles can be charged if the system is not at its peak, the need for future investments may be reduced.

Distribution Networks

Distribution networks in the Jakarta region mainly consist of 20-kilovolt networks and 400-volt networks connected to each other by 20 kV/400 V transformers. The distribution networks consist of both overhead lines and underground cables. Different from transmission networks, distribution networks can be expanded rather quickly and can rely on a shorter load forecast. In order to keep up with the current demand increase in Indonesia, PLN is continually investing in new distribution networks and reinforcing existing networks (Figure 33).

---

[48] PLN. 2019. *Memaknai Tantangan, Meningkatkan Layanan: Laporan Tahunan 2019* (Redefining Challenges, Enhancing Services: Annual Report 2019). https://web.pln.co.id/statics/uploads/2021/02/PLN_AR_2019_Rev_010221_Hires.pdf.

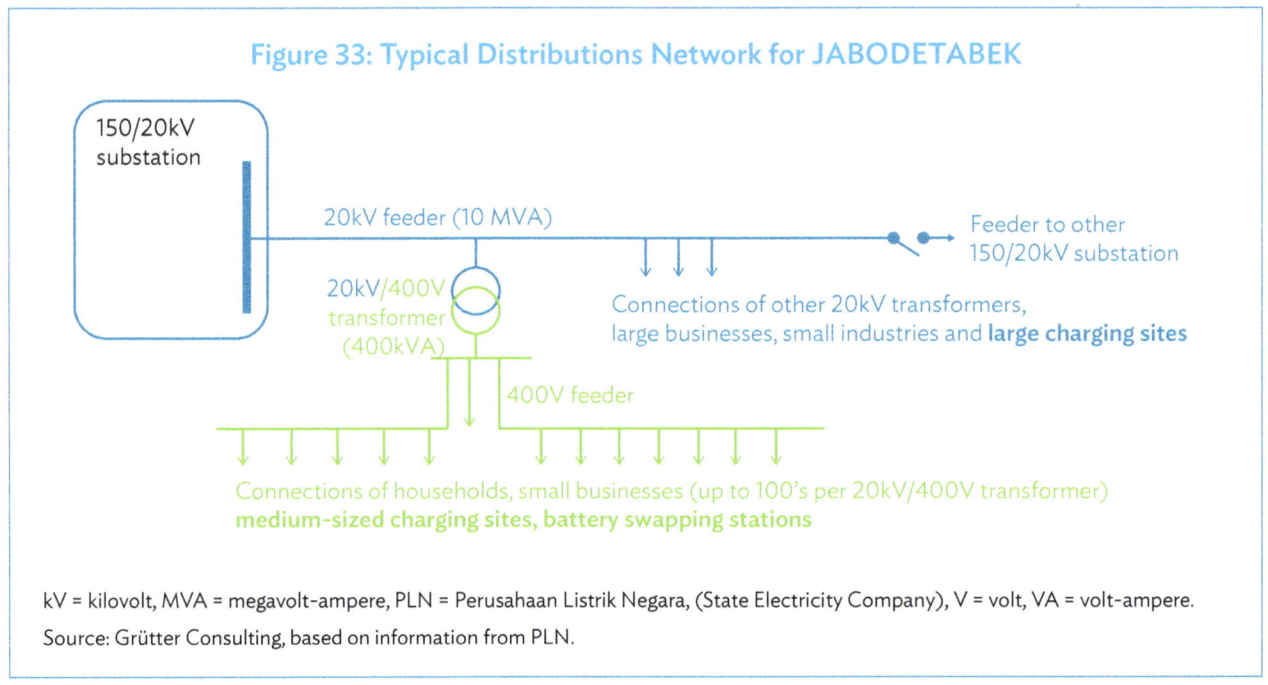

Figure 33: Typical Distributions Network for JABODETABEK

kV = kilovolt, MVA = megavolt-ampere, PLN = Perusahaan Listrik Negara, (State Electricity Company), V = volt, VA = volt-ampere.
Source: Grütter Consulting, based on information from PLN.

Considering that the expected load of even the large charging sites will not exceed 1,000 kW, charging sites will be connected to the distribution grids and typically directly to the 400 V networks. However, large charging sites may be connected via one or more dedicated transformers to the 20 kV network.

On an aggregated level, the load increase in distribution networks caused by charging e-motorcycles will follow the same path as transmission and generation. However, there may be large differences between areas with respect to charging activity and consequently some distribution networks may require more e-motorcycle charging reinforcements that others. For example, connecting a large charging site with a load of 1 megawatt may well be possible within the reserve margin of typical 20-kilovolt feeders with a capacity of 10 megavolt-amperes, but if several large charging sites will be connected to this feeder, a new one may be required.

On a smaller scale, a similar issue may happen with medium-sized charging sites and swapping stations. Connecting one or a few of these charging sites to the 400-volt networks will usually not require reinforcements. However, if several charging sites with a load of 15–100 kW will be connected to a 400-volt distribution feeder, the 20 kV/400 V transformer with a capacity of 400 kilovolt-amperes (kVA) may become overloaded and new transformers need to be added to the network.

The need for more 20 kV/400 V transformers may even be triggered by home chargers, which is likely not because of the size of their individual load, but because of the number of e-motorcycles that should be charged. It must be noted that e-motorcycles are becoming increasingly popular and that households may own more than one e-motorcycle.[49] Furthermore e-motorcycle owners tend to start home charging when they return from work, which takes several hours. Consequently, evening loads in distribution networks may increase significantly and may add to the already high residential load in peak hours.

---

[49] Based on CLASP/IPSOS 2020 it is estimated that in the entire country, half the households with a power connection up to 1,300 volt-amperes owns one motorcycle and one-quarter owns two motorcycles.

To put this in context, the impact on the distribution system cannot be seen separately from the total demand increase. It is noted that, because of the government's and PLN's promotion of electricity use, there will also be an autonomous growth of the consumption of households by adapting more electrical appliances. Furthermore, it is anticipated that the impact of electric four-wheelers will add load as well. As the additional loads of e-motorcycles are small compared to the total load increase, the impact of electrifying two-wheelers will be that reinforcements will need to be realized earlier than without e-motorcycles. This adds to PLN's workload and investments in distribution networks (Rp27 trillion/$1.9 billion in 2019 for Indonesia) (footnote 48). Box 2 and Section 11.3 provide considerations on the use of "smart charging," aiming for reducing the investments in Indonesia.

Box 1: An Introduction to Smart Charging

In practice, charging a battery is not always time-critical. For example, when plugging in an e-motorcycle at the office in the morning, a commuter may only be interested in a sufficiently charged battery that allows reaching home in the afternoon. This provides flexibility in when to charge and with how much power. Implementation of so-called "smart charging" makes use of this flexibility by adapting charging times and power to the system dynamics.

Many countries that foresee a large increase of electric transport consider the application of smart charging. Its main characteristic is that the charging process can be adapted in such a way that it reduces the impact of the load to the power system. In some implementations, smart charging even contributes to the power system needs. The objective of smart charging is to reduce the power system cost, related both to operational expense by, e.g., charging in hours when electricity is produced at low cost, and to capital expense by reducing the need for additional investments in generation and networks. A recent German study suggests that "managed charging" of four-wheelers results in 50% lower reinforcement cost for distribution networks than "unrestricted charging."[a] Governments (e.g., the United Kingdom, city of Rotterdam) support an efficient power system and require the use of smart charging for the charging points that they funded.[b]

Smart charging can be triggered by an incentive that affects a customer's decision on when to start charging. For example, a household subject to a time-of-use tariff may be eager to start charging in hours with a low tariff. The implementation of these examples may be as simple as using time clocks for starting the charge and/or limiting the charging power through an adjustable "mode 2" charger.

In a more sophisticated implementation, smart charging may be implemented as a large-scale optimization of many electric vehicle chargers that considers real-time electricity price (forecasts), network constraints, charge information of vehicles, etc. In this implementation, continuous communication between a central system and all chargers is required. The implementation of this kind of smart charging is largely foreseen for four-wheelers that apply "mode 3" chargers.

Although both examples share the same objective to reduce power system cost, the optimizations are on different parts of the power system. More advanced implementations may provide additional features that further optimize the power system. For example, in some European countries, aggregated portfolios including electric vehicle chargers provide fast-acting reserves that respond to a failure in the power system, a service that is traditionally provided by a generation plant.[c]

[a] K. Burges. 2020. Infrastructure for Charging Electric Vehicles and Renewables—How Much Do We Need to invest? Presentation at the 4th E-Mobility Power System Integration Symposium. 3 November.
[b] *Government of the United Kingdom*. 2018. Government Funded Electric Car Chargepoints To Be Smart by July 2019. 14 December. https://www.gov.uk/government/news/government-funded-electric-car-chargepoints-to-be-smart-by-july-2019; *Government of Rotterdam*. 2021. 1,500 Nieuwe Laadpunten Voor Elektrische Auto's in Rotterdam (1,500 New Charging Points for Electric Cars in Rotterdam). 8 April. https://persberichtenrotterdam.nl/persbericht/1500-nieuwe-laadpunten-voor-elektrische-autos-in-rotterdam/.
[c] TenneT. 2018. End Report FCR Pilot: Just A Matter of Balance. 28 June. https://www.tennet.eu/fileadmin/user_upload/SO_NL/FCR_Final_report_FCR_pilot__alleen_in_Engels_.pdf.

Source: Grütter Consulting.

> ### Box 2: Smart Charging in Indonesia
>
> For household and business customers who own electric four-wheelers, the State Electricity Company (PLN) introduced a discounted off-peak tariff for additional electricity consumption between 10 p.m. and 4 a.m. PLN also developed a smart charging system in which the home chargers communicate with a central system. A smartphone app takes care of charging control by the customer and providing information to the customer. PLN's objectives with this initiative include supporting the government program to accelerate the use of electric vehicles and obtaining data on the charging behavior of electric four-wheeler owners.
>
> For e-motorcycles, PLN does not consider smart charging. As discussed, the additional load by e-motorcycles is only a small share of the total load increase. However, since it adds to the load, it may also add to the peak load and consequently require investments in the power system. To put this in perspective, a comparison is made with the year 2019 in which the sales in electricity increased by 12.3 TWh/year. To catch-up with the demand increase, PLN required investments in the power system of Rp105 trillion in 2019.[a] Although not all of these investments were related to keep up with the load increase, it may be assumed that a significant portion of them were. In scenario 2, the e-motorcycle charging load will increase to 21 TWh/year in 2030, i.e., more than the load increase in 2019. It may therefore be concluded that, without smart charging, e-motorcycle charging may require investments of around Rp100 trillion ($7 billion). This figure provides an indication of the potential investment savings of e-motorcycle smart charging for Indonesia. It may therefore be considered to implement some kind of smart charging for e-motorcycles as well. Section 11.3 therefore also includes smart charging possibilities for the different sites and the mitigating impact on the load of different parts of the power system.
>
> PLN = Perusahaan Listrik Negara (State Electricity Company), TWh = terawatt-hour.
>
> [a] PLN. 2020. *Memaknai Tantangan, Meningkatkan Layanan: Laporan Tahunan 2019* (Redefining Challenges, Enhancing Services: Annual Report 2019). https://web.pln.co.id/statics/uploads/2021/02/PLN_AR_2019_Rev_010221_Hires.pdf.
>
> Source: Grütter Consulting.

10.2 Connections

This section describes the connections of the different charging sites and their impact on the grid.

Connections for Large Charging Sites

The connection of large charging sites (1,000 chargers, 1,000 kW) will typically take place via one or more dedicated transformers connected to the 20-kilovolt feeders. This connection may be realized in a compact substation, which is a small building that includes a transformer, switchgear, electrical protection, and metering equipment. In general, PLN should be able to realize a connection for the chargers within their target of 75 days. Within this time, PLN needs to identify a 20-kilovolt feeder with sufficient capacity, cut this cable, and install the compact station and a connection cable. If there is insufficient capacity, it may be necessary to install new 20-kilovolt feeders from the 150/20 kV substation.

Chapter 9 shows that large charging sites are mainly operated during the day and hardly during the night. However, at many of these charging stations, for example, at sites where commuters are working the entire day, there is no need to charge the battery as fast as possible but should only be completed by the end of the working day. This would provide the flexibility to distribute the charging load over the day instead of creating a peak in the morning hours when people plug in their e-motorcycles.

This can be achieved by smart charging (Box 1). In this case, smart charging may be as simple as choosing for a lower installed capacity of each of the chargers at the site. By using, for example, 300 W chargers instead of 1 kW chargers, the charging load may be spread out over the day. Accordingly, the peak load for 1,000 chargers is reduced from 1,000 kW to 300 kW. This would reduce the need for dedicated 20-kilovolt to 400-volt transformers from three 400 kVA transformers to only one 400 kVA transformer. Similarly, fewer reinforcements in the 20 kV distribution network may be required.

A more advanced implementation of smart charging may be by centrally controlling (groups of) charging sites. Different from the first implementation, this implementation could also actively reduce the contribution of the chargers to system peaks, e.g., at midday in JABODETABEK. By doing this, the benefits for the power system are further increased, but so are the implementation costs and complexities.

It is further noted that the impact of smart charging of even a large charging site (1–2 megawatts) may seem to be small. However, it needs to be considered that, according to scenario 2, up to 50 million e-motorcycles can connect in 2030 to thousands of large charging sites. In that case, the figures grow to thousands of megawatts, which is in the same order of magnitude to the size of a large generation plant.

Connections for Medium-sized Charging Sites and Battery Swapping Stations

Medium-sized charging sites (50–100 chargers) and battery swapping stations (10–30 chargers) will be connected directly to PLN's low voltage grid (400 V). In practice, this may require extensions to these 400-volt networks and, in some cases, reinforcements of the 20 kV/400 V transformers and 400-volt cables as previously discussed.

The potential for smart charging for medium-sized charging stations used by commuters is similar to the potential for large charging stations and may be worth exploring. The potential of smart charging for other medium-sized charging stations may be limited though. For example, at shopping centers or at other sites where people reside only for a short period of time, there is little flexibility to shift the charging time. However, in theory, it would be feasible to implement price differentiation or (fixed) hours with limited availability of charge.

As shown in Chapter 9, swapping stations will operate continuously between 6 a.m. and 10 p.m. A battery will start charging immediately after plugging in so that it can be fully charged as soon as possible, typically within 1 hour. Consequently, the required power for the swapping station will be constantly high during the day and evening and low at night. Because of this load pattern, there is only limited flexibility for postponing charging. However, since the battery swapping stations will be highly IT-driven, connected in real time with central IT systems and with operators that will likely operate many swapping stations, the cost for smart charging may be limited as well. Consequently, if the right incentives are in place (e.g., time of use tariff), there may be a business case for smart charging.

Household Connection

PLN offers different standard household connections. While historically the smallest connection of 450 VA was the choice of most household customers, in recent years many customers upgraded to 900 VA, 1,300 VA, 2,200 VA, 3,500–5,500 VA or >6,600 VA.[50] Figure 34 shows that in 2021, approximately three-fourths of the customers in Jakarta and Bali had a connection capacity of not more than 1,300 kVA.

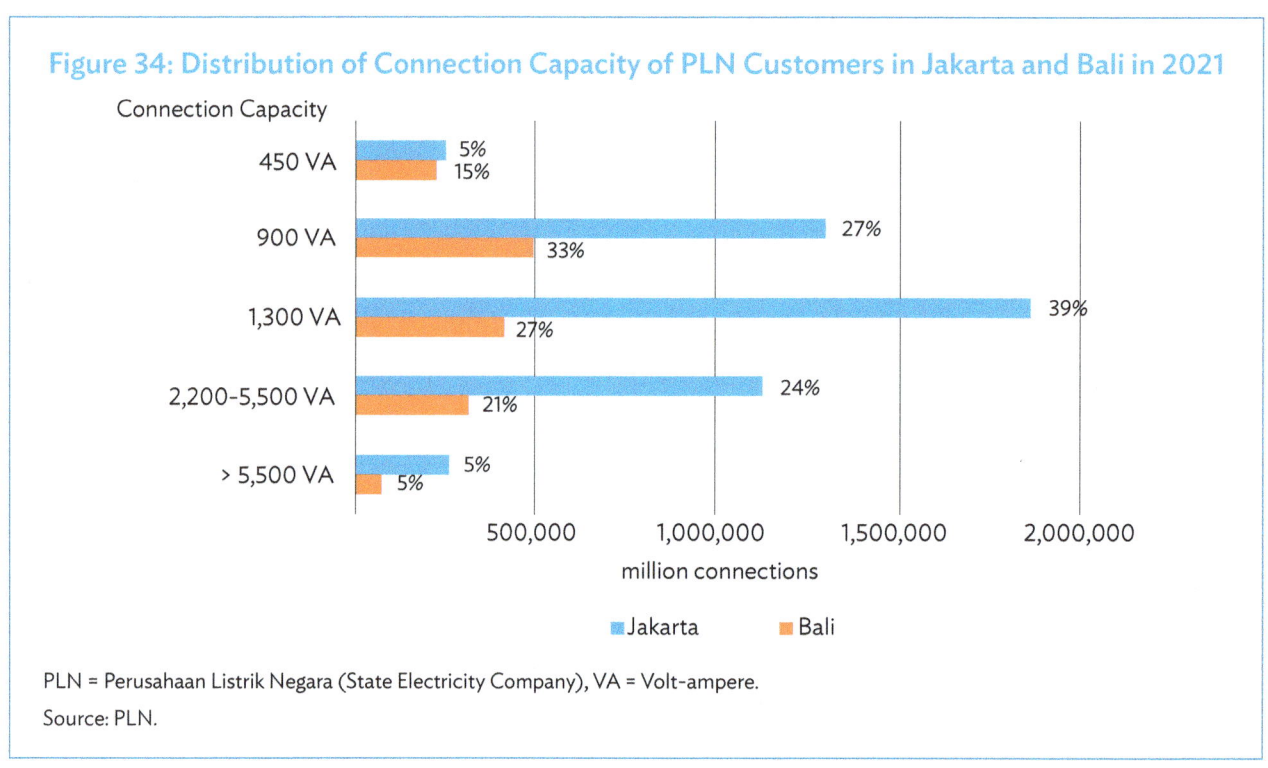

Figure 34: Distribution of Connection Capacity of PLN Customers in Jakarta and Bali in 2021

PLN = Perusahaan Listrik Negara (State Electricity Company), VA = Volt-ampere.
Source: PLN.

In 2018, household customers had an average power consumption of 4 kWh/customer/ day (footnote 48). PLN's "Electrifying Life Style" Program aims to increase the use of electricity in daily life to optimize PLN's available capacity and to use more environmentally friendly electrical equipment. This program includes discounted fees for connection capacity upgrades for users of electric stoves and electric vehicles.

An e-motorcycle battery charger for household use will usually connect to a normal power point behind the household power connection and typically has a capacity of up to 1 kW. Particularly for households with a connection capacity of 450 VA and 900 VA, the charging load may exceed the connection capacity. For connections with a capacity up to 1,300 VA, charging load may compete with other household appliances that require similar amounts of power. This may be especially the case during the residential peak load periods in the evening and if a household owns more than one e-motorcycle that needs to be charged.

---

[50] Government of Indonesia, MEMR. 2019. Regulation No. 19 of 2019 Concerning the Third Amendment to MEMR Regulation No. 28 of 2016 Concerning Electricity Tariffs Provided by PLN.

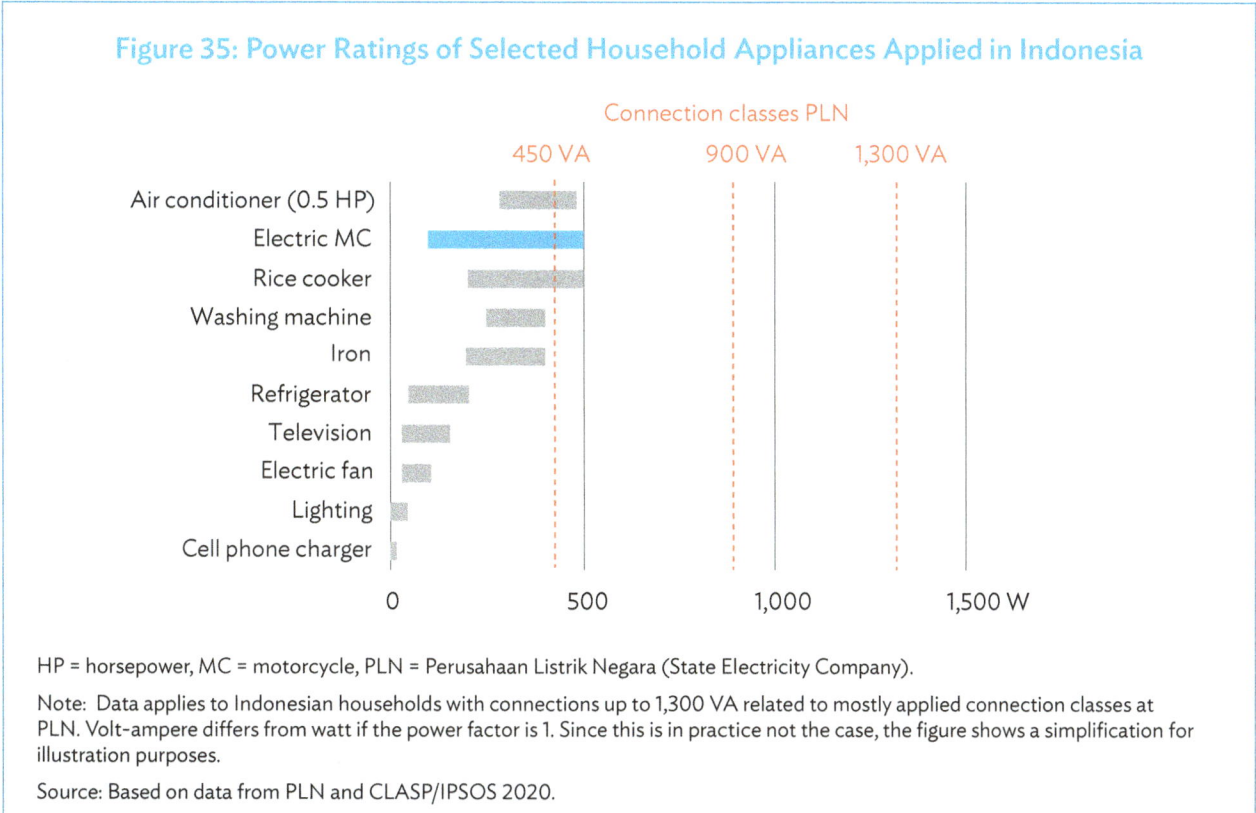

Figure 35: Power Ratings of Selected Household Appliances Applied in Indonesia

HP = horsepower, MC = motorcycle, PLN = Perusahaan Listrik Negara (State Electricity Company).

Note: Data applies to Indonesian households with connections up to 1,300 VA related to mostly applied connection classes at PLN. Volt-ampere differs from watt if the power factor is 1. Since this is in practice not the case, the figure shows a simplification for illustration purposes.

Source: Based on data from PLN and CLASP/IPSOS 2020.

Figure 35 shows several household appliances with connections up to 1,300 VA, including their typical range of power ratings. The figure shows that the power rating of a two-wheeler charger is in the same range as the power rating of small (0.5 horsepower) air conditioners, rice cookers, washing machines, and irons, for example. However, e-motorcycle chargers may be applied for more hours per day than most of these appliances. Moreover, there may be several e-motorcycles per household that need to be charged. The figure also indicates the connection classes of PLN and shows that, especially for connections of 450 VA or 900 VA, charging the motorcycle at the same time as using other electrical appliances may easily overload the connection and consequently trip the main micro circuit breaker. To prevent this, an upgrade to a higher connection class may be required unless the household is managing to charge the battery at hours with low electricity consumption, e.g., at night. This may be considered a form of smart charging, which is discussed below. For households with several e-motorcycles, upgrading to a higher capacity seems unavoidable, but smart charging could limit the required upgrade.

The connection capacity of many Indonesian households may be especially tight on capacity if charging starts when e-motorcycles arrive home in the evening when it adds to the already high evening load of households. Charging e-motorcycles during the evening could therefore increase the peak load of single households and residential areas. This would likely require an increase of the connection capacity of individual households and may require reinforcements of networks in residential areas in JABODETABEK and Bali (e.g., more or larger 20 kV/400 V transformers).

However, home charging is quite flexible. For example, a commuter requires that his e-motorcycle is charged sufficiently when he leaves home the next morning. It is not important to this commuter when and with what power his e-motorcycle is charged. It is this flexibility that provides an opportunity for smart charging. If it would be possible to shift the home charging load from the evening to the night, there may be less need to increase connection capacities or reinforce distribution networks in residential areas.

The term "smart charging" covers a wide range of implementations. Customer-controlled smart charging can be triggered by incentives that affect a customer's decision on when to start charging. In Indonesia, the connection upgrading fee (about Rp500,000 for upgrading from 900 VA to 1,300 VA) provides an incentive to reduce the load peak and consequently avoid the upgrade. Another example of an incentive scheme is a tariff system that provides incentives to reduce the household peak load by a progressive electricity tariff ($/kWh) that increases with the connection capacity. These incentives could lead to household decisions to charge their e-motorcycles at night. Households could quite easily realize this by applying a time clock on each charger and making sure that the e-motorcycle batteries are charged when no other applications are used. In addition, they can limit the charging power through an adjustable "mode 2" charger.

10.3 Quality of Power Supply

Reliability of Power Supply

Increasing power supply reliability is one of the main objectives of PLN and the government. In 2019, the Minister of Energy and Mineral Resources issued a regulation that provides an incentive to PLN to increase reliability.[51] This regulation stipulates that PLN is required to pay their customers a compensation payment for each outage, dependent on the duration of the outage (events of force majeure are exempted).

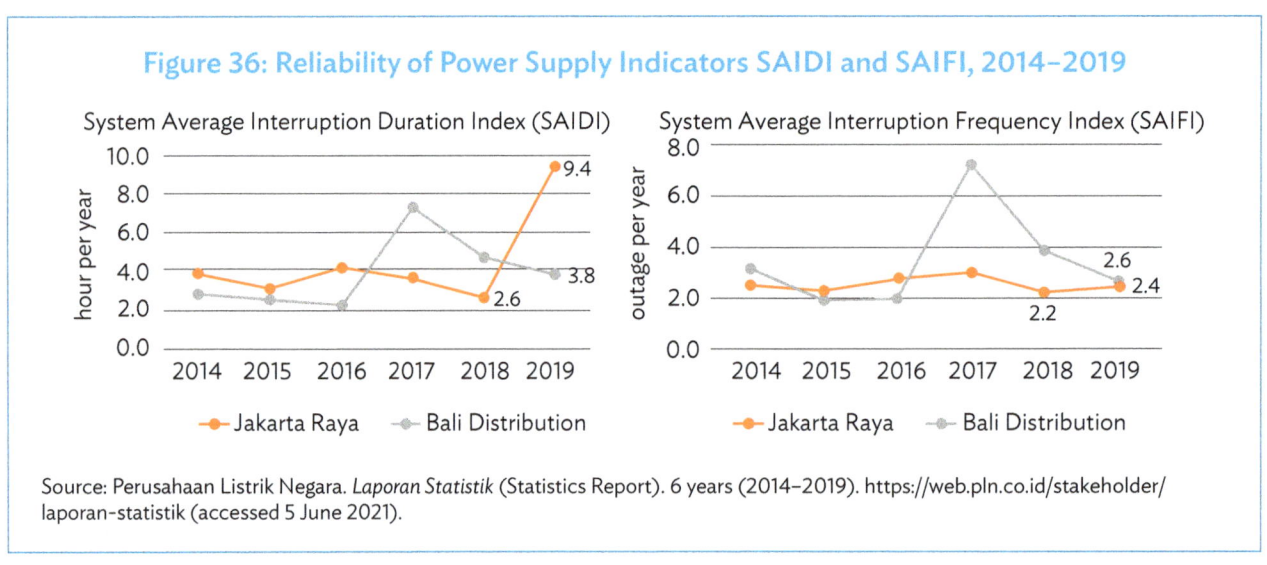

Figure 36: Reliability of Power Supply Indicators SAIDI and SAIFI, 2014–2019

Source: Perusahaan Listrik Negara. *Laporan Statistik* (Statistics Report). 6 years (2014–2019). https://web.pln.co.id/stakeholder/laporan-statistik (accessed 5 June 2021).

---

[51] Government of Indonesia, MEMR. 2019. Permen 18/2019. Jakarta.

Since electrical vehicles rely totally on electricity, the reliability of the power supply is important. PLN reports that their customers in Jakarta faced in 2019 on average 2.4 outages (SAIFI) with a total duration of 9.4 hours (SAIDI). A significant factor in this figure was the large blackout on 4 August 2019 that lasted for many hours and affected 22 million customers in the Greater Jakarta area and parts of West and Central Java (footnote 48). Figure 36 shows that 2018 is a more representative year, when customers in Jakarta were on average without power for 2.6 hours distributed over 2.2 outages. On average, an outage took 72 minutes.

For Bali, the customers were interrupted in 2019 on average for 3.8 hours distributed over 2.6 outages. On average, an outage took 87 minutes.

Neglecting the large outages, the reported reliability figures should not be an issue for electric two-wheeler charging.

It shall be noted though that large incidents such as the blackout that happened on 4 August 2019 may occur again. In these—hopefully rare—circumstances, it will not be possible to charge e-motorcycles. Additionally, recovery of the power supply may need to consider that electric vehicle owners want to recharge their batteries immediately and all at the same time. Centrally controlled smart charging (Box 1) could help PLN in preventing an immediate overload after recovery of an outage.

Connection Requirements, Standards, and Power Quality

E-motorcycle chargers will only function well if the technical quality of the voltage in the power system—the so-called power quality—is on a sufficient level. The Distribution Code of Indonesia establishes the rules on the minimum power quality of PLN's service. On the other hand, vehicle chargers may also impact the quality of the power system themselves. The Distribution Code therefore also includes requirements for connections and connected equipment to limit this impact.

Most prominently, chargers may affect the voltage level (i.e., the deviation from the 230 V/400 V) and harmonic distortion are affected (Box 3). The Distribution Code includes minimum quality levels for voltage and harmonic distortion.[52] To meet these standards, the distribution code also specifies limits for the impact on harmonic distortion by connected equipment (Table 34). There are no strict limits on the power factor of equipment, which affects the voltage level.[53] However, PLN in practice requires a minimum power factor of 0.85 (lagging), which should be manageable by the charging sites.

The Distribution Code also refers to Indonesian standards and—where national standards do not exist —to international standards for connected equipment. The focus of the Directorate General of Electricity (DJK) is on implementing IEC standards for chargers up to 150 kW, standards which are (being) adopted as Indonesian standards.

---

[52] Distribution Code CC3.0: Deviation in normal situation not more than -10% or +5% of nominal voltage; Distribution Code CC3.0: 3% in Voltage of individual harmonics, not more than 5% in total – THD.
[53] However, section SC 2.0 of the Distribution Code stipulates that if the monthly average power factor is less than 0.9 lagging in some classes of consumers, an excess charge for reactive power is charged according to the tariff applicable.

> **Box 3: What is Harmonic Distortion?**
>
> The voltage in a non-disturbed grid looks like a sine wave, as in the grey line in the picture below. Customer appliances like classic light bulbs or water heaters (linear loads) do not influence the shape of the wave. Conversely, appliances that are controlled by electronics, like LED lights and electric vehicle-chargers (nonlinear loads, often including alternating and direct currency converters) do influence the wave form. In the following figure, the red line shows an example of resulting harmonic distortion, which looks abnormal compared to the grey sine wave. The more the wave form diverts from a sine wave, the more the harmonic distortion.
>
>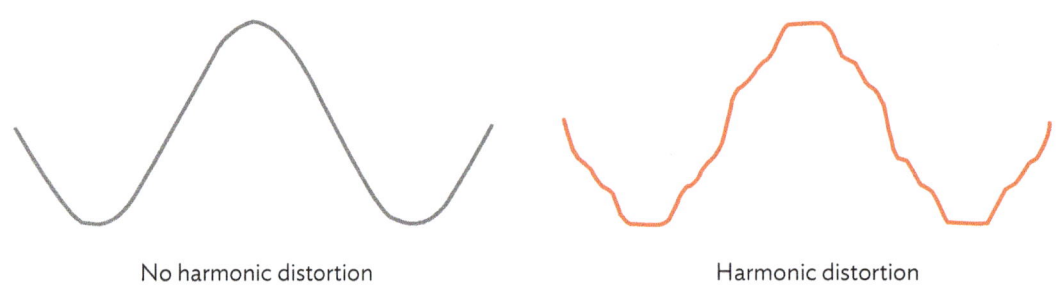
>
> No harmonic distortion   Harmonic distortion
>
> Source: Grütter Consulting.

Table 34: Limit of Harmonic Distortion—Flow in Indonesian Distribution Code CC3.0

Harmonics Odd, h	h<11	11<h17	17<h<23	23<h<35	35<h<	TDD
Harmonic Distortion -Current (%)	4,0	2,0	1,5	0,6	0,3	5,0

ESDM = Ministry of Energy and Mineral Resources, h = harmonics Odd, TDD = Total Demand Distortion.
Source: ESDM.

Chargers for e-motorcycles may also result in an asymmetrical load on the power system. However, if battery swapping stations and large and medium-sized charging sites, which typically have three-phase connections, are loaded in a balanced way, this issue should, in practice, be limited.

The impact of the chargers on power quality will add to the impact of other equipment, including air conditioners, chargers, metro, trains, and light rail. A poor power quality may in itself affect the functioning of the equipment, including chargers. Consequently, PLN shall monitor the power quality in distribution networks. PLN already monitors the power quality in 150/20 kV substations. It is recommended to extend this measurement program by also monitoring a sample of 20-kilovolt and 400-volt nodes within different distribution networks. By monitoring several nodes regularly, PLN would gain knowledge on the trend of the voltage quality in their network.

10.4 Summary and Conclusion on Grid Impact

Table 35 summarizes the power grid impact of the four types of charging sites.

Table 35: Impact of Chargers on the Electricity Network

Area	Home Charging	Swapping Stations	Medium-sized Charging Sites	Large Charging Sites
Number of chargers	1–5	10–30	50–100	1,000
Total power of chargers	100–2,500 W	15–40 kW	50–100 kW	1,000 kW
Required connection	Increase with at least 450 VA	20–50 kVA	60–120 kVA	1,200 kVA
Typically connected to	400 V network (single phase)	400 V network (three-phase)	400 V network (three-phase)	20 kV network (via own transformer)
Contribution to the system peak load (if not controlled by smart charging)	Charging expected during evening/nights	Charging during the day 6 a.m.–10 p.m.		
Impact on system demand	In 2030, e-motorcycle charging load may form 4% of PLN's electricity sales.			
Impact on Generation	Sufficient reserve margin in Java/Bali subsystem until at least 2025. Investments after 2025 may be significantly reduced by smart charging.			
Impact on Transmission Grid	Large investments in Transmission Grids completed and planned. Investments in future may be significantly reduced by smart charging.			
Impact on distribution grid	Investments may be significantly reduced by smart charging.			
Realization of Connection	New connection may be realized within 75 days			
Smart charging – flexibility	incentives may help to shift the peaks to the night	Limited flexibility to shift load	Potential to reduce connection cost and power system cost by shifting load from peak	
Smart charging – potential benefit	Large for connections and distribution networks	Limited	Large for connections, distribution networks and generation	
Reliability of Supply	For Jakarta: On average, 2.2 outages per year, with approx. 2.6-hour duration For Bali: On average, 2.6 outages per year, with approx. 3.8-hour duration			
Power Quality	Distribution Code rules are in line with international standards International standards apply			

kVA = kilovolt-ampere, kW = kilowatt, PLN = Perusahaan Listrik Negara (State Electricity Company), V = volt, W = watt.
Source: Grütter Consulting.

10.5 Investments Required

Table 36 provides an estimate on investment costs for upgrading the power system that are required to serve the additional load of e-motorcycles. It is not expected that upgrades in generation and transmission, in addition to the already planned reinforcement, will be required until 2025. Furthermore, the related investment cost may be significantly reduced by applying smart charging. The investment levels are to be understood as initial approximation to indicate the order of magnitude.

Table 36: Expected Investment Related to Charging Infrastructure for E-Motorcycles in Indonesia

Parameter	2022	2023	2024	2025	2026	2027	2028	2029	2030
e-motorcycles (million)	0.8	2.9	7.2	12	18	26	35	45	56
Electricity usage (GWh)	304	1,054	2,676	4,427	6,696	9,555	12,864	16,437	20,553
Distribution investment (Rp billion)	700	1,640	2,600	3,190	4,450	5,870	6,990	7,690	8,980
Transmission investment (Rp billion)	0	0	0	0	5,570	7,340	8,740	9,610	11,230
Generation investments (Rp billion)	0	0	0	0	5,320	7,020	8,360	9,190	10,740
Total investments (Rp billion)	700	1,600	2,600	3,200	15,300	20,200	24,100	26,500	31,000
Total investments ($ million)	50	110	180	220	1,070	1,410	1,690	1,850	2,170

GWh = gigawatt-hour, PLN = Perusahaan Listrik Negara (State Electricity Company), Rp = Indonesian rupiah.

Source: Grütter Consulting; based on PLN Annual Report 2019 and assumption that 80% of investments in 2018 and 2019 were for system expansion (6% for transmission and generation, sales increase for distribution).

11. Reusing and Recycling Battery

In the transition to electric mobility around the world, one of the main concerns is the use of batteries once they have reached the end of their useful life in the vehicle. This is a valid concern as most countries do not have yet specific regulations for the proper treatment of lithium batteries from electric vehicles, along with other types of batteries that not recycled, presenting a serious threat to health and the environment. In Australia, for example, only 3% of lithium batteries are recycled. The rest goes to landfill, where toxic materials leach into the soil.

Batteries are hazardous materials, so reusing and recycling are important aspects of their life cycle. Batteries have a limited technical life and during their life, the energy capacity slowly decreases. This has an effect on the electric vehicle range. At a certain point, the number of kilometers on a full battery charge is too low for daily operation. The battery may still be used, e.g., for another stationary application (i.e., reuse or second life). When the battery is at its end of life (or damaged), recycling is needed according to safe and environmentally friendly methods (Figure 37).

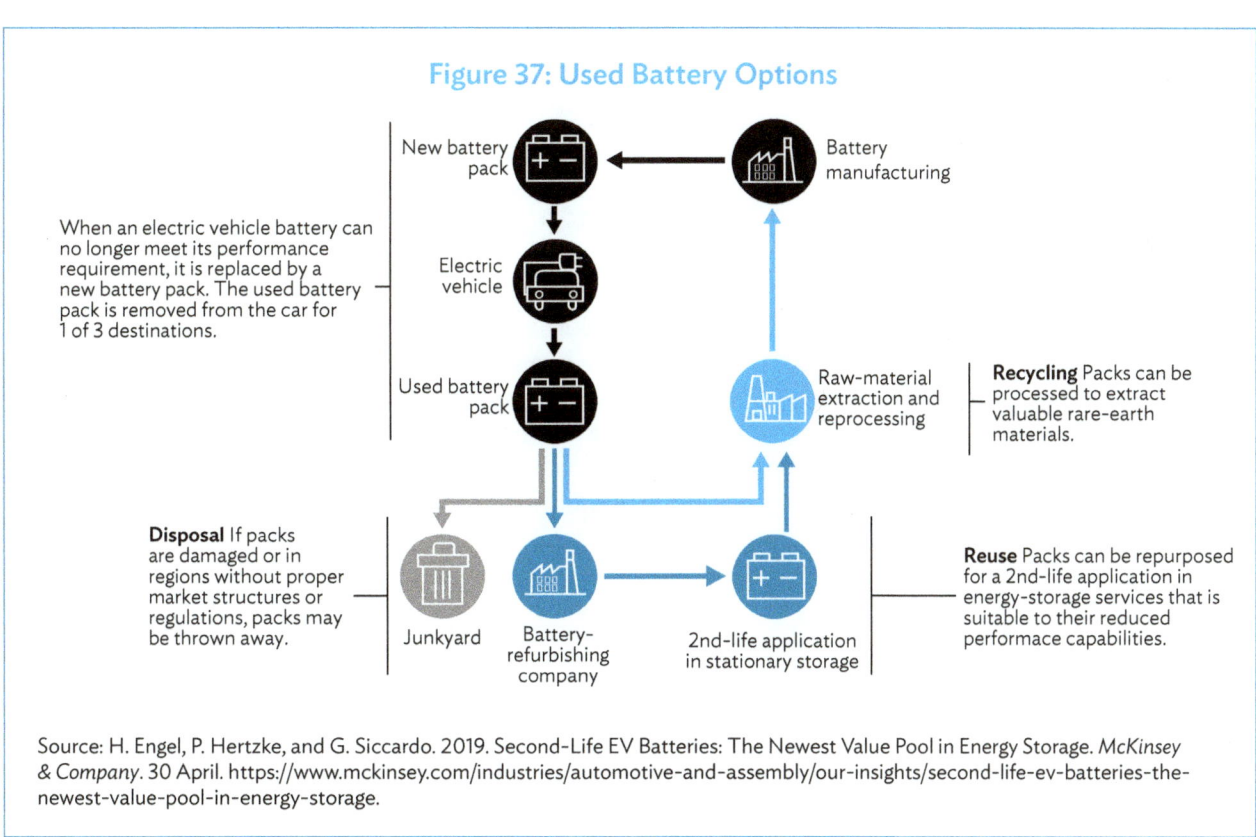

Figure 37: Used Battery Options

Source: H. Engel, P. Hertzke, and G. Siccardo. 2019. Second-Life EV Batteries: The Newest Value Pool in Energy Storage. *McKinsey & Company*. 30 April. https://www.mckinsey.com/industries/automotive-and-assembly/our-insights/second-life-ev-batteries-the-newest-value-pool-in-energy-storage.

Disposal in illegal landfills or dumps is naturally the least desirable. It occurs in countries where there is no regulation regarding battery disposal or where the body that would oversee these practices is weak. In cases where the battery pack is damaged in a collision, the battery will also have to be disposed of. Damage to the battery can cause the electrolyte to spill and can lead to fires. This already happens in scrap yards or landfills.[54]

Energy Storage

With a growing share of renewable energy, especially solar, the demand for storage options is also increasing significantly. In addition, with the rapid adoption of electric vehicles and the number of batteries reaching their end of life, a significant secondary market is emerging. According to a McKinsey study, it is estimated that the supply of secondary batteries for stationary applications will exceed 200 GWh by 2030. The market value is estimated to be more than $30 billion. But certain challenges also need to be addressed to realize this potential.

For the batteries to be used in a stationary manner, they must first be adapted. To do so, different procedures will be required instead of a standardized one. Another challenge will be to remain competitive with new batteries, the price of which is falling rapidly. The lack of standards and regulations for the use of stationary batteries presents one of the most important obstacles. There are no guarantees in terms of performance quality, safety, efficiency, etc. However, there are already manufacturers establishing alliances with energy companies to secure their place in the emerging energy storage market.[55]

If reuse of electric vehicle batteries is applied (probably mainly in small-scale stationary applications), the battery should still be in a proper technical condition. For four-wheeled cars, the battery is at its economic end of life at a state-of-health (SOH)—the remaining capacity as a percentage of the original capacity—of 70%. The battery can still be used safely until an SOH of around 50%, either inside the electric vehicle or in a second-life, stationary application. Below 50% SOH, the performance drops and also safety issues could arise. The explanation above shows that, for second use to become a success, it is very important to accurately know the battery's SOH. The main issue with the declining SOH is the proportional reduction of the driving range. So, at a certain point, the driver is not satisfied with the range anymore and would like to have a new battery in the electric vehicle, although the battery can still be useful in another application. The main electric car manufacturers expect that the battery will live as long as the vehicle in the near future.

It is expected that a battery for e-motorcycles or e-scooters is used intensively, i.e., for many kilometers per day and with one or even more recharging cycles per day. This means that the battery will reach a low SOH and be at its technical and economic end of life within a few years without value left for second use. In some cases, a second life for an electric vehicle battery might make sense, e.g., because the first use was benign. However, in such a case, the second-life battery still needs to compete with new batteries that have declined in price in the meantime. This is another reason why second use of electric vehicle batteries is expected to be a small market in the future.

---

[54] P. Kramliczek. 2019. E-Mobilität: Warum Das Batterie-Recycling So Schwierig Ist (E-Mobility: Why Battery Recycling Is So Difficult). BR24. 8 November. https://www.br.de/nachrichten/wissen/e-mobilitaet-warum-das-batterie-recycling-so-schwierig-ist,RYeQPYR.

[55] H. Engel, P. Hertzke, and G. Siccardo. 2019. Second-Life EV Batteries: The Newest Value Pool in Energy Storage. McKinsey & Company. 30 April. https://www.mckinsey.com/industries/automotive-and-assembly/our-insights/second-life-ev-batteries-the-newest-value-pool-in-energy-storage.

Recycling

Lithium-ion batteries are composed of different high-value materials. However, the profitability of recycling will depend on the costs of collection, transport, storage, sorting, dismantling, etc. Some lithium recyclers in the PRC, which are operating today, are operating at an attractive profit margin and are expected to grow substantially. In Europe, most electric vehicle batteries have not yet reached the end of their useful life, so there is not yet a competitive recycling market.[56]

The battery recycling process is complex. Almost all disassembly occurs manually and there are very few options to automate it.[57] In addition, the amount of materials in each battery is different according to the model, which also makes manual processes necessary. This is why high volumes are required to be cost-effective. Generally, vehicle manufacturers have agreements with battery suppliers so that they fulfill their extended producer responsibility. Just because a country has good recycling practices for lead-acid batteries, such as for internal combustion vehicles, does not mean that the same can be done for lithium batteries.

11.1 International Electric Vehicle Battery Standards

European Union

Collection and recycling of used batteries in the European Union (EU) is arranged by the EU Batteries Directive.[58] The successor of this Directive, the EU Batteries Regulation, is under development.[59] These regulations require proper waste management of batteries, including collection, take-back programs, disposal, and recycling. Also, targets for waste battery collection rates are set. One of the key points in the regulation is that EV batteries should not be disposed in landfills. The regulation requires EU countries to maximize the separation of batteries from regular municipal waste and requires spent batteries to be collected separately. Recycling and collection targets are called for so that fewer batteries end up in landfills. The actual legal implementation is each country's own responsibility. EU Member States are required to provide collection sites that are accessible and free of charge. Battery distributors may be required to provide this and manufacturers may not refuse to take back waste batteries from end-consumers.

In practice, EU manufacturers or importers of batteries need to make sure they have applied the legal framework to their company. For collection and recycling of used batteries, the battery industry in most EU countries has set up a national organization that includes recycling factories. In many countries, this is separate for the automotive industry (part of car and motorcycle recycling, including starter batteries and electric vehicle propulsion batteries) and for general industrial and household batteries.[60] In the EU, it is a common rule that retailers of products with a battery (e.g., toys or e-bikes) must take back the waste batteries and send them to a recycling organization.

The largest battery recycling company in the EU is Umicore.[61] This company recycles all battery chemistries and extracts all valuable materials from the batteries. Like its European competitors, it produces new battery materials and sub-components that are manufactured from the recycled materials.

---

[56] Avicenne Energy. 2018. *Worldwide Rechargeable - Battery Market 2017-2030 - 2018 edition.*
[57] D. M. Steward. 2019. Economics and Challenges of Li-Ion Battery Recycling from End-of-Life Vehicles. *Procedia Manufacturing.* 33. pp. 272–279.
[58] EU. 2006. Directive 2006/66/EC of the European Parliament and of the Council of 6 September 2006 on Batteries and Accumulators and Waste Batteries and Accumulators. http://data.europa.eu/eli/dir/2006/66/oj.
[59] The EU has a proposed regulation on batteries and waste batteries. EU. Waste and Recycling. Batteries and Accumulators. https://environment.ec.europa.eu/topics/waste-and-recycling/batteries-and-accumulators_en.
[60] The automotive organization in NL is ARN, arn.nl/en/; the general battery collection organisation is Stibat, stibat.nl/en/.
[61] Umicore. Industries. umicore.com/en/industries.

In the EU Member States, the battery industry is responsible for the cost of battery collection and recycling and it must facilitate the collection of waste batteries from end-users. This means that in many shopping areas, collection boxes are present for consumers to return their waste batteries. Batteries of electric bikes and scooters must be returned to the bike or scooter retailer.

There is a big difference between the business case of modern lithium-ion battery recycling versus conventional lead-acid battery recycling: the lead from the lead-acid batteries is more valuable than the cost of recycling, so the company will pay a small sum for the waste battery and still earn money. Therefore, recycling lead-acid batteries is good business. The materials of lithium-ion batteries, however, are less valuable than the cost of recycling. This means that additional incentives or more stringent legislation are needed to ensure a high rate of lithium-ion battery recycling. In Europe, this is arranged such that your electric vehicle dealer will take back the battery and arrange the recycling through the national recycling organization. The associated low cost of a few tens of euros is added up front to the electric vehicle price.

Reuse of batteries, especially automotive batteries, is still at an early stage of development in Europe and the rest of the world. Some car manufacturers do not promote battery reuse and want to collect all their electric vehicle batteries themselves.

North America

The rechargeable battery industry has formed the Rechargeable Battery Recycling Corporation (RBRC), which operates a battery recycling program called Call2Recycle throughout Canada and the US.[62] RBRC provides businesses with prepaid shipping containers for rechargeable batteries of all types while consumers can drop off batteries at numerous participating collection centers. It claims that no component of any recycled battery eventually reaches a landfill. Other programs, such as the Big Green Box, offer a recycling option for batteries.[63]

The People's Republic of China

In the PRC, regulations on the second life of electric vehicle batteries have become clearer and stricter in recent years. The Ministry of Industry and Information Technology in 2018 issued a series of interim measures to strengthen the management of battery recycling or stationary use. These measures require manufacturers to establish channels for battery recycling and collection points. These mechanisms are similar to extended producer responsibility. In addition, they require batteries to be traceable, to ensure that they are properly treated and in case they are not, to know who is responsible. However, there are no sanctions for manufacturers in case of noncompliance. Another interim measure is to promote the standardization of batteries, to make recycling processes simpler and thus more cost-effective. A list of five manufacturers that meet the required standards was established and put on a priority list. However, according to Avicenne Energy, with all regulations in place, the recycling of lithium vehicle batteries in the PRC still leaves something to be desired. Dismantling happens illegally and under non-standardized procedures. Moreover, the companies that do exist expect the government to give them subsidies.[64]

---

[62] Call2Recycle. call2recycle.org.
[63] Big Green Box. biggreenbox.com.
[64] Avicenne Energy. 2018. *Worldwide Rechargeable Battery Market 2017–2030*. 2018 edition.

11.2 Regulations in Indonesia

In the Presidential Decree 55/2019, a section on environmental protection was established. It mentions that used battery waste must be handled by recycling and/or waste management in accordance with the waste handling and management law and that further regulation will be administered by the Ministry for the Environment and Forestry. A state-owned enterprise subsidiary, PT Nasional Hijau Lestari, has also been tasked to participate in the battery recycling program as part of the battery industry ecosystem in Indonesia.

12. Proposed Policies and Actions

Actors

Transport policy and decision making in Indonesia involve stakeholders at the national, provincial, and city or district level. In some cases, the policy formulation also involves nongovernmental actors such as international development agencies. Table 37 provides an overview of the roles and responsibilities of organizations within the central government related to the transport sector policy and decision making.[65]

At the national level, the overall planning process is headed by BAPPENAS, in coordination with the other ministries. As the policy framework goes into a more detailed level, the Ministry of Transport is responsible for formulating a national policy that provides guidelines for local governments. Within this ministry, the responsibilities are split between several different general directorates: road transportation, sea transportation, civil aviation, and rail transportation. High-level transport policies are formulated in a document called the National Transportation System, which acts as a guide for the transport system integration and transport planning system in general. Electric vehicles, especially electric two-wheelers, are under the road transportation general directorate.

Regulatory and Policy Framework

Indonesia has taken initial steps to promote the deployment of electric vehicles in its transportation system. Presidential Decree 55 of 2019 provides the framework legislation for the introduction of electric vehicles, charging infrastructure, and battery technology in Indonesia. Of key importance is the development of charging infrastructure based on projections for electric transportation deployment and the availability and reliability of grid-based electricity service, as well as conducive electricity tariffs for electric transportation.

The Presidential Decree 55/2019 serves as the legal framework for accelerating electric vehicle adoption for land transport in Indonesia for both two- or three-wheelers and four-wheelers. The decree emphasizes:

- accelerating the development of local electric vehicle-related industry as per the road map set by the relevant ministry;
- encouraging electric vehicle technology research, development, and innovation collaboration between corporation, university, research institute, and government;
- setting a gradually increasing local content requirement for electric vehicles in Indonesia to support the development of a local related industry;

---

[65] S. E. Wijaya and M. Imran. 2019. *Moving the Masses: Bus-Rapid Transit (BRT) Policies in Low Income Asian Cities.* https://link.springer.com/book/10.1007/978-981-13-2938-8.

- regulating the usage of conventional vehicles in stages;
- possible incentives that can be provided by the government to all stakeholders;
- charging infrastructure deployment, mandating PLN as state-owned utility to spearhead the initial deployment;
- electricity tariff regulation for charging, to be set by the relevant ministry;
- technical requirement for electric vehicles in Indonesia, including type test requirement;
- environmental protection concerning the electric vehicle ecosystem, including battery waste, to be regulated by the relevant ministry; and
- creation of a coordinating team for the acceleration program, headed by the maritime minister.

Table 37: Overview of Central Government Agencies' Roles and Responsibilities Related to the Transport Sector

Organization	Roles and Responsibilities
Ministry of National Development Planning (BAPPENAS)	• Formulate and develop national development planning as a guideline for central, provincial, and city government • Control and review regional development planning • Coordinate and control national and international programs • Decide budget allocations for programs, together with the MoF
Ministry of Transport	• Prepare national transport policy that provides guidelines to provincial and city governments • Manage the operation of public transport facilities and infrastructure
Ministry of Public Works and Housing	• Formulate national policy for public works infrastructure including roads and bridges • Develop and construct public works infrastructure
Ministry of State-Owned Enterprise	• Develop national policy for the operation of transport infrastructure • Manage the operation of national transport infrastructure and public transport services
Ministry for the Environment and Forestry, including National Council on Climate Change	• Develop national policy and guidelines for environmental management and control of pollution • Control and review environmental problems • Provide guidelines on climate change in Indonesia • Coordinate and negotiate with international agencies dealing with climate change
Ministry of Home Affairs	• Coordinate national, provincial, and city government programs and activities for development • Supervise national and regional government to improve development practices
Coordinating Ministry for Economic Affairs	• Formulate national economic policy, planning and implementation procedures • Coordinate and create synergy in economic policy that relates to urban transport policy among line ministries
Ministry of Finance (MoF)	• Formulate national policy on economic growth • Allocate a budget for road and public transport infrastructure projects, together with BAPPENAS

Source: S. E. Wijaya and M. Imran. 2019. *Moving the Masses: Bus-Rapid Transit (BRT) Policies in Low Income Asian Cities.* https://link.springer.com/book/10.1007/978-981-13-2938-8.

Several derivative regulations have been made following the presidential decree to support the acceleration program, as summarized in Table 38.

Other relevant regulations have been released as well, as described in Table 39. The central government officials have also repeatedly made a statement that they will push the adoption of electric vehicles starting with government fleets and encouraging state-employed staff to use electric vehicles as much as possible.

Table 38: Derivative Regulations from Presidential Decree 55/2019

Regulation	Description
MoHA Ministerial Regulation 8/2020	• This provides a legal framework for regional or local government to set the electric vehicle tax and vehicle return duty with maximum rate limit stated. • Compared with the conventional ICE vehicle tax rate, the maximum rate limit for private electric vehicles is similar. But for electric vehicles used for public transport (yellow licensed plate), the maximum rate limit is lower.
MoT Ministerial Regulation 44/2020	• This regulates the type test specific for any electric vehicle to be operated in Indonesia, including two- or three-wheelers, which will be the basis for later releasing the vehicle registration. • The type test also covers additional complementary equipment such as chargers for electric vehicles.
MoT Ministerial Regulation 87/2020	• This regulates the type of test specific for electric vehicles to be operated in Indonesia, including two- or three-wheelers, which will be the basis for releasing the vehicle registration. • It also regulates how and by whom the type test shall be carried out. • This regulates the test for batteries, protection of direct and indirect contact, and insulation resistance. • This regulates the noise required for safety reason.
MEMR Ministerial Regulation 13/2020	• This regulates the deployment of charging infrastructure, including charging station and battery swapping facilities. • Private charger is not allowed to be used for buying and selling electricity or charging services, while public chargers can do so. • Owners of public chargers must have a license for buying and selling electricity, similar to the license owned by the utility, and owners must have chargers in more than one province. • Battery swapping facility owners do not have to own a license for buying and selling electricity. • Several possible business schemes for public chargers and battery swapping facilities are described here. • PLN is mandated to spearhead the initial charging infrastructure deployment, with the possibility to collaborate with other SOEs and business entities and is required to create a deployment road map for both charging stations and battery-swapping facilities. • Electricity tariffs for charging infrastructure are also regulated here, covering wholesale electricity from the utility to the charging infrastructure owner, private chargers (as per normal tariff), and electricity sales from the infrastructure owner to the user. • Incentives such as a reduced connection cost, subscription guarantee fee, and minimum payment for the first 2 years are provided to the charging infrastructure owner.
MoI Ministerial Regulation 27/2020	• This provides a classification of electric vehicles based on the specification of the components such as drivetrain and battery capacity, according to the ministerial regulation. • Road map for development of electric vehicle-related industries is provided here and planned for the national motorized vehicle industry. • Method for calculating the local content requirement number, verification, and certification process is specified under this regulation. • This also establishes the tentative targets for electric two- or three-wheeler production, sales, and export.
MoI Ministerial Regulation 28/2020	• This regulates import and manufacturing of electric vehicles in the form of completely knocked down and semi-knockdown.
MoTr Ministerial Regulation 100/2020	• This regulates the importation of lithium as raw material for the battery industry to support the national electric vehicle-related industry.

ICE = internal combustion engine, MEMR = Ministry of Energy and Mineral Resources, MoHA = Ministry of Home Affairs, MoI = Ministry of Industry, MoT = Ministry of Transport, MoTr = Ministry of Trade, PLN = Perusahaan Listrik Negara (State Electricity Company), SOE = state-owned enterprise.

Source: Asian Development Bank.

Table 39: Other Relevant Regulations Concerning Electric Vehicles

Regulation	Key Points
Regulation 65/2020	• This regulates the conversion of ICE motorcycles to e-motorcycles.
MoT Ministerial Regulation 45/2020	• This regulates other type of electric motor-based vehicle not specified in the MoT Ministerial Regulation 44/2020, dubbed as specific vehicle which includes electric scooter, hoverboard, unicycle, otopet, and electric bike. • Instead of type test, safety equipment requirements are regulated here.
MoT Ministerial Regulation 65/2020	• This regulates conversion of conventional motorcycle to e-motorcycle. • It covers the requirement for the licensed workshop, and the conversion certification process to signify that the motorcycle is allowed to operate.
Government Regulation 73/2019	• This specifies zero value added tax for luxury goods (tariff 15%, tax base 0%) for electric vehicle under the fuel consumption or emission threshold. • The regulation will come into effect 2 years after the date of release, in October 2021.
MoF Ministerial Regulation 72/2020	• This specifies that the government's procurement for electric vehicles will be based on the available market price to facilitate using them as operating vehicles.
Regulation from MoF and Indonesia Investment Coordinating Board (IICB)	• This establishes income tax reduction for companies in the electric vehicle-related industry, with different duration depending on the amount of investment as long as the requirement is met.

Regulation from Financial Services Authority (OJK)	• OJK made a press release summarizing incentives provided for electric vehicle ecosystem, as follows:
	  – Financing for electric vehicle purchase or development of relevant upstream industry (battery, charging station, component) can be categorized as implementation of sustainable financing.
	  – Financing for electric vehicle manufacturing and the supporting infrastructure can be categorized as a government program with maximum credit limit exemption.
	  – Credit quality scoring for electric vehicle purchase or development of relevant upstream industry with upper limit up to Rp5 billion can be based only on principal and/or interest payment punctuality.
	  – Financing for electric vehicle purchase or development of relevant upstream industry is eligible for lower risk weight (75% instead of the usual 100%) during the assessment.

Regulation from Bank of Indonesia	• This allows zero down payment for the purchase of vehicle considering its environmental impact.

ICE = internal combustion engine, MoF = Ministry of Finance, MoT = Ministry of Transport.
Source: Asian Development Bank.

At the local government level, several provinces have started rolling out the regulations to support the acceleration program. The Ministry of Home Affairs has also repeatedly pushed the provincial governments to release the local regulation to provide incentives for the electric vehicle ecosystem, such as vehicle tax and return duty rates which are under the jurisdiction of the provincial government. Table 40 summarizes regulations released by the local government in Jakarta and Bali. Consistent with the central government, the local government officials are also trying to push electric vehicle adoption starting from government fleets and encouraging state-employed staff to use them as much as possible.

Table 40: Local Government Regulations on Electric Vehicles in Jakarta and Bali

Regulation	Key Points
Jakarta's Governor Regulation 3/2020	• The regulations states 0% return duty rate for electric vehicles in Jakarta.
Jakarta's Governor Regulation 88/2019	• The vehicle restriction based on the last digit in the vehicle plate (odd/even restriction) is not applicable to electric vehicles
Bali's Governor Regulation 9/2019	• The regulation states 10% return duty rate for the first owned electric vehicle. For the second and the following, a 1% return duty rate applies.
Bali's Governor Regulation 48/2019	• The regulation lists a strategy and action plans for accelerating electric vehicle adoption in Bali. • The regulation includes requirements for local material and service usage for an electric vehicle industry in Bali. • The regulation lists options and recipients of incentives that can be provided. • Electric vehicles must pass a type test and a periodic test administered by the local government or an authorized private company licensed by the Ministry of Transport. • The regulation lists options for an action plan to limit conventional vehicles that later can be implemented are listed in this regulation. • Battery waste must be recycled and managed by authorized institutions.
Bali's Governor Instruction 11 / Transport Department / 2021	• Government bodies and SOEs are asked to procure electric vehicles wherever applicable. • Electric vehicles must have passed the type test stated by the law. • Government staff are urged to switch to electric vehicles. • Government bodies and SOEs shall prepare the charging infrastructure. • Head of Transport Department in Bali shall facilitate any electric vehicle procurement.

SOE = state-owned eneterprise.
Source: Asian Development Bank.

Beside the regulations that are already released as listed in the previous tables, Indonesia expects more derivative and related regulations to be released as part of the acceleration program stated in the presidential decree. The list, together with the responsible government bodies, is in Table 41.

Table 41: Expected Regulations Concerning Electric Vehicles to be Released

Institution	Description
MoF, MEMR, DEN	• Regulation concerning subsidy shift to the electric vehicle purchaser
MoI, National Standardization Agency (BSN)	• Regulation concerning battery standardization to support battery swapping
MoEF, MoI, MoTr	• Regulation concerning used battery management and governance
Local Government	• More regulations regarding incentives (financial or nonfinancial) to be released by the local government

DEN = Dewan Energi Nasional (National Energy Council), MEMR = Ministry of Energy and Mineral Resources, MoEF = Ministry for the Environment and Forestry, MoF = Ministry of Finance, MoTr = Ministry of Trade.
Source: Government of Indonesia, MEMR.

Table 42 summarizes the current incentives for electric vehicles, both financial and nonfinancial. Beside the incentives provided as per the list of regulations mentioned in the previous tables, there are also additional incentives provided by PLN and by credit facility providers. Most of the incentive providers are SOEs that have been mandated by the government to support the acceleration program.

Table 42: Summary of Incentives for Electric Vehicles

Type	Recipient	Provider	Incentives
Financial	Electric Vehicle Purchaser	Central Government	• For private electric vehicles, the tax rate is similar to conventional vehicles, but the rate for electric vehicles is set as a maximum limit, giving local government room to provide incentives. • For public transport electric vehicles, the vehicle tax rate maximum limit is lower. • Zero value added tax for luxury goods • Zero down payment for financing electric vehicle purchase • More relaxed credit scoring evaluation for electric vehicle purchase
		Local Government	• Zero return duty rate for electric vehicles in Jakarta • 10% return duty rate for a first electric vehicle and 1% for subsequent electric vehicles in Bali
		Credit Provider	• Besides the zero down payment, a lower interest rate and longer credit duration are provided
	Charging Infrastructure Developer	Central Government and PLN	• MEMR mandated PLN to provide incentives in the form of connection cost reduction, subscription guarantee fee reduction, and minimum payment exemption for the first 2 years. • Tariff discount provided by PLN for charging during the non-peak load time (10 p.m. to 4 a.m.). • More relaxed credit scoring evaluation for charging infrastructure development.
	Electric Vehicle-Related Industry	Central Government	• Income tax reduction with various duration for investment in Indonesia that met the requirement
Non-Financial	Electric Vehicle User	Local Government	• Exemption from odd–even license plate restrictions in Jakarta

MEMR = Ministry of Energy and Mineral Resources, PLN = Perusahaan Listrik Negara (State Electricity Company).

Sources: Government of Indonesia, MEMR; Government of Indonesia, Ministry of Maritime and Investment; and various government regulation documents.

Proposed Policies

E-motorcycles are attractive for society due to lowering emissions and noise. However, compared to their fossil-fuel-based counterparts, they only have a limited attractiveness for users:

- For private users, fossil-fuel-based motorcycles are more attractive due to having more power and unlimited range. An e-motorcycle with more or less comparable power to a 110 cc petrol version i.e., with 3,500 W, costs around three times more than the fossil-fuel-based version plus requires a costly battery replacement after 2–3 years and only has a range of 50 km. Even if operational costs are lower with an e-motorcycle, the incremental investment is not recovered during its lifespan. E-motorcycles in a comparable price range are much lower powered. While this power rationally is not required for urban purposes, customers do cherish it and will continue choosing fossil-fuel-based units. The limited range is not really a large issue for urban usage but motorcycles are also often used outside the urban zone.
- For commercial users, the limited power is of less concern as 1,500–2,000 W motorcycles also have sufficient power to transport two passengers or goods at typical urban speeds. The main problem why e-motorcycles are not attractive to commercial users is their business model based on the drivers supplying the motorcycle, which increases flexibility and reduces costs of the delivery company, while drivers cherish that a part of

their motorcycle cost is being paid. Drivers will not purchase e-motorcycles as they prefer a gasoline version. Battery swapping would need to be established at the company level.

Without regulatory intervention, e-motorcycles will remain in the short and medium term confined to low-powered scooters used especially by students. This is also clearly reflected in other large motorcycle markets such as Viet Nam, where e-motorcycles are confined to students that use the low-powered units without registration.

Taipei,China is a good example of a market-based intervention with large purchase incentives for e-motorcycles plus financial support in the establishment of a dense battery swapping infrastructure. The financial support for high-powered e-motorcycles allowed them to compete with fossil-fuel-based versions. But even with this support, the market share of newly registered e-motorcycles did not surpass 20% and with a reduction of subsidies has dropped to 10%, i.e., even with close-to-purchase-cost parity for high-powered e-motorcycles and with a high density of swapping stations, customers still preferred fossil-fuel-based units.

In contrast, the PRC has a huge market for e-motorcycles. This is, however, only due to not permitting the registration and usage of fossil-fuel-based motorcycles in most urban areas of the country.

Technically, low- to medium-powered e-motorcycles (1,000–2,000 W) are fast and strong enough for any urban trips including ride-hailing services, and have lower lifetime costs than fossil-fuel-based units and a comparable capital expenditure. While some charging infrastructure is required, this can be tailor-made for commercial services. The preference of customers for power and speed and the business models of ride-hailing and delivery services are the barriers. Economic incentives for private users will not change this picture fundamentally and will result in a very limited impact while costing large amounts of money. Subsidizing commercial companies to move to e-motorcycles while they enjoy huge profits is not justified. Thus, from a policy perspective the message is clearly that the government should not embark of giving financial incentives for the purchase of e-motorcycles or for the establishment of charging infrastructure as such policies are neither efficient, effective, nor sustainable. The policy proposed to spur usage of e-motorcycles is to regulate the usage of fossil-fuel-based motorcycles and thereby reduce their attractiveness. Usage of fossil-fuel-based motorcycles should be restricted with a clear pathway. To avoid sunk investments, this should be announced with a sufficient time-lag, as motorcycles are used for various years. Suggested pathways are:

- **Pathway 1.** Gradual expansion of electric-only zones for motorcycles. Initially, urban downtown areas could be limited to only usage of e-motorcycles and then this could be gradually expanded, e.g., from 2023 onward, only e-motorcycles can enter downtown; by 2025, the zone is then expanded to the entire JABODETABEK.
- **Pathway 2.** Focus on commercial services: This can be by allowing only e-motorcycles for certain operating zones (similar to pathway 1) or by demanding that e-motorcycles be a certain share of the fleet. This is, however, far more difficult to control, especially as ride-hailing and delivery services generally do not own the motorcycles. For motorcycle rental services, e.g., in Bali, this approach could, however, be used by demanding that their fleet be 25% electric by end-2022, with shares increasing 25% every year to reach 100% by end-2025.

Restricting fossil-fuel-based motorcycle usage is the pathway that has been followed successfully by the PRC. In Viet Nam, Hanoi and Ho Chi Minh City have also announced bans on fuel-powered motorbikes entering their downtown areas starting in 2025.[66]

---

[66] C. F. Wu. 2020. Gogoro's EV Dream Facing Major Headwinds. *Common Wealth Magazine*. 24 July.

Asking commercial ride-hailing companies to go electric if they want to keep their licenses is also being applied, e.g., by California.[67] The California Air Resources Board has approved ambitious emissions-reductions goals for ride-hailing services, effectively requiring companies like Uber and Lyft to go all-electric by the end of the decade.[68] The new rules require ride-hailing companies to start ramping up electrification in 2023 (2% of all miles), continuing to 50% of all miles by 2027 and to ensure that 90% of vehicle miles are electric by 2030. "Ensure" is the key word here, as the business models of Uber and Lyft rely on drivers supplying their own cars. Instead of looking at vehicles themselves, compliance will be determined by vehicle miles traveled. Thus, ride-hailing and delivery companies will effectively no longer be able to shield themselves behind the excuse of not owning vehicles. Such a system could well be applied also by the Government of Indonesia, demanding that service companies, ride-hailing, or delivery companies become fully electric within a given time period based on their service miles.

Restricting the usage of fossil-fuel-based motorcycles is justified in economic and social terms as:

- trips can be made also with e-motorcycles with comparable convenience levels;
- financially, e-motorcycles have a comparable cost or are even less expensive than fossil-fuel-based units;
- the environmental impact of fossil-fuel-based motorcycles is highly negative due to emission of air pollutants, GHGs, and high noise levels; and
- in the absence of such policies, private and commercial users will continue using fossil-fuel-based motorcycles due to the preference for high-powered, high-speed units and due to commercial ventures that maximize profits without taking into consideration the environment and the well-being of society.

For low-income, motorcycle-dependent residents that live within or commute to areas with restrictions, the government can establish an initial purchase subsidy paid against scrapping of the fossil-fuel-based motorcycle on a one-time basis.

Policies to standardize batteries are not recommended. Private e-motorcycles will be charged at home and at the destination. Battery swapping is not a necessity for private users nor a big advantage, except perhaps for long-distance rides. For commercial users, battery swapping has an advantage as daily mileage is higher and battery swapping reduces the recharging time. While uniform battery technologies would facilitate battery swapping and reduce costs at least initially, this is not a necessity as smaller battery swap stations can be used with different battery types. It is not deemed realistic that manufacturers will agree on a specific battery type given that it is a main distinctive component of an e-motorcycle. Uniform battery types could also hamper competition and thus avoid innovation and further development of this technology.

Additional incentives could be given next to regulatory measures. However, these are not needed. The customers will purchase lower-powered e-motorcycles, which are around 40% more expensive than gasoline units but these incremental costs are quickly recovered. Using a standard bank loan with standard interest rates, the monthly payment for finance together with energy and maintenance cost will be lower for e-motorcycles than for gasoline units. Providing subsidized loans is thus not recommended and not necessary within a regulatory framework that demands the usage of electric units. Without regulatory measures, subsidized interest rates will not be a sufficient measure to increase demand for e-motorcycles (Section 9.7).

---

[67] S. Edelstein. 2021. California Approves EV Mandate for Uber and Lyft. *Green Car Reports*. 24 May. https://www.greencarreports.com/news/1132348_california-approves-ev-mandate-for-uber-and-lyft.
[68] California Air Resources Board. 2021. *Proposed Clean Miles Standard*. https://ww2.arb.ca.gov/our-work/programs/clean-miles-standard.

13. Outline Road Map for Electric Motorcycles in Indonesia

Electric motorcycles or e-motorcycles will outpace fossil-fuel-based units in terms of market share of newly sold units by 2030. Indonesia has taken decisive steps to significantly increase the market share of e-motorcycles based on a phased approach of limiting access to urban areas in favor of e-motorcycles and gradually expanding the restricted areas.

This long-term vision builds upon the following aspects:

(i) E-motorcycles result in less air pollution, GHGs, and noise compared to fossil-fuel-based units. This improves the health and social well-being of citizens.

(ii) E-motorcycles are already technically and financially a feasible alternative, especially for urban trips and commercial services including ride-hailing and delivery services.

(iii) Conversion of old gasoline motorcycles to electric units is not recommended and not a strategy that will have market success. Conversion results in old motorcycles with new but non-guaranteed electric components at a price tag comparable to a new gasoline motorcycle and only 50% below the price of a new electric unit, while having many old components, no manufacturer guarantee, and potential malfunctions. This is not what customers will demand and electric vehicle conversion has failed in all vehicle categories, except for special utility vehicles.

(iv) Medium-powered e-motorcycles are on the market, are convenient especially for urban usage, and have comparable life-time costs to gasoline motorcycles. Clients, however, prefer fossil-fuel-based motorcycles due to higher power and speed, although this is not required in urban settings.

(v) The experiences of the PRC; Taipei,China; and Viet Nam, with a significant market share of electric two-wheelers is that, in the absence of significant subsidies or of regulations, only low-powered electric scooters will be sold. E-scooters do not require a license and are thus convenient for students. However, they will replace bicycles and public transport.

(vi) The dissemination of e-motorcycles requires government policies that clearly favor the usage of e-motorcycles. Fossil-fuel-based motorcycles result in costs to society that are not being born by the user.

(vii) In the absence of either massive subsidies (about Rp5–10 million per motorcycle) or of regulations that favor e-motorcycles, gasoline motorcycles will continue to dominate the market and the targets of Indonesia on having 2 million e-motorcycles operating by 2025 will not be reached. The proposed carbon tax will have no measurable influence on the sale of e-motorcycles as the resultant lifetime cost saving is less than 1%. Incentives such as preferential interest rates are insufficient and will not convince clients to purchase e-motorcycles since the main issues are the high incremental price tag, the limited driving range, and the limited speed and power.

(viii) A subsidy policy like that realized in Taipei,China, for example, would require an investment of around $1.1 billion (Rp$1.6*10^{13}$) to reach the target of 2 million e-motorcycles by 2025. The same target could be reached without financial investment and without costs to the private sector by regulating the usage of fossil-fuel-based motorcycles, as was done very successfully in the PRC.

(ix) Limiting usage of fossil-fuel-based motorcycles is the most effective and efficient policy to promote usage of electric two-wheelers. The usage of motorcycles in urban areas should be limited to electric units. Electric vehicle zone areas could be gradually expanded. The same approach could be made for islands such as Bali.
(x) For ride-hailing and delivery services, regulations can be applied asking for a certain share of e-motorcycles (including not only company-owned, but all vehicles operating under their brand) or a share of electric mileage of services provided by or through the company, with gradually increasing targets. Such a policy has for example been implemented recently by the state of California obliging that all ride-hailing and service delivery companies effectuate 90% of their mileage electric by 2030.
(xi) The regulatory policy proposed requires no government subsidies. Private parties invest in e-motorcycles, battery swapping stations, and destination chargers within JABODETABEK with their own financial means. To accommodate for additional electric vehicles and their chargers, investments in the distribution network worth cumulative Rp9 trillion are required by 2030, as well as investments in transmission (starting 2025, worth Rp11 trillion) and generation (starting 2025, worth Rp11 trillion). Total cumulative grid investments costs of Rp31 trillion can be significantly reduced by applying smart charging. These are long-term investments which can be recovered through the energy bill.
(xii) The Indonesian motorcycle industry can profit by having a strong and growing domestic market demanding e-motorcycles, thereby positioning themselves in a future growth market.

Target Users

The users targeted are commercial and private users of electric two-wheelers (Figure 38).

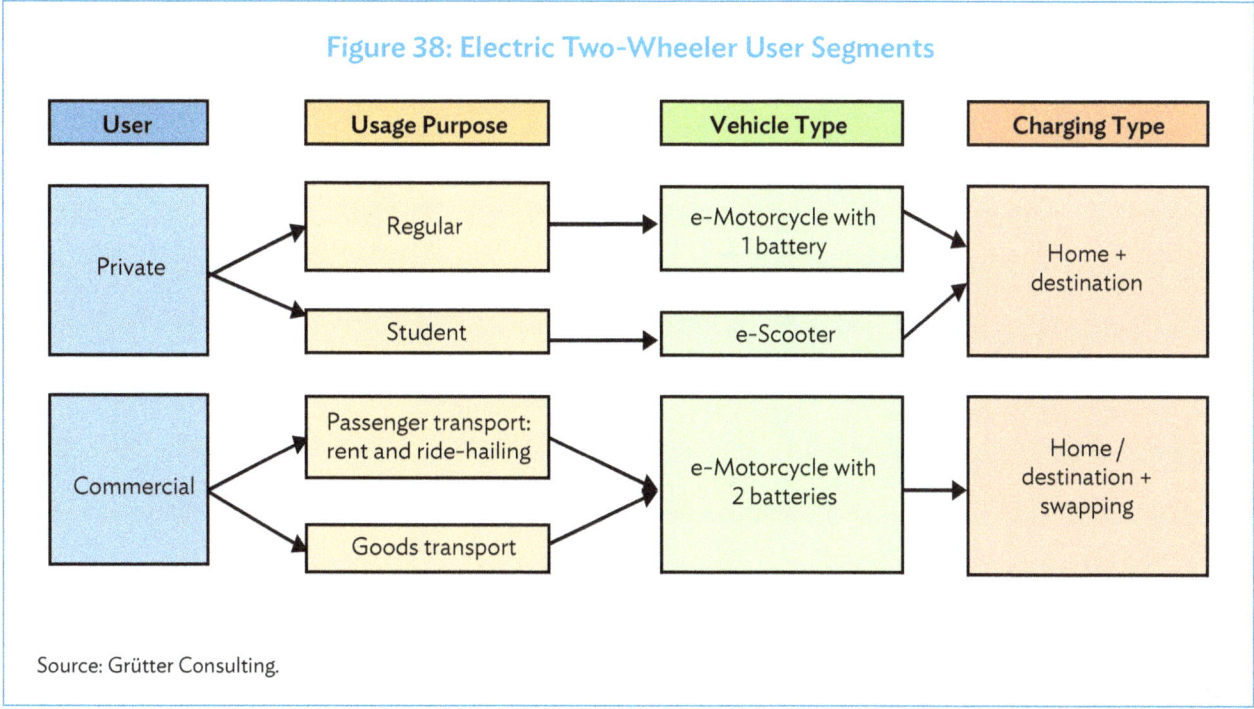

Figure 38: Electric Two-Wheeler User Segments

Source: Grütter Consulting.

E-scooters used by students replace often bicycles or public transport and not fossil-fuel-based units. Commercial users targeted include ride-hailing services, rental services, and delivery services. This sector is growing at a two-digit pace and will result in significant emissions damaging the health of citizens if not aligned with environmental policies.

E-Motorcycles and Charging Systems

E-motorcycles for urban usage are available today in Indonesia. The technical and financial characteristics of such motorcycles compared to fossil-fuel-based units are shown in Table 43.

Many lower-powered electric scooters are available in the market with 500- to 800-watt engines and speeds of 25–30 km/h. However, they do not have sufficient power and speed to be considered comparable to gasoline units and are not targeted by this road map.

Table 43: Targeted Electric versus Gasoline Motorcycles for Private and Commercial Urban Usage

Parameter	Gasoline motorcycle	Electric motorcycle	Comment
Engine	110–125 cc engine with 6 to 9 kW power	1,800–2,500 W engine with peak power of 5–7 kW and speeds of 50–70 km/h	Lower powered e-scooters are not considered to be comparable and are thus not included; higher powered e-motorcycles such as the Niu NGT are not included due to having triple investment cost of a fossil-fuel-based motorcycle.
Batteries	---	Lithium-ion of 1.2–1.5 kWh with a lifespan of 2–3 years (1,000 cycles)	Electric motorcycles are offered in general with the option of one or two batteries; 2–3 hours are required for a full charge at home
Driving range	150 km	40–70 km with one battery; 80–140 km with two batteries	Average distance per day for an urban Jakarta private user: 40–50 km; Average distance per day for commercial user: 80–100 km
Popular brands	Honda, Yamaha, Suzuki	Gesits, Swag Type X, United T1800,	Brands as sold in Indonesia currently
CAPEX	Rp17–21 million	Rp24–28 million with 1 battery	Battery cost around Rp5 million. The battery cost is declining annually 5%–10%
OPEX private user	Rp3.4 million per year or Rp240 per km	Rp1.0 million per year or Rp70 per km	Based on annual mileage of 14,000 km; includes maintenance and energy cost; excludes finance cost
OPEX commercial user	Rp5.9 million per year or Rp250 per km	Rp1.6 million per year or Rp70 per km	Based on annual mileage of 24,000 km; includes maintenance and energy cost; excludes finance cost
Total Cost of Ownership	Private: Rp550 per km Commercial: Rp470 per km	Private: Rp556 per km Commercial: Rp520 per km	Includes CAPEX (including battery replacement), OPEX and finance cost; 5-year lifespan of motorcycle private and 4-year commercial usage

CAPEX = capital expenditure, cc = cubic centimeter, km = kilometer, kmh = kilometer per hour, kW = kilowatt, OPEX = operating expenditure, Rp = Indonesian rupiah, W = watt.

Source: Grütter Consulting; JABODETABEK Commuter Statistics, 2019.

Charging

Three systems for charging are used potentially by e-motorcycle owners: home charging, destination charging, and battery swapping stations.

Home charging. All e-motorcycles will be charged at home on a regular basis from home connections. Home charging will primarily occur in the evening/at night. The household might have various e-motorcycles and thus various units are connected. A typical e-motorcycle battery charger for household use will require 200 to 500 W and will connect to a normal power point within the household power connection. An e-motorcycle battery will typically require approximately 1 kWh per charge, which means that the e-motorcycle will be recharged in 2 to 5 hours. Home charging or overnight charging is used by private as well as commercial users of e-motorcycles.

Destination charging. Sites can be designed for charging 100 to 1,000 motorcycles. They are used primarily by private e-motorcycle users and have as characteristic that the motorcycle is at the site for various hours and can thus be charged with the battery on-board the vehicle. This allows recharging fully the battery or topping-up the battery if only parked for a short time, thus reducing the need for a spare battery and thus reducing range anxiety. Typically, a low fee is levied, which includes space utilization, electricity consumed, and the service offered. To foster usage of e-motorcycles, institutions and companies could offer free energy provision.

Battery swapping stations. These will allow swapping a low battery with a new fully loaded one. This system is basically used by commercial users. Standardized batteries facilitate battery-swapping; it is, however, also feasible to operate with various battery types and sizes, either within the same swapping site or at different locations if the number of e-motorcycles is large enough. Typically, such sites handle 10–30 batteries and are densely distributed (having a swap point every 4–6 km). Business models used for swapping often include monthly subscriptions or payments per swap, with batteries often owned by the swapping company or the motorcycle manufacturer.

Market Projections

The projections are based on following a policy clearly favoring e-motorcycles by restricting usage of fossil-fuel-based motorcycles, initially in urban areas and thereafter also outside urban areas. This can be pushed quicker for commercial motorcycles than for private units, but the assumption used for projections is that this is realized simultaneously. Figure 39 shows the projected market share of e-motorcycles for Indonesia until 2030 under such a strategy.

The market share increases slowly due to vehicle survival rates. However, with the proposed policies, by 2030, 80% of newly sold motorcycles would be electric and their share in the total stock of vehicles would be around 45%, representing some 55 million units.

Figure 40 shows the projected number of e-motorcycles in JABODETABEK and Bali. For both sites, an e-motorcycle market share of 45% is targeted for 2030.

By 2030, nearly 8 million e-motorcycles are expected to circulate in JABODETABEK and close to 2 million units in Bali. It is assumed that around 10% are commercial and 90% private e-motorcycles.

Charging is differentiated, as mentioned, among home charging, destination charging, and battery swapping, with the latter being used basically by commercial users. Home charging would be a feature for all e-motorcycles.

Figure 39: Projected E-Motorcycle Market in Indonesia

Source: Grütter Consulting, based on regulatory policies favoring e-motorcycles.

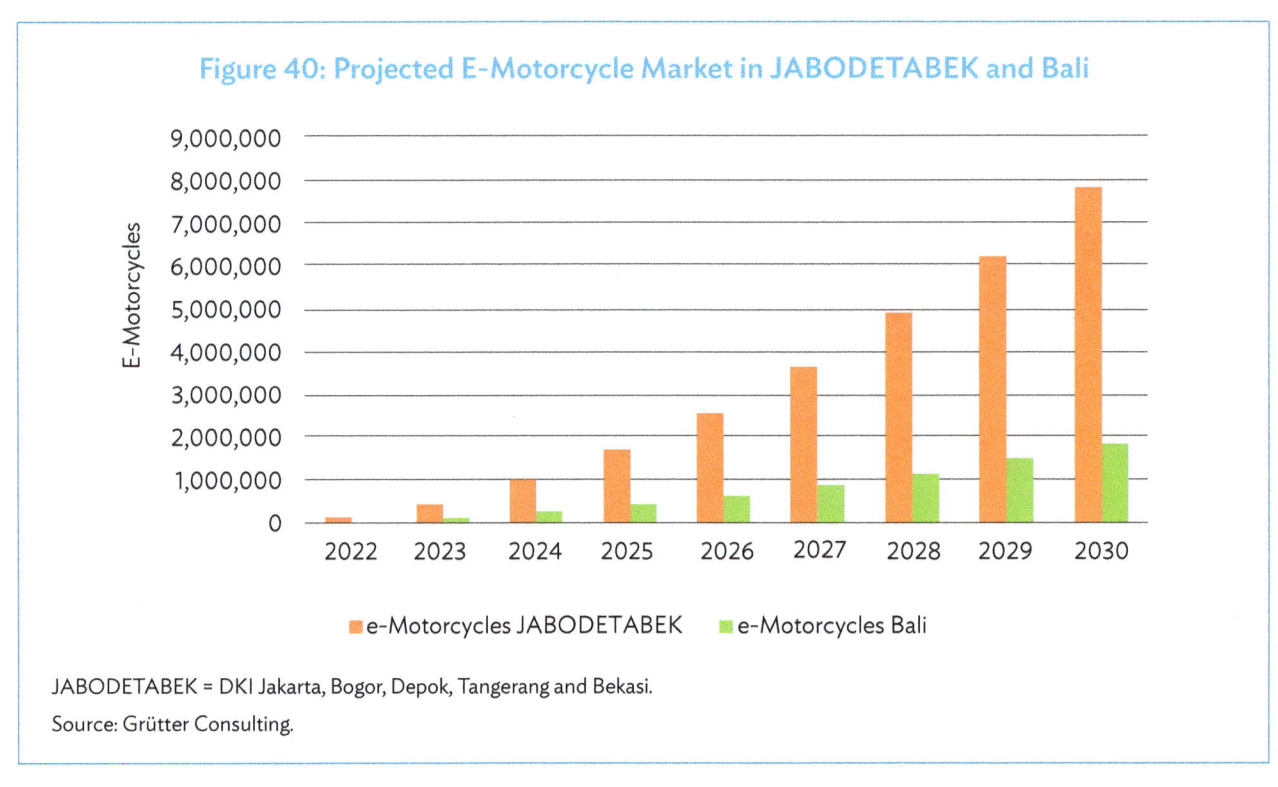

Figure 40: Projected E-Motorcycle Market in JABODETABEK and Bali

JABODETABEK = DKI Jakarta, Bogor, Depok, Tangerang and Bekasi.
Source: Grütter Consulting.

However, not all e-motorcycles are charged simultaneously and every day, with some households possibly having multiple units being charged at the same time. Charging at home or at work could be done just by plugging into the wall socket with no need for a dedicated charging infrastructure.

Figure 41 shows the projected numbers of destination electric vehicle chargers for JABODETABEK and Bali in relation to the e-motorcycle projections mentioned above. If, on average, each destination has some 100 chargers, one can get an idea of the number of destination charging sites.

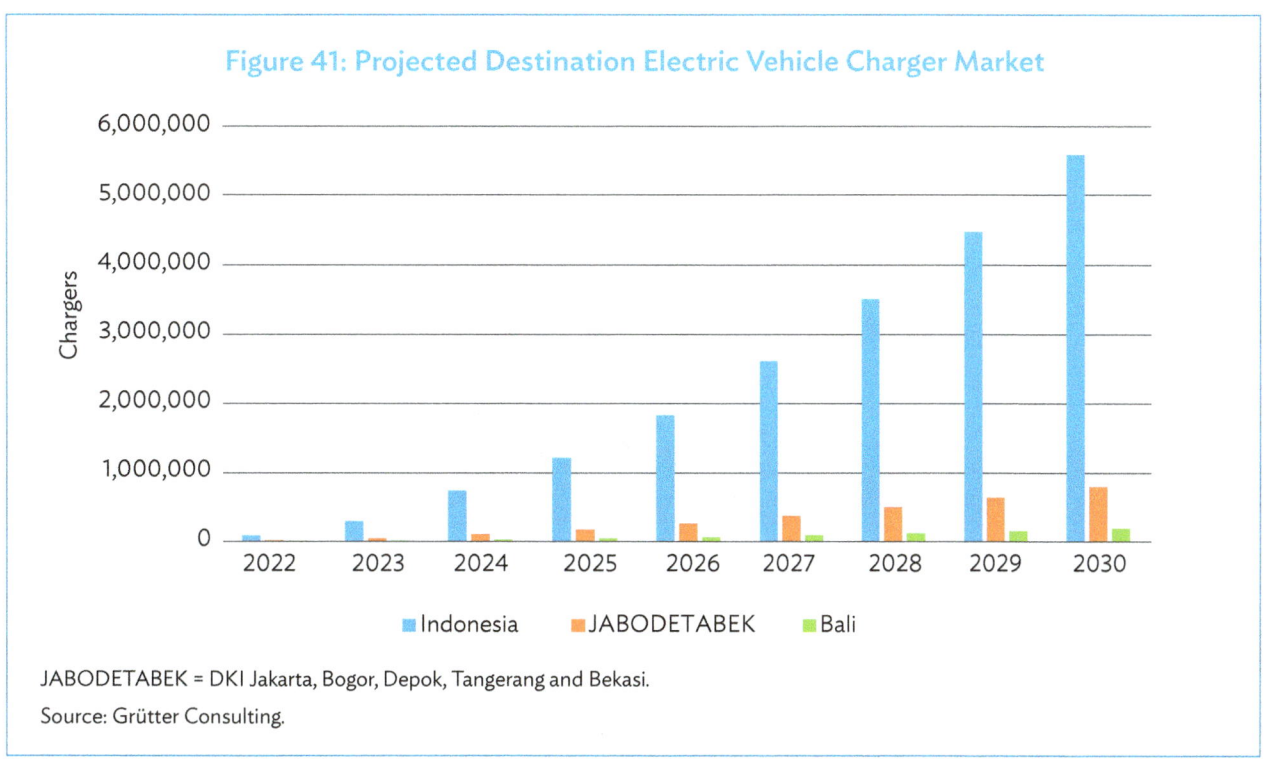

Figure 41: Projected Destination Electric Vehicle Charger Market

JABODETABEK = DKI Jakarta, Bogor, Depok, Tangerang and Bekasi.
Source: Grütter Consulting.

In total, some 5.5 million destination chargers would be required by 2030; of these, some 800,000 are needed in JABODETABEK and about 200,000 in Bali.

Figure 42 shows the projections on the number of swapping stations for JADOBETABEK and Bali, which levels out once a certain density is reached and is related to the number of e-motorcycles. Thereafter, it is assumed that swapping stations grow in number of slots rather than in number of swap sites. The projections assume that batteries are not standardized and that three battery types are used. This requires a larger number of swapping sites so that each customer can, within 4–6 km, reach a swap site commensurate with the battery used on his motorcycle.

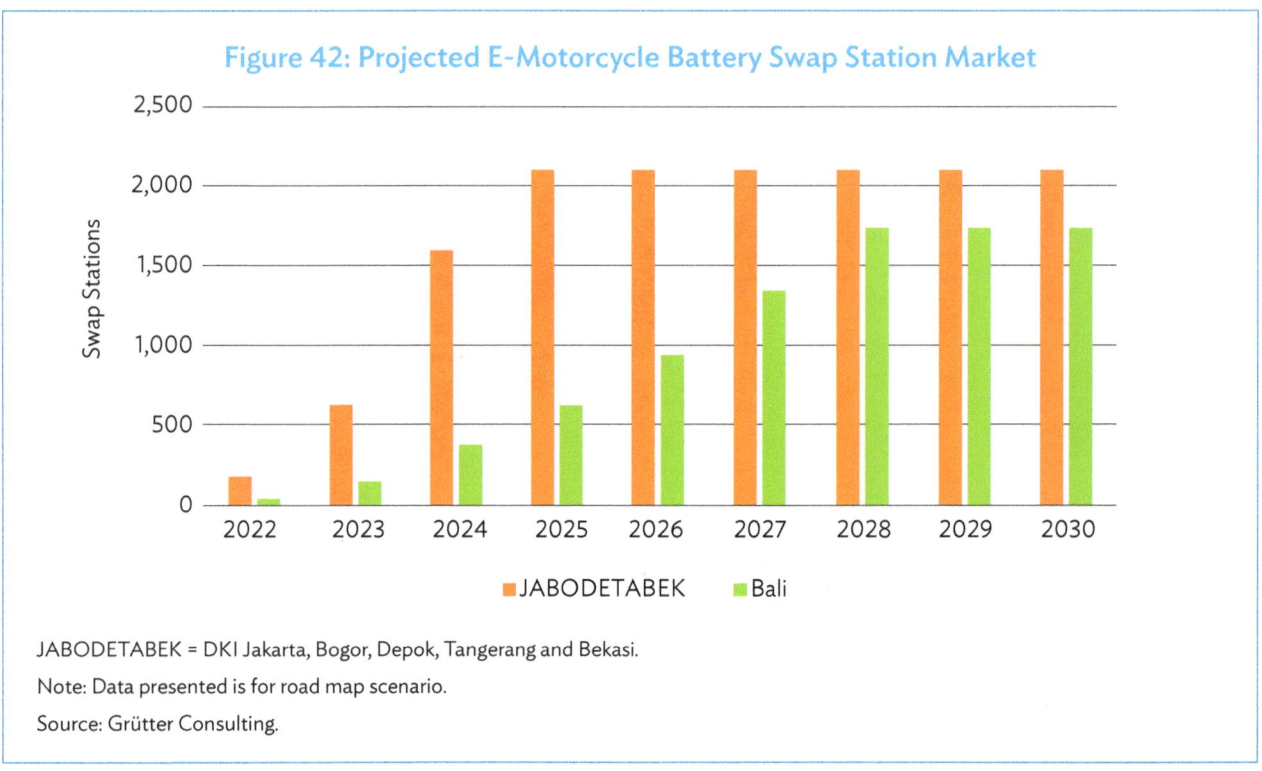

Figure 42: Projected E-Motorcycle Battery Swap Station Market

JABODETABEK = DKI Jakarta, Bogor, Depok, Tangerang and Bekasi.
Note: Data presented is for road map scenario.
Source: Grütter Consulting.

At both sites, a smaller area is targeted initially, e.g., DKI Jakarta for JABODETABEK and Kota Denpasar for Bali (Maps 2 and 3). This allows reaching a sufficient density of swap stations. The area is then increased. Between 2025 and 2027, a sufficient density of swap stations would be achieved, i.e., a station would be available every 4–6 km and stations would primarily grow in size. In case of regulations standardizing battery types, a higher density of swap stations would be achieved earlier.

Policies and Measures

In the absence of policies fostering e-motorcycles, the market uptake will be very limited and confined primarily to low-powered scooters with a maximum speed of 25–30 km/h which do not require a license. E-motorcycles are technically and financially feasible but not sufficiently attractive for private users due to limitations on speed and range (both are, however, under rational reasons, not a hindering factor for urban usage).

Financial incentive instruments as used in Taipei,China for example have proven to be very costly and with limited impact and sustainability. This is not considered to be an effective and efficient policy instrument. On the other hand, regulations limiting the usage of fossil-fuel-based motorcycles in urban operations have been very effective without limiting mobility mode choices of residents and with negative financial effects on neither private nor commercial users. This is therefore the recommended policy intervention.

The following policy steps are proposed:

- **By 2023.** Only allow e-motorcycles to operate in selected urban downtown areas of Jakarta and other large cities. Motorcycle rental services in Bali and selected other islands must have an electric fleet of minimum 20% of their total fleet offered for rental.

Outline Road Map for Electric Motorcycles in Indonesia 95

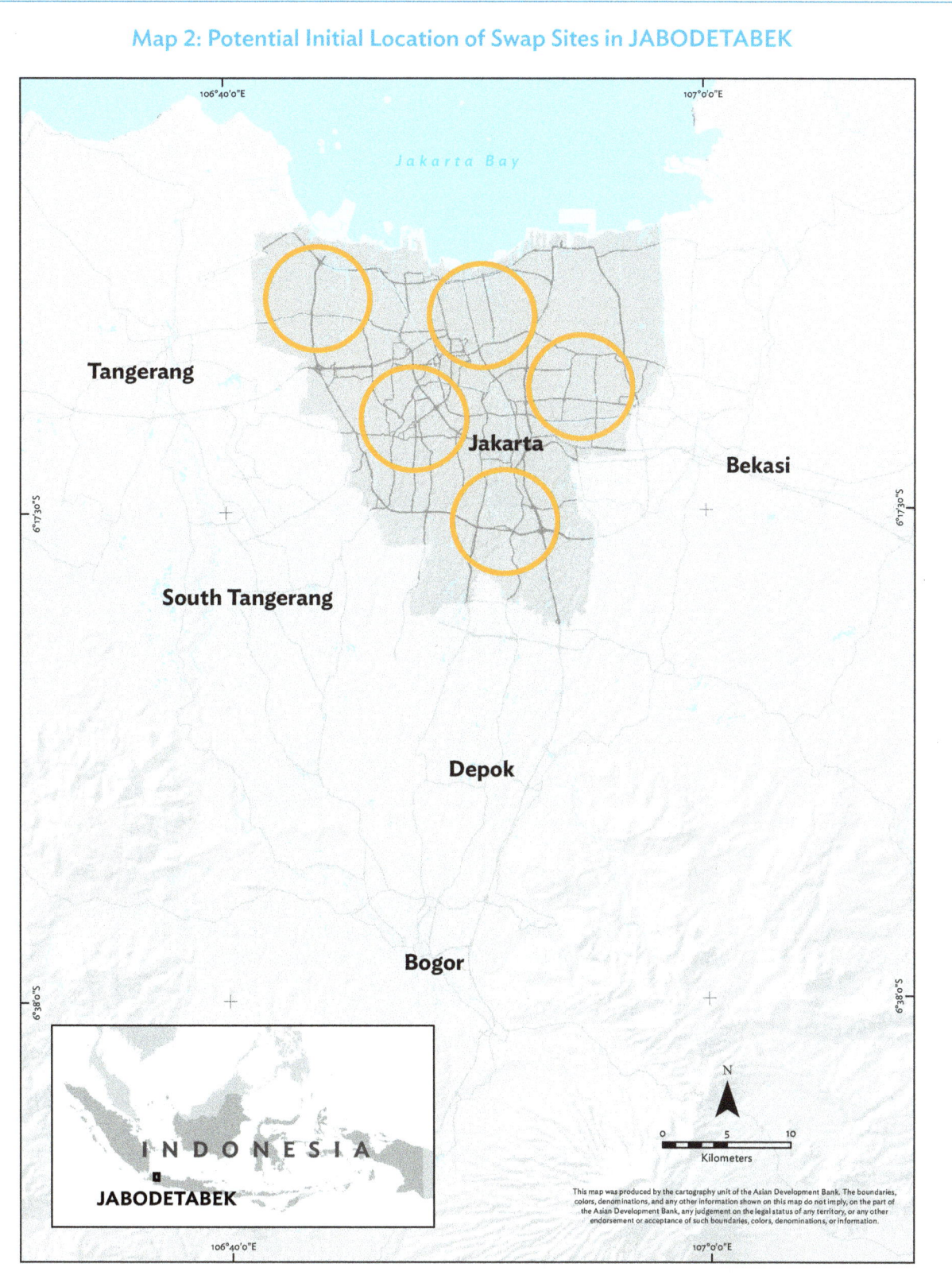

Map 2: Potential Initial Location of Swap Sites in JABODETABEK

JABODETABEK = DKI Jakarta, Bogor, Depok, Tangerang and Bekasi.
Source: Det Norske Veritas.

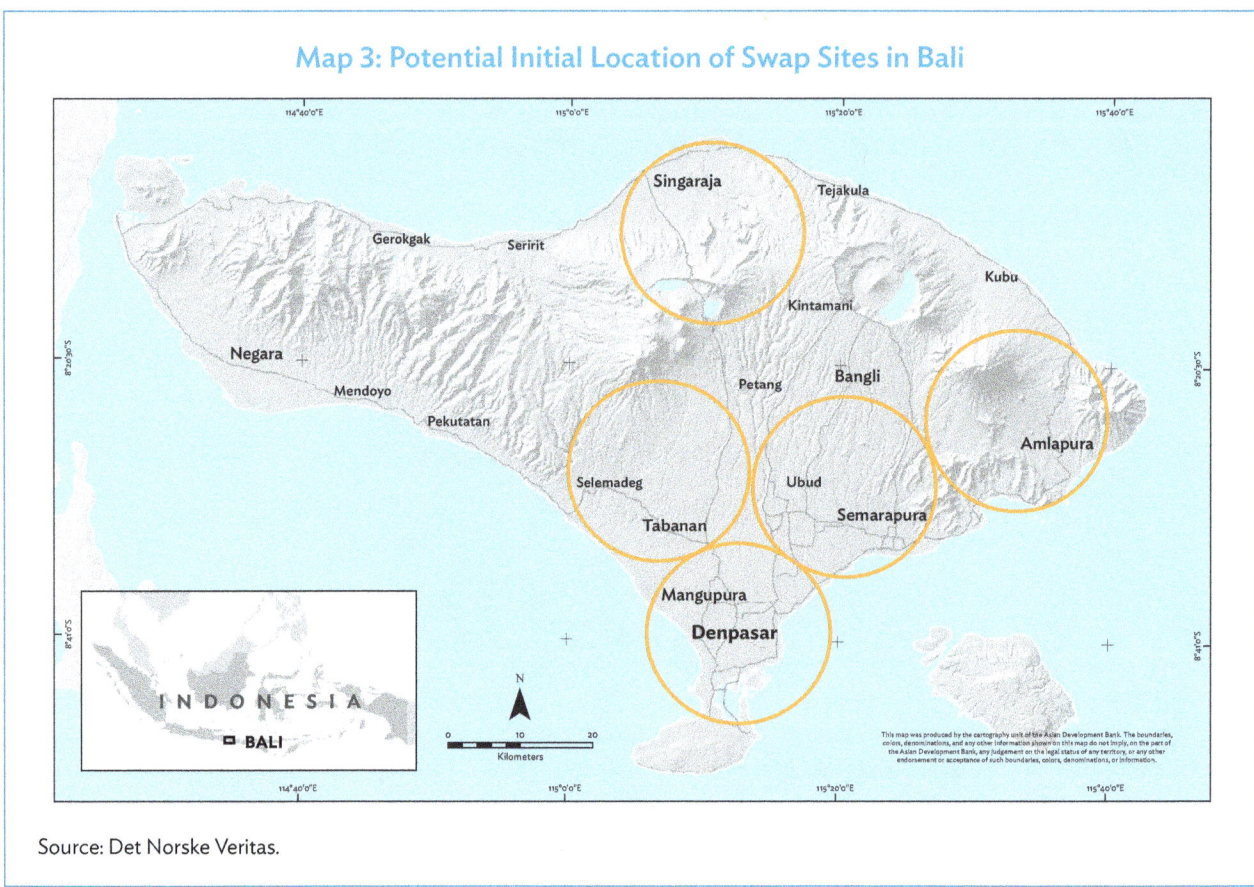

Map 3: Potential Initial Location of Swap Sites in Bali

Source: Det Norske Veritas.

- **By 2025.** Only allow e-motorcycles to operate in urban areas of Indonesia and the island of Bali plus selected other islands.
- **By 2030.** Only allow e-motorcycles to be newly registered.

Additionally, for commercial operations, a minimum share of e-motorcycles operating in urban areas is requested. This shall be applied to all motorcycles under contract or owned by the company or brand, i.e., it applies for all motorcycles which deliver at least one service during 1 year for the brand, independent of the ownership. The service company must have records on the number of motorcycles and their mileage, which are managed under the brand. The following targets are proposed:

- **By 2023.** A minimum 10% of motorcycles operating in JABODETABEK and in Bali within each ride-hailing or delivery company must be electric.
- **By 2024.** A minimum 20% of motorcycles operating in JABODETABEK and in Bali within each ride-hailing or delivery company must be electric.
- **By 2025.** A minimum 35% of motorcycles operating in JABODETABEK and in Bali within each ride-hailing or delivery company must be electric.
- **By 2026.** A minimum 60% of motorcycles operating in JABODETABEK and in Bali within each ride-hailing or delivery company must be electric.
- **By 2027.** A minimum 80% of motorcycles operating in JABODETABEK and in Bali within each ride-hailing or delivery company must be electric.
- **By 2028.** All motorcycles operating in JABODETABEK and in Bali within each ride-hailing or delivery company must be electric.

13.1 Environmental and Economic Benefits

Figure 43 shows the environmental impacts of the e-motorcycles under the road map scenario for Indonesia.

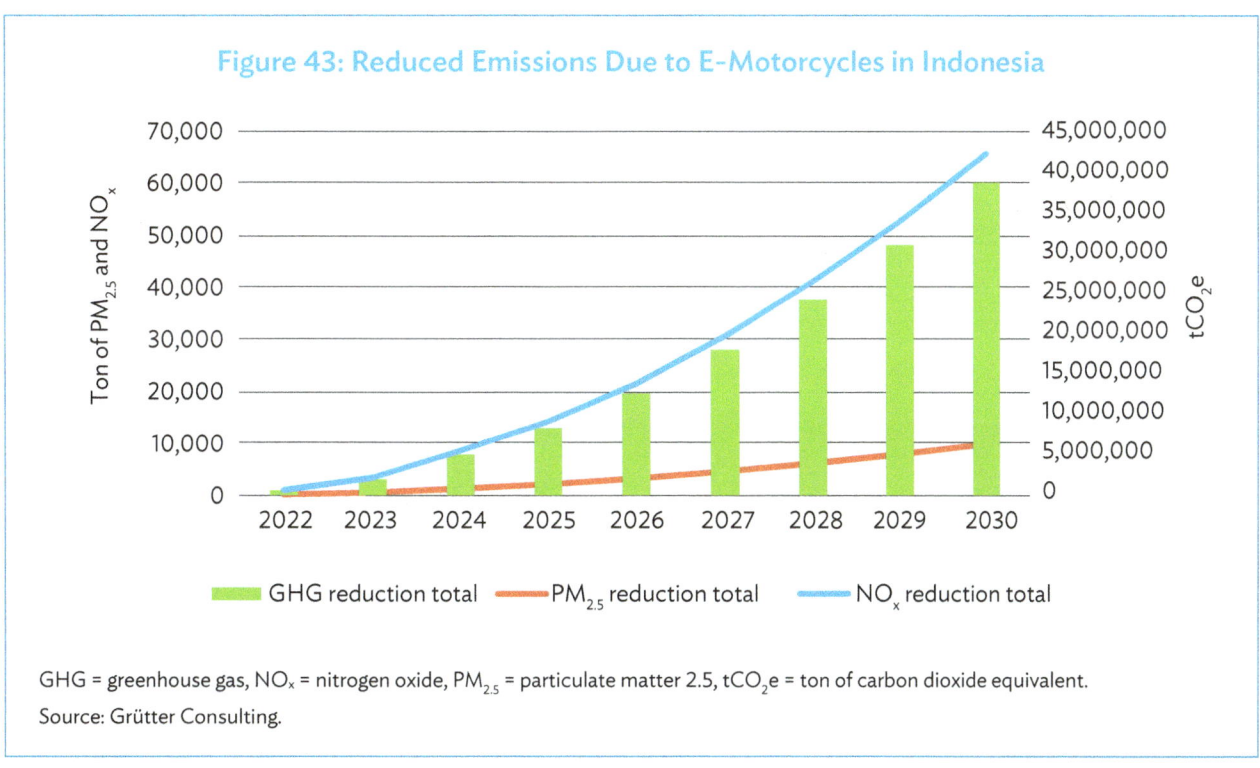

Figure 43: Reduced Emissions Due to E-Motorcycles in Indonesia

GHG = greenhouse gas, NOx = nitrogen oxide, PM$_{2.5}$ = particulate matter 2.5, tCO$_2$e = ton of carbon dioxide equivalent.
Source: Grütter Consulting.

Total electricity demand in 2030 would be around 21 TWh or 4% of national consumption. By 2030, e-motorcycles could reduce around 39 million tons of CO_2, around 10,000 tons of particulate matter 2.5 ($PM_{2.5}$), and 65,000 tons of nitrogen oxides (NOx), thus reducing significantly emissions and especially improving urban air quality.[69] This results in economic benefits of annually Rp50,000 billion ($3.4 billion) due to reduced emissions.

Reducing GHG emissions by 39 MtCO$_2$e is highly relevant for Indonesia, taking into account that 2018 total transport emissions were 154 MtCO$_2$e and would be around 301 MtCO$_2$e by 2030 assuming the same average annual growth rate as in the period 1990 to 2018; this would represent a 13% reduction relative to a BAU GHG scenario.

Figure 44 shows the main results for JABODETABEK.

JABODETABEK could reduce 5.4 million tons of CO_2 annually by 2030, 1,400 tons of $PM_{2.5}$, and more than 9,000 tons of NO$_x$ emissions, thereby improving the air quality. This would cost the area nearly $0.5 billion less in terms of air pollution costs per year (Figure 45).

---

[69] GHG reductions in practice might be more, as the carbon grid factor of Indonesia is reducing.

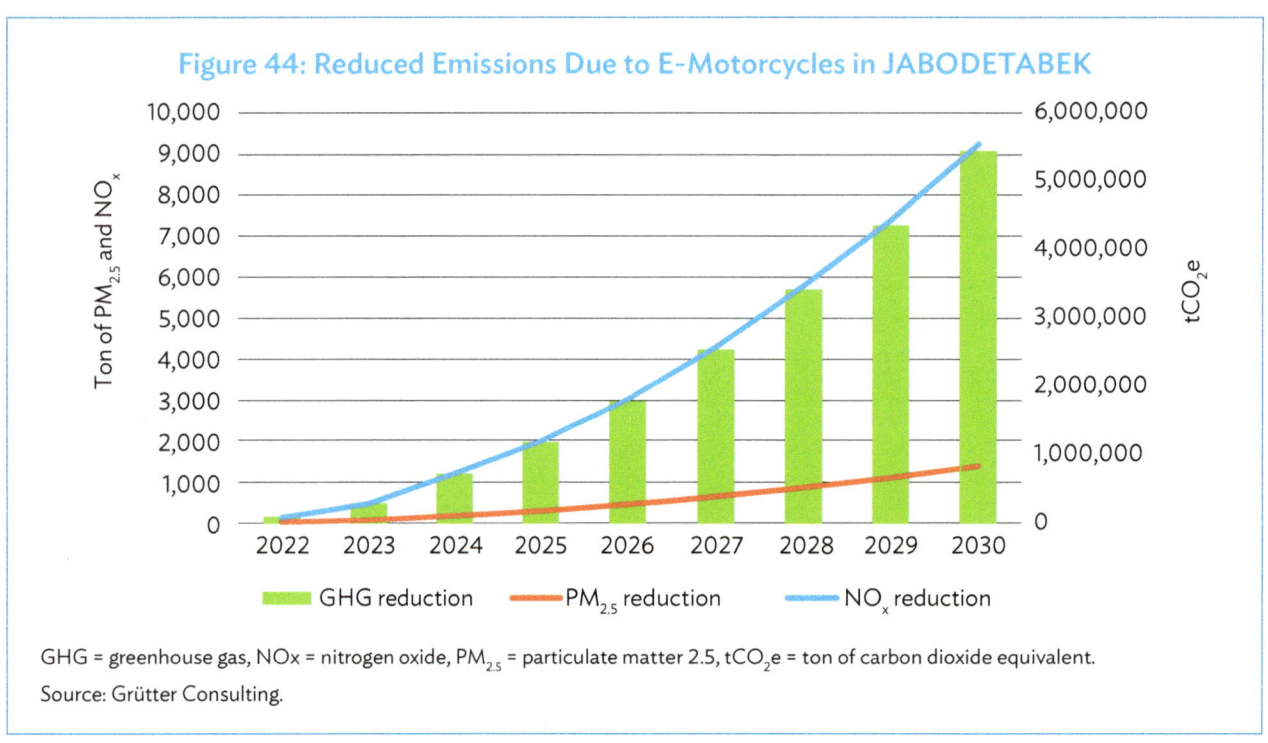

Figure 44: Reduced Emissions Due to E-Motorcycles in JABODETABEK

GHG = greenhouse gas, NOx = nitrogen oxide, $PM_{2.5}$ = particulate matter 2.5, tCO_2e = ton of carbon dioxide equivalent.
Source: Grütter Consulting.

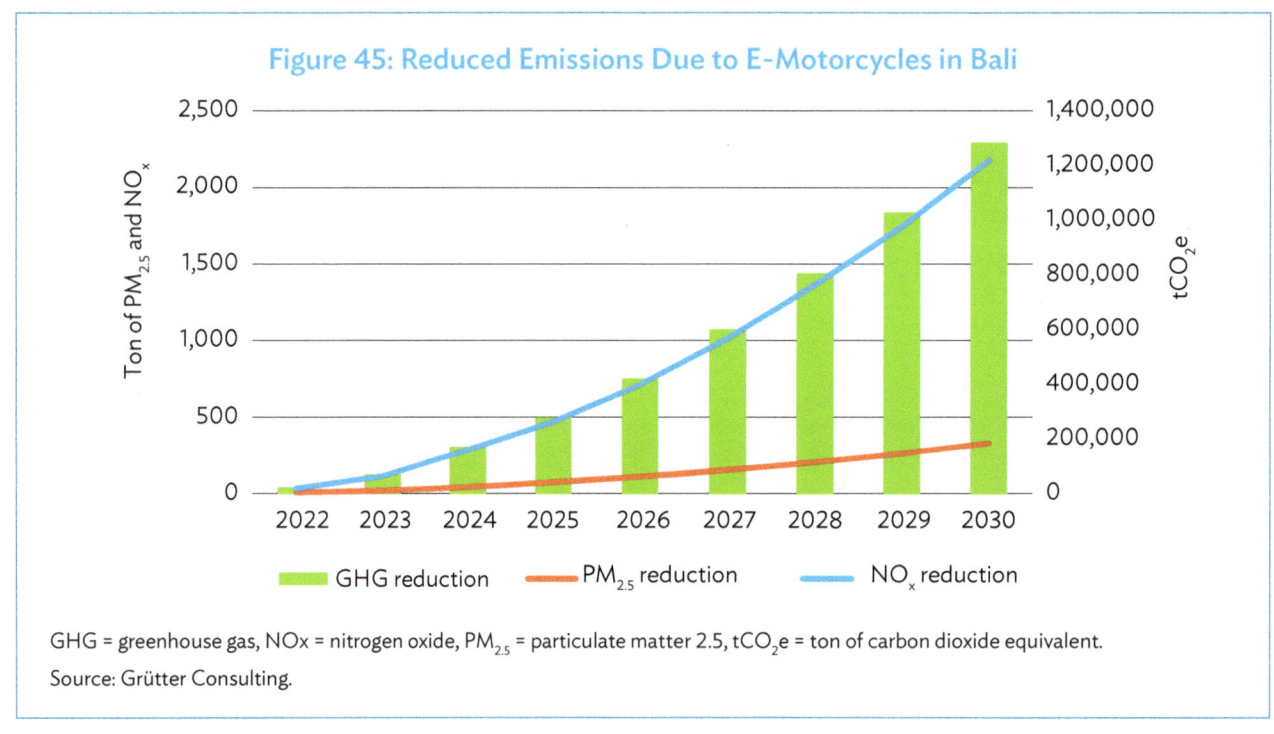

Figure 45: Reduced Emissions Due to E-Motorcycles in Bali

GHG = greenhouse gas, NOx = nitrogen oxide, $PM_{2.5}$ = particulate matter 2.5, tCO_2e = ton of carbon dioxide equivalent.
Source: Grütter Consulting.

Bali could reduce 1.3 million tons of CO_2 annually by 2030, 330 tons of $PM_{2.5}$, and 2,200 tons of NO_x emissions, thereby improving the air quality and the environmental reputation of the island. This would bring economic benefits in terms of avoided pollution costs worth more than $100 million per year.

Appendix 1: Standards

Standards for light electric vehicle, direct current (DC) charging <120 volts (V), including battery swap systems.

International Electrotechnical Commission (IEC) 61851-3 subseries is under development and is intended to cover electric vehicle supply equipment with a DC output not exceeding 120 V where reinforced or double insulation or class III is used as the principal means of protection against electric shock (information on scope as available on 312016).

- Part 3-1: Electric vehicles conductive power supply system - Part 3-1: General Requirements for Light Electric Vehicles (LEV) alternating curent (AC) and DC conductive power supply systems.
- Part 3-2: Electric vehicles conductive power supply system - Part 3-2: Requirements for Light Electric Vehicles (LEV) DC off-board conductive power supply systems.
- Part 3-3: Electric vehicles conductive power supply system - Part 3-3: Requirements for Light Electric Vehicles (LEV) battery swap systems.
- Part 3-4: Electric vehicles conductive power supply system - Part 3-4: Requirements for Light Electric Vehicles (LEV) communication.
- Part 3-5: Electric vehicles conductive power supply system - Part 3-5: Requirements for Light Electric Vehicles communication - Pre-defined communication parameters.
- Part 3-6: Electric vehicles conductive power supply system - Part 3-6: Requirements for Light Electric Vehicles communication -Voltage converter unit.
- Part 3-7: Electric vehicles conductive power supply system - Part 3-7: Requirements for Light Electric Vehicles communication - Battery system.

Appendix 2: Data Details

Table A2.1: General Parameters used for Calculations of the Impact of E-Motorcycles

Parameter	Value	Source
NCV of gasoline	44.3 MJ/kg	IPCC, 2006, table 1.2
CO_2 emission factor of gasoline	69.3 gCO_2/MJ	IPCC, 2006, Guidelines for National Greenhouse Gas Inventories Intergovernmental Panel on Climate Change
Density of gasoline	0.741 kg/l	International Energy Agency IEA, 2005, Energy Statistics Manual
Well-to-tank mark-up factor gasoline	19%	UNFCCC (2014), CDM Methodological Tool: Upstream leakage emissions associated with fossil fuel usage, Version 02.0 United Nations Framework Cionvention on Climate Change
Carbon grid factor Indonesia	0.825 $kgCO_2$/kWh	Organisation for Economic Co-operation and Development/IEA (2018) for CO_2 emissions and IEA for electricity production minus losses
Economic cost per ton NO_x emissions	\$1,334/t	
Economic cost per ton $PM_{2.5}$ emissions	\$180,330/t	
Economic cost of CO_2	\$40/t	International Monetary Fund (2014), Getting Prices Right
Battery manufacturing emissions	110 $kgCO_2$/kWh	ICCT (2018), Effects of battery manufacturing on electric vehicle life-cycle greenhouse gas emissions International Council on Clean Transportation
Conversion kWh to MJ	3.6 MJ/kWh	Energy Fundamentals. Units of Energy. https://home.uni-leipzig.de/energy/energy-fundamentals/03.htm#:~:text=Power%20.
$PM_{2.5}$ emissions MC	0.012 g/km	European Environmental Agency (2019), Air pollutant emission inventory guidebook update December 2019
NO_x emissions MC	0.080 g/km	
Exchange rate, May 2021	Rp14,300 = \$1	Currency Converter | Foreign Exchange Rates | OANDA

g/km = gram/kilometer, gCO_2 = gram Carbon Dioxide, kg = kilogram, $kgCO_2$ = kilogram Carbon Dioxide, kWh = kilowatt-hour, l = liter, MJ = Mega-joule, t = ton.

Source: ADB.

Table A2.2: Environmental Impact per E-Motorcycle Lifespan

Parameter	Value
GHG reduction	3.2 tons
$PM_{2.5}$ reduction	0.82 kg
NO_x reduction	5.47 kg
Economic value of emission reduction	\$284.00

GHG = greenhouse gas, NO_x = nitrogen oxides, $PM_{2.5}$ = particulate matter 2.5.

Source: Calculation by Grutter Consulting.

Table A2.3: Cost of Gasoline Fueled Motorcycles

Parameter	Value	Details
CAPEX gasoline motorcycle	Rp17,000,000	Honda Beat 110cc
Gasoline consumption	2.5 l/100 km	Average value monitored e.g., Viet Nam
Annual maintenance	Rp600,000	IESR, 2020
Lifespan motorcycle	5 years	Same as electric

CAPEX = capital expenditure, cc = cubic centimeter, IESR = Institute for Essential Services Reform, km = kilometer.
Source: ADB.

Table A2.4: Projections of Cost of e-Motorcycles of Same Power as Gasoline Motorcycles Used Currently

Parameter	2021	2022	2023	2024	2025	2026	2027	2028	2029	2030
CAPEX	40,000,000	36,426,635	33,172,494	30,209,058	27,510,359	25,052,745	22,814,680	20,776,551	18,920,496	17,230,250
TCO electric	862	800	740	680	630	590	550	510	480	450
TCO fossil	550	550	550	550	550	550	550	550	550	550
TCO fossil with carbon tax	554	554	554	554	554	554	554	554	554	554
Relative FIRR (%)	(35%)	(32%)	(27%)	(22%)	(15%)	(4%)	14%	69%		

CAPEX = capital expenditure, FIRR = financial internal rate of return, TCO = total cost of ownership.
Source: Calculations by Grutter Consulting.

Table A2.5: Impact on Total Cost of Ownership of Applying a Carbon Price in Indonesia

Parameter	Value
Carbon price	Rp75,000/tCO$_2$
Impact per liter of gasoline	Rp171
Increase in gasoline price	2%
Impact per kilometer	Rp4
Impact per annum	Rp58,350
New FIRR (%)	(5)
Old FIRR (%)	(35)
TCO old fossil	Rp550/km
TCO new fossil	Rp554/km

FIRR = financial internal rate of return, km = kilometer, l = liter, Rp = Indonesian rupiah, TCO = total cost of ownership, tCO$_2$ = tons of carbon dioxide.
Source: Calculations by Grutter Consulting.

Table A2.6: Projected Number of E-Motorcycles in Total Indonesia with a BAU Scenario, an Urban Regulation Scenario and a Financial Incentive Scenario

Parameter	2019	2020	2021	2022	2023	2024	2025	2026	2027	2028	2029	2030
Total motorcycles (million)	113	119	123	127	130	131	131	131	131	131	131	131
Additional units		6	5	4	3	1	0	0	0	0	0	0
Sales market	**6.0**	**6.5**	**7.0**	**7.6**	**8.2**	**8.8**	**9.5**	**10.3**	**11.1**	**12.0**	**13.0**	**14.0**
EV target GSE cumulative	0.0	0.5	1.3	2.7	4.6	7.6	11.8	12.0	12.3	12.5	12.8	13.0
EV target GSE per annum new	0.0	0.5	0.9	1.3	2.0	3.0	4.1	0.2	0.2	0.2	0.2	0.2
EV target as share of sales (%)	0	7	13	17	24	34	44	2	2	2	2	2
Market share (%)	0	0	1	2	4	6	9	9	9	10	10	10
EV target BAU RUEN national energy target cumulative	0.0	0.0	0.0	0.2	0.5	1.1	2.1					
EV target BAU RUEN national energy target annual	0.0	0.0	0.0	0.2	0.3	0.6	1.0					
EV target as share of sales (%)	0	0	0	3	4	7	11	0	0	0	0	0
Market share (%)	0	0	0	0	0	1	2	0	0	0	0	0
RUEN optimistic scenario							100	100	100	100	100	100
No government intervention BAU EV share sales (%)	0	0	1	2	3	4	5	6	7	8	9	10
Sales of EVs BAU	0	0	0.1	0.2	0.2	0.4	0.5	0.6	0.8	1.0	1.2	1.4
Cumulative EVs BAU	0	0	0.1	0.2	0.5	0.8	1.3	1.9	2.7	3.6	4.8	6.2
Market share (%)	0	0	0	0	0	0	0.04	0.05	0.05	0.06	0.07	0.08
Urban regulation strategy (%)	0	0	1	10	25	50	50	60	70	75	75	80
Sales of EVs regulations	0.00	0.00	0.07	0.76	2.04	4.41	4.76	6.17	7.77	9.00	9.72	11.19
Cumulative EVs regulations	0.00	0.00	0.07	0.83	2.87	7.27	12.04	18.20	25.98	34.97	44.69	55.88
Market share (%)	0	0	0	1	2	6	9	14	20	27	34	43
High economic incentives (like Taipei,China) EV sales share (%)	0	0	0	2	4	7	11	15	20	25	35	50
Sales of EVs high finance incentives RUEN SCENARIO	0	0.0	0.0	0.2	0.3	0.6	1.0	1.5	2.2	3.0	4.5	7.0
Cumulative Evs high incentive benefits	0	0	0.0	0.2	0.5	1.1	2.1	3.7	5.9	8.9	13.4	20.4
Market share (%)	0	0	0	0	0	1	2	3	5	7	10	16
2019 Data[a]	2019	2020	2021	2022	2023	2024	2025	2026	2027	2028	2029	2030
CAGR MCC 2015 to 2019 (%)	6	5.00	4.00	3.00	2.00	1.00	0.00	0.00	0.00	0.00	0.00	0.00
Expected CAGR 2030 (%)	1.0											

BAU = business-as-usual, CAGR = compound annual growth rate, EV = electric vehicle, GSE = grand strategy for energy, RUEN = Rencana Umum Energi Nasional (National Energy Masterplan), STD = statistik transportasi darat (land transportation statistics).

Notes:

1. Assumed decreasing CAGR due to saturation of market reaching populaiton growth by 2030
2. Replaced units based on 5 year usage and then replaced based on old data of new units plus additional ones

Source: STD, 2019, table 3.3.

Table A2.7: Motorcycle Total and E-Motorcycle Sales Projections

Parameter	2021	2022	2023	2024	2025
Motorcycle sales	7.0	7.6	8.2	8.8	9.5
RUEN base target	0.0	0.2	0.3	0.6	1.0
GSE target	0.9	1.3	2.0	3.0	4.1
BAU scenario	0.1	0.2	0.2	0.4	0.5
Financial incentives scenario	0.0	0.2	0.3	0.6	1.0
Regulation scenario	0.1	0.8	2.0	4.4	4.8

BAU = business-as-usual, GSE = grand strategy for energy, RUEN = Rencana Umum Energi Nasional (National Energy Masterplan).
Source: Grutter Consulting.

Table A2.8: Estimated Subsidy Requirement to Achieve Target of 2.1 Million E-Motorcycles by 2025

Parameter	Value
Subsidy differential investment cost per motorcycle year 1 based on 50%	Rp10 million
Subsidy differential expected year 5	Rp5 million
Number of e-motorcycles targeted in 5 years by RUEN	2.1 million
Motorcycle estimated subsidy	Rp1.58E+13
Number of motorcycles per charging station based on relation in Taipei,China	200
Cost per swapping station excl. Land	Rp71.5 million
50% subsidy charging station	Rp35.75 million
Total number of charging stations	10,500
Subsidy charging station based on subsidizing 25% of units	Rp93,844 million
Total subsidy	Rp1.58E+13
Motorcycle estimated subsidy	$1,101 million
Subsidy charging station	$6.56 million
Total subsidy	$1,108 million
Subsidy per motorcycle	Rp7.5 million
Economic value of reduced GHG emissions	Rp1.8 million
Economic value of reduced air pollutants	Rp2.2 million
Economic value of reduced emissions total	Rp4.1 million

GHG = greenhouse gas, Rp = Indonesian rupiah, RUEN = Rencana Umum Energi Nasional (National Energy Masterplan).
Source: Calculations by Grutter Consulting.

Table A2.9: Scenarios of Number of Swapping Stations for E-Motorcycles in JABODETABEK

Parameter	2022	2023	2024	2025	2026	2027	2028	2029	2030
BAU e-motorcycles	2,809	4,213	5,617	7,021	8,426	9,830	11,234	12,638	14,043
Scenario 1: RUEN / DEN with subsidies	21,228	67,079	153,739	300,813	517,412	829,316	1,250,386	1,887,043	2,869,315
Scenario 2 e-motorcycles: GSE with regulations	115,966	402,539	1,021,536	1,690,054	2,556,453	3,648,115	4,911,324	6,275,590	7,847,224
Total motorcycles	17,847,907	18,204,865	18,386,913	18,386,913	18,386,913	18,386,913	18,386,913	18,386,913	18,386,913
Swap stations scenario 1	33	105	240	470	808	1,296	1,954	2,949	4,483
Area swap stations scenario 1	211	67	29	15	9	5	4	2	2
Area assumed non-standardization	633	200	87	45	26	16	11	7	5
Actual number of swap station non-standardized	33	105	240	470	808	1,296	1,954	2,100	2,100
Swap stations scenario 2	181	629	1,596	2,641	3,994	5,700	7,674	9,806	12,261
Area swap stations scenario 2	39	11	4	3	2	1	1	1	1
Actual number of swap stations standardized	181	629	700	700	700	700	700	700	700
Area assumed non-standardization	116	33	13	8	5	4	3	2	2
Actual number of swap station excluding standardization	181	629	1,596	2,100	2,100	2,100	2,100	2,100	2,100
Area targeted	10	10	10	10	10	10	10	10	10

BAU = business-as-usual, DEN = National Energy Council, GSE = grand strategy for energy, JABODETABEK = DKI Jakarta, Bogor, Depok, Tangerang and Bekasi, RUEN = Rencana Umum Energi Nasional (National Energy Masterplan).

Notes:
1. Non-standardization assumed with three battery types
2. Actual number assumed that density is not more than targeted area i.e., swap stations get bigger

Source: Calculations by Grutter Consulting.

Table A2.10: Scenarios of Number of Swapping Stations for E-Motorcycles in Bali

Parameter	2022	2023	2024	2025	2026	2027	2028	2029	2030
BAU e-motorcycles	662	993	1,325	1,656	1,987	2,318	2,649	2,980	3,312
Scenario 1: RUEN / DEN with subsidies	5,006	15,818	36,254	70,937	122,015	195,567	294,863	444,998	676,635
Scenario 2 e-motorcycles: GSE with regulations	27,347	94,926	240,896	398,545	602,857	860,290	1,158,177	1,479,895	1,850,514
Total motorcycles	4,208,852	4,293,029	4,335,959	4,335,959	4,335,959	4,335,959	4,335,959	4,335,959	4,335,959
Swap stations scenario 1	8	25	57	111	191	306	461	695	1,057
Area swap stations scenario 1	742	235	102	52	30	19	13	8	5
Area assumed non-standardization	2,225	704	307	157	91	57	38	25	16
Actual number of swap station excl. standardization	8	25	57	111	191	306	461	695	1,057
Swap stations scenario 2	43	148	376	623	942	1,344	1,810	2,312	2,891
Area swap stations scenario 2	136	39	15	9	6	4	3.2	2.5	2.0
Actual number of swap stations standardized	43	148	376	580	580	580	580	580	580
Area assumed non-standardization	407	117	46	28	18	13	10	8	6
Actual number of swap station excl. Standardization	43	148	376	623	942	1,344	1,740	1,740	1,740
Area targeted	10	10	10	10	10	10	10	10	10

BAU = business-as-usual, DEN = National Energy Council, GSE = grand strategy for energy, RUEN = Rencana Umum Energi Nasional (National Energy Masterplan).

Notes:
1. Non-standardization assumed with three battery types
2. Actual number assumed that density is not more than targeted area i.e., swap stations get bigger

Source: Calculations by Grutter Consulting.

Table A2.11: Destination Chargers

Parameter	2022	2023	2024	2025	2026	2027	2028	2029	2030
Indonesia	82,581	286,654	727,453	1,203,515	1,820,492	2,597,883	3,497,435	4,468,951	5,588,138
JABODETABEK	11,597	40,254	102,154	169,005	255,645	364,811	491,132	627,559	784,722
Bali	2,735	9,493	24,090	39,854	60,286	86,029	115,818	147,990	185,051

JABODETABEK = DKI Jakarta, Bogor, Depok, Tangerang and Bekasi.
Note: Data based on 10% of e-motorcycles.
Source: Calculations by Grutter Consulting.

Table A2.12: Scenario Calculations

Parameter	2022	2023	2024	2025	2026	2027	2028	2029	2030
JABODETABEK	181	629	1,596	2,100	2,100	2,100	2,100	2,100	2,100
Bali	43	148	376	623	942	1,344	1,740	1,740	1,740

JABODETABEK = DKI Jakarta, Bogor, Depok, Tangerang and Bekasi.
Source: Calculations by Grutter Consulting.

Table A2.13: Scenario Calculations

Indonesia	2022	2023	2024	2025	2026	2027	2028	2029	2030
Total e-motorcycles (cumulative)	825,811	2,866,545	7,274,529	12,035,152	18,204,919	25,978,826	34,974,347	44,689,509	55,881,377
Private (90%)	743,230	2,579,890	6,547,076	10,831,637	16,384,427	23,380,943	31,476,912	40,220,558	50,293,239
Commercial (10%)	82,581	286,654	727,453	1,203,515	1,820,492	2,597,883	3,497,435	4,468,951	5,588,138
Electricity usage total MWh	303,733	1,054,315	2,675,572	4,426,529	6,695,769	9,555,012	12,863,565	16,436,802	20,553,170
Electricity usage private MWh	254,185	882,322	2,239,100	3,704,420	5,603,474	7,996,283	10,765,104	13,755,431	17,200,288
Electricity usage commercial MWh	49,549	171,993	436,472	722,109	1,092,295	1,558,730	2,098,461	2,681,371	3,352,883
GHG reduction total	571,652	1,984,312	5,035,657	8,331,110	12,602,017	17,983,359	24,210,341	30,935,482	38,682,844
$PM_{2.5}$ reduction total	146	506	1,284	2,125	3,214	4,586	6,175	7,890	9,866
NO_x reduction total	972	3,374	8,562	14,165	21,426	30,576	41,163	52,598	65,770
Economic benefit million (Rp)	721,483	2,504,402	6,355,506	10,514,699	15,905,013	22,696,808	30,555,886	39,043,690	48,821,640
Economic benefit ($ million)	50	175	444	735	1,112	1,587	2,137	2,730	3,414

JABODETABEK	2022	2023	2024	2025	2026	2027	2028	2029	2030
Total e-motorcycles (cumulative)	115,966	402,539	1,021,536	1,690,054	2,556,453	3,648,115	4,911,324	6,275,590	7,847,224
Private (90%)	104,369	362,285	919,383	1,521,048	2,300,807	3,283,303	4,420,192	5,648,031	7,062,502
Commercial (10%)	11,597	40,254	102,154	169,005	255,645	364,811	491,132	627,559	784,722
Electricity usage total MWh	42,652	148,054	375,721	621,602	940,263	1,341,777	1,806,385	2,308,162	2,886,209
Electricity usage private MWh	35,694	123,901	314,429	520,199	786,876	1,122,890	1,511,706	1,931,627	2,415,376
Electricity usage commercial MWh	6,958	24,152	61,292	101,403	153,387	218,887	294,679	376,535	470,833
GHG reduction total	80,275	278,650	707,140	1,169,908	1,769,657	2,525,340	3,399,773	4,344,161	5,432,095
$PM_{2.5}$ reduction total	20	71	180	298	451	644	867	1,108	1,385
NO_x reduction total	136	474	1,202	1,989	3,009	4,294	5,780	7,386	9,236
Economic benefit million (Rp)	101,315	351,684	892,481	1,476,542	2,233,485	3,187,233	4,290,855	5,482,767	6,855,850
Economic benefit ($ million)	7	25	62	103	156	223	300	383	479

Bali	2022	2023	2024	2025	2026	2027	2028	2029	2030
Total e-motorcycles (cumulative)	27,347	94,926	240,896	398,545	602,857	860,290	1,158,177	1,479,895	1,850,514
Private (90%)	24,612	85,433	216,807	358,690	542,571	774,261	1,042,359	1,331,906	1,665,463
Commercial (10%)	2,735	9,493	24,090	39,854	60,286	86,029	115,818	147,990	185,051
Electricity usage total MWh	10,058	34,914	88,602	146,585	221,731	316,415	425,978	544,305	680,619
Electricity usage private MWh	8,417	29,218	74,148	122,672	185,559	264,797	356,487	455,512	569,588
Electricity usage commercial MWh	1,641	5,696	14,454	23,913	36,171	51,617	69,491	88,794	111,031
GHG reduction total	18,930	65,711	166,756	275,885	417,316	595,520	801,727	1,024,430	1,280,984
$PM_{2.5}$ reduction total	5	17	43	70	106	152	204	261	327
NO_x reduction total	32	112	284	469	710	1,013	1,363	1,742	2,178
Economic benefit million (Rp)	23,892	82,933	210,463	348,195	526,695	751,606	1,011,860	1,292,934	1,616,731
Economic benefit ($ million)	2	6	15	24	37	53	71	90	113

GHG = greenhouse gas, JABODETABEK = DKI Jakarta, Bogor, Depok, Tangerang and Bekasi, MWh = megawatt hour, NO_x = nitrogen oxides, $PM_{2.5}$ = particulate matter 2.5, Rp = Indonesian rupiah.

Source: Calculations by Grutter Consulting.

Table A2.14: Charging Infrastructure

General assumptions for the swapping and charging infrastructure

Parameter	Commercial Usage	Private Usage
Number of batteries per EV	2	1
Number of km driven daily (km)	80	46
Energy usage (kWh/km)	0.025	0.025
Battery useable capacity (kWh/battery)	1	1
EV swaps per day	1.5	0
Share of motorcycles (%)	10	90
Charging power (kW)	1	
Slots in swap station (minimum)	10	
Number of operating hours	16	
Average recharge time per battery (hour)	1	
Maximum station utilization (number of batteries)	160	
Station utilization (% of slots x operating hours)	60	
Number of battery swaps per station per day	96	
Number of e-motorcycles served per day	64	

Overview JABODETABEK

Parameter	2022	2025	2030
Land area JABODETABEK (km²)	7,000		
Land area DKI Jakarta (km²)	660		
Number of citizens	37,630,356	41,458,000	42,131,000
Total number of motorcycles	17,847,907	18,386,913	18,386,913
Motorcycles used for ride-hailing	1,784,791	1,838,691	1,838,691
Number of e-Motorcycles			
BAU e-motorcycles	2,809	7,021	14,043
Scenario 1 : RUEN / DEN with subsidies	21,228	300,813	2,869,315
Scenario 2 e-Motorcycles: GSE with regulations	115,966	1,690,054	7,847,224

BAU = business-as-usual, DEN = National Energy Council, EV = electric vehicle, GSE = grand strategy for energy, JABODETABEK = DKI Jakarta, Bogor, Depok, Tangerang and Bekasi, km = kilometer, km² = square kilometer, kW = kilowatt, kWh = kilowatt-hour, RUEN = Rencana Umum Energi Nasional (National Energy Masterplan).

Source: Calculations by Grutter Consulting.

Table A2.15: Scenarios for 2025 in JABODETABEK

Parameter	BAU	Scenario 1: RUEN / DEN with Subsidies	Scenario 2: GSE with Regulations
Number of e-motorcycles	7,021	300,813	1,690,054
Total number of battery swaps	1,053	45,122	253,508
Number of swap stations	11	470	2,641
Service area per swap station standardized			
JABODETABEK (km^2)	638	14.9	2.7
Jakarta (km^2)	60.2	1.4	0.25
Service area JABODETABEK non-standardized (km^2)	1,914	45	8

Overview Bali

Parameter	2022	2025	2035
Land area Bali (km^2)	5,800		
Land area Kota Denpasar (km^2)	124		
Number of residents	4,500,000	4,700,000	4,900,000
Number of tourists on island peak time	100,000	100,000	100,000
Kota Denpasar	700,000	900,000	1,000,000
Number of (combustion) motorcycles	4,208,852	4,335,959	4,335,959
Rental (25% of peak tourists)	25,000	25,000	25,000
Number of e-Motorcyles			
BAU e-motorcycles	662	1,656	3,312
Scenario 1 : RUEN / DEN with subsidies	5,006	70,937	676,635
Scenario 2 e-MCs: GSE with regulations	27,347	398,545	1,850,514

BAU = business-as-usual, DEN = National Energy Council, GSE = grand strategy for energy, JABODETABEK = DKI Jakarta, Bogor, Depok, Tangerang and Bekasi, km^2 = square kilometer, RUEN = Rencana Umum Energi Nasional (National Energy Masterplan).

Source: Calculations by Grutter Consulting.

Table A2.16: Scenarios for 2025 in Bali

Year 2025	BAU	Scenario 1: RUEN / DEN with Subsidies	Scenario 2: GSE with Regulations
Number of e-motorcycles	1,656	70,937	398,545
Total number of battery swaps	248	10,641	59,782
Number of swap stations	3	111	623
Service area per swap station*/**			
Bali (km^2)	2,242	52.3	9.3
Kota Denpasar (km^2)	47.9	1.1	0.2
Service area JABODETABEK non-standardized (m^2)	6,726	157	28

BAU = business-as-usual, DEN = National Energy Council, GSE = grand strategy for energy, km^2 = square kilometer, m^2 = square meter, RUEN = Rencana Umum Energi Nasional (National Energy Masterplan).

* Distance between swap locations on Bali (average): urban 6 km; suburban 20 km.

Source: Calculations by Grutter Consulting.

Further Reading

Avicenne Energy. 2018. *Worldwide Rechargeable - Battery Market 2017-2030 - 2018 Edition.*

European Commission. 2019. *Commission Staff Working Document on the Evaluation of the Directive 2006/66/EC on Batteries and Accumulators and Waste Batteries and Accumulators and Repealing Directive 91/157/EEC.*

International Monetary Fund. 2014. *Getting Energy Prices Right.*

Swartenbroux, L. V. 2018. *Belgium: Enviroment & Climate Change LAW 2019.*

Government of Indonesia. 2016. *Nationally Determined Contribution.*

Motilal Oswal. 2021. *Sector Update 19.3.2021 Automobiles: Disruption from e-2Ws ahead, e-3Ws near an inflection point.*

www.ingramcontent.com/pod-product-compliance
Lightning Source LLC
Chambersburg PA
CBHW042044240426
4366°CB0004°B/2997